Dowding's Eagles

Dowding's Eagles

Accounts of Twenty-five Battle of Britain Veterans

Norman Franks

Pen & Sword
AVIATION

First published in Great Britain in 2015 by
Pen & Sword Aviation
an imprint of
Pen & Sword Books Ltd
47 Church Street
Barnsley
South Yorkshire
S70 2AS

ISBN 978 1 47384 420 9

Typeset in Ehrhardt by
Mac Style Ltd, Bridlington, East Yorkshire
Printed and bound in the UK by CPI Group (UK) Ltd,
Croydon, CR0 4YY

Pen & Sword Books Ltd incorporates the imprints of Pen & Sword
Archaeology, Atlas, Aviation, Battleground, Discovery, Family
History, History, Maritime, Military, Naval, Politics, Railways, Select,
Transport, True Crime, and Fiction, Frontline Books, Leo Cooper,
Praetorian Press, Seaforth Publishing and Wharncliffe.

For a complete list of Pen & Sword titles please contact
PEN & SWORD BOOKS LIMITED
47 Church Street, Barnsley, South Yorkshire, S70 2AS, England
E-mail: enquiries@pen-and-sword.co.uk
Website: www.pen-and-sword.co.uk

Contents

Acknowledgments

My thanks go to Paul Baillie for archive help with decoration citations, etc. Also to the staff of the Reference Department of the Ilkeston Library Derbyshire. Photographs have come from many sources quite apart from my own archive built up over fifty years, but also from friends and fellow aviation historians Chris Shores, Wojtek Matusiak and Chris Thomas. Most of the rest came from many of the former pilots I met or corresponded with over the years.

Foreword

Every year the British people celebrate the anniversary of the Battle of Britain. Ever since Group Captain Douglas Bader DSO DFC led a group of surviving pilots from that important victory, on 15 September 1945, there has always been some form of commemoration on this day, known as Battle of Britain Day. Over the years many RAF stations opened their gates to the general public, holding flying events, church services, dinners, and so on. The 25th and 50th anniversaries were celebrated a little more lavishly and no doubt the 75th will be the same.

On Battle of Britain Day we always remember the 544 men of Fighter Command who died during the Battle, which is as it should be, but we must also remember those who survived after the end of October 1940. Many went on to continue fighting with the RAF over the next few years, many of them falling in various parts of the world, but many survived the war. Those who did survive have now reached the twilight of their years; indeed only a comparative handful remain alive today. As one famous actor in an equally famous film said: 'The problem with being one of the few is that we get fewer and fewer.'

As this 75th anniversary arrives, this book commemorates and remembers a few of the Few, so named by Winston Churchill in the House of Commons on 20 August 1940. His now famous speech included the words: *Never in the field of human conflict was so much owed by so many to so few.* The mini-biographies in this book detail the service of some of those pilots, most of whom did survive the war, each with distinguished war service. Sadly most have now departed this world, but their names are remembered with pride.

There are two main reasons why I chose the ones I did: a number of them I had the privilege to meet; while others had incredible adventures in the RAF and I felt that their achievements had been overlooked by historians. Their stories are exceptional, as you will read. However, let us not forget that these are, or were, just ordinary men, but men who had that little bit of extra skill and luck. We shall not see their like again.

Chapter 1

Flying Officer N leC Agarzarian

I said in the foreword that this book remembers survivors of the Battle of Britain and the war, and this first story deals with a pilot who did not survive to see peace, although his Spitfire did survive, and is still with us today. I have always been fascinated with this particular pilot.

Noel LeChevalier 'Aggy' Agazarian was born on 26 December 1916, the son of an Armenian father, Berge Agazarian, and a French mother,

Flying Officer Noel LeC Agazarian RAuxAF, flew with 609 Squadron in the Battle of Britain. Many of his sorties were in Spitfire R6915 which today hangs in the Imperial War Museum, Lambeth, London.

Jacqueline Marie-Louise le Chevalier. Berge Agazarian had come to England in 1911 to escape persecution and had set up what became a very successful electrical business.

Noel was the third of four brothers, and there were also two sisters. All four brothers were educated at Dulwich College, where Noel excelled as an athlete. He was in the first Rugby XV, captained the swimming and boxing teams and was awarded the *Victor Ludorum* for his sporting achievements. In 1935 he went to Wadham College, Oxford, taking an honours degree in jurisprudence three years later.

While at university, he was one of many who joined the university Air Squadron. Upon leaving, he joined the Royal Air Force Volunteer Reserve, being commissioned in February 1939. The three brothers who each served with the RAF may well have had their interest in aviation stimulated by their mother who, soon after the end of the First World War, purchased a war surplus Sopwith Pup fighter aeroplane for the ridiculous sum of £5 at a Croydon auction and had it brought home and installed in the family's back garden so that her children could play with it.

When war was declared in September 1939 Noel was immediately called up and went to No. 3 Initial Training Wing at Hastings on the Sussex coast. Here he was to meet a similarly minded young college graduate, Richard Hillary, later the famed author of the book *The Last Enemy*. In his book Hillary described Noel as having a 'pleasantly ugly face' and being 'cosmopolitan by nature, intelligent and a brilliant linguist'. Hillary also described Noel's flying as '… rough, slap-dash, and with touches of brilliance'.

That November they were both posted to No. 15 Flying Training School at RAF Lossiemouth, and having completed the course moved to No. 1 School of Army Co-operation at Old Sarum in early May 1940. This might well have led to a career in Army Co-operation, but fortunately they both showed promise as fighter pilots, so on 23 June Agazarian went to No. 5 Operational Training Unit at Aston Down, converting to single-seat fighters, namely Spitfires. Once converted, and with the Battle of Britain having started, Noel was posted to No. 609 Squadron at RAF Middle Wallop. Hillary, in turn, went to 603 Squadron. Both were auxiliary squadrons, one of a number formed to be manned by 'weekend' airmen. 609 was known as the West Riding Squadron, that began life at RAF Yeadon, Yorkshire as a bomber unit in 1936 but by 1939 had been reorganised to day fighters.

No. 609 Squadron was to be heavily involved in the Battle of Britain, under the command of Squadron Leader H S Darley DSO, and was to have a number of very successful fighter pilots among its complement. John Dundas was one, John Bisdee (qv), Johnnie Curchin, Frankie Howell, David Crook, Keith Ogilvie and James McArthur were others of note. Later in the Battle, 609 received three early American volunteers fighting alongside them, Andy Mamedorf, Red Tobin and Vern Keough. The squadron, while it continued to have Middle Wallop as its main base, often used Warmwell, located south-east of Dorchester and north-east of Weymouth. When German raiders were expected to come into the Weymouth or Portland areas, 609 would fly down and operate from here and return to Wallop each evening.

Noel Agazarian (right) with his flight commander, Frank Howell. Howell won the DFC in 1940 but later in the war became a Japanese prisoner of war. He survived captivity only to die in 1948 in a tragic accident whilst filming Vampires taking off at Odiham, being hit by the wing tip of one.

Noel, although he would never know it, was to gain fame by flying a number of sorties during 1940 in Spitfire R6915. Why was this so special? It was due to the fact that this particular Spitfire survived the war and now hangs in the Imperial War Museum in Lambeth, south London. It has done so for many years. In fact Noel would fly it on twenty-five operational sorties in 1940.

However, he was not flying it on 11 August, the day he claimed his first combat victory, his victim being a Messerschmitt 110C twin-engined fighter which he shot down over the sea south of Portland. These aircraft came from I/ZG2 and they suffered heavily at the hands of 609. They, and aircraft from II Gruppe, were on a mid-morning operation and were intercepted by fighters from 609, 213, 1 and 145 Squadrons. It is always difficult to be certain who got who, but 609 claimed four of the five lost, and a further five fighters damaged. One source indicates that Argazarian shot down that flown by Major Ott, the *I Gruppe Kommandeur*, with his gunner Fw. Zimehl. Dundas, Crook, Bisdee and McArthur were also amongst the victorious claimants of these 110s. It had been the squadron's first 'big show' and it had been ordered off at around 11.30 am. After climbing to 25,000 feet they spotted this large formation of 110s and the CO led his pilots down into the attack. After a terrific dog-fight 609 began to drift back to Warmwell where, surprisingly, everyone returned. McArthur had been heavily engaged by two German fighters but avoided them by spinning down to 5,000 feet. He landed more than a little shaken by the experience.

The next day Noel knocked pieces off another 110 south of Portland as bombers raided Portsmouth docks, then waded into several Me109 single-seaters, claiming two destroyed. These were fighters from III Gruppe of JG53, while the 110s were of III/ZG76. Noel's next claim came on the 25th, sharing the destruction of another 110 with Pilot Officer G N Gaunt. This 110 came from 1/ZG2 and crashed at Priory Farm, East Holme, Dorset. The Messerschmitts had been escorting Ju88s of KG51. Unteroffizier Siegfried Becker and his gunner, Obergerfreiter Walter Wöpzel were taken prisoner, the latter having been wounded. 609 Squadron had become heavily engaged with 110s and 109s that came from II/ZG2, V/LG1 and III/JG2, over Portsmouth and the Isle of Wight. 609 certainly accounted for three 110s and at least two 109s. On 15 September, Noel appears to have been involved, along with several other pilots, in attacking a formation of Dornier 17 bombers from KG76 north of Hastings at 15.30, one of which was shot down.

Noel's next combat successes did not occur until late September, by which time he was regularly flying R6915. However, in this machine, he was hit and the Spitfire damaged by return fire from a Heinkel 111 he was attacking. The Spitfire was hit in the oil sump and had to be force landed at RAF White Waltham at around 6 pm. Noel was not hurt and R6915 was quickly repaired.

On 25 September Noel, in company with Johnnie Curchin, shot down a He111 of 7/KG55 near Swanage. It crashed into a house east of Poole Harbour, in Westminster Road, Branksome Park, at 12.08 pm. Oberleutnant Hans Bröcker and four of his crew all died, the survivor being Gefreiter Kurt Schraps, the wireless operator, who baled out. Bröcker was the unit's *Staffelkapitän*. On the 26th, again in R6915, Noel shot down a 109 over Southampton, and claimed damaging hits on two Dornier 17 bombers.

Spitfire R6915 in the Imperial War Museum, taken by the author in the 1970s.

After making his pass on the Dorniers he engaged the 109, and his combat report reads:

'I then climbed up to attack a Me109 when I saw one diving past me – I turned and dived after it. It zoomed and I followed, getting in a short burst from about 400 yards. I then gave my machine full throttle and revs, and caught up [with] the 109 hand over fist. When about 50 yards away and directly behind I gave him the rest of my ammunition. He went onto his back and spun down – I followed him down – the spin straightened out into a vertical dive so that I could not long keep up with him. I lost interest and climbed up at about 3,000 feet and went home.'

The following day he was in action again, this time shooting down a Me110 twenty miles south of Portland. 110s of LG1, ZG26 and ZG76 suffered heavy losses this day. Noel and R6915 finished the month damaging another 110 on the 30th, but again return fire caught him. This time R6915 was hit in the glycol tank but luckily Noel was not far from his base and managed to get back and down before his engine seized through overheating.

Although the Battle had begun to slacken, enemy incursions over southern England continued, mostly with Me109s carrying bombs. The RAF engaged them in cloudy autumn skies that proved dangerous. However, Noel knocked down one Me109 on 15 October north-west of Southampton. The squadron had been somewhat surprised by a number of 109s of JG2 that suddenly came down on them. David Crook spotted them coming and yelled a warning, and the Spitfires scattered. Despite this, John

He111 of 7/KG55 caught by the camera gun in R6915 on 25 September 1940 with Agazarian at the controls.

Dundas' Spitfire took several hits, but without serious damage. To everyone's surprise, when the squadron scattered, Noel and Tadeusz Nowierski, a Polish pilot with 609, had pulled round and stayed at height, but as Noel manoeuvred round his Spitfire (X4539) he was hit by several bullets too, one actually crashing through the cockpit hood three inches above his head. He then saw two 109s calmly flying off, not paying him the slightest attention. He chased after them and shot down the rear one. Nowierski also shot down a 109, this one from JG2's 4th Staffel, its pilot crashing near Lymington, where Gefreiter Alois Pollach was taken prisoner. JG2 lost two aircraft and had a third written off in a crash at base, its pilot returning wounded.

His last claim for 1940 came on 2 December, sharing a Dornier 17 damaged, again with Flying Officer T Nowierski flying with him. It seems they may have identified this machine as a Me110, something that often happened as both aircraft had twin rudders. However, it was a Dornier, probably a machine of Kü.Fl.Gr.606 (Küstenfleigergruppe), which subsequently crashed into the sea near Brest, killing Leutnant Helmut Anders and his crew. The German unit, as its named suggests, were formed to attack coastal targets but often went for inland targets over Britain in 1940 too.

With victory in the air over Britain secured, everyone waited to see what would happen in 1941, once the spring weather made operations more favourable for both sides. However, the war in the Middle East was hotting up, and Fighter Command were seeking volunteers to go out to the Western Desert, or even Malta, and Noel apparently volunteered. He was shipped out in January 1941 and assigned to No. 274 Squadron on 6 April, based at Amiriya (LG39) in the Western Desert. The downside to this was that his new squadron flew Hurricanes, somewhat different to the Spitfire he had become used to. Combat was just as fierce in North Africa, where blue skies and brilliant sunshine could make things difficult for fighter pilots. However Noel, fighting over the beleaguered garrison coastal town of Tobruk on 1 May 1941, shot down a Me109. This, and another 109 claimed by a fellow pilot, while confirmed by ground observers, may well have been crashing RAF aircraft, shot down in a fight with JG27.

Sadly, Noel Agazarian was not to survive for much longer. The RAF squadrons were heavily engaged in Operation 'Battleaxe' that involved many ground attack sorties, fighters strafing German troops and transports. On 16 May, 274 Squadron was intercepted on an early morning sortie by Me109s of JG27, and Noel and Flying Officer Clostre failed to return to base. One fell to a 109; the other is thought to have been hit by ground fire. In any event, both men were killed. Noel is buried in Knightsbridge war cemetery, at Acroma, Libya. If he was shot down by a 109, its pilot was Fw. Elles.

* * *

One of Noel's brothers, Flight Lieutenant Jack Charles Stanmore Agazarian, was a British espionage agent with SOE in France during the war, having been recruited from the RAF where he had been a wireless operator. He was captured by the Germans and shot by them on 29 March 1945 whilst in Flossenberg concentration camp. He was 29. His wife Francine also worked with SOE in France. Another brother, Leven, also served in the RAF and became a Thunderbolt pilot in Burma.

One sister, Monique, became a much respected name in aviation. During the war she flew with the Air Transport Auxiliary delivering wartime aeroplanes from factories to RAF units. She had earlier been a VAD nurse. After the war she gained a commercial pilot licence, flying for Island Air Services, becoming its managing director, and later chairperson and chief pilot. She died in 1981.

Spitfire 1 R6915 was part of a batch of 450 ordered from Vickers-Supermarine on 9 August 1939, and made its first test flight on 11 July 1940 in the hands of George Pickering. Pickering was an experienced test pilot with Vickers, a former RAF pilot, and had also tested aircraft with the Marine Aircraft Experimental Establishment at Felixstowe. While there, Reginald Mitchell, designer of the Spitfire, noted his qualities and potential.

R6915 had its pre-service checks at No. 6 Maintenance Unit at Brize Norton, Oxfordshire, and once signed off was given to 609 Squadron on 21 July, at Middle Wallop. Checked again by 609's maintenance staff, it had the squadron codes of PR painted on the fuselage, and the aircraft's individual letter 'O' aft of the fuselage roundel. Ten days later it suffered some minor damage but was soon back on strength.

Records show it flew 58 operational sorties during the Battle of Britain, 25 in the hands of Noel Agazarian, with 13 more by Flying Officer Piotr Ostaszewski-Ostaja, a Polish pilot with 609. The other 20 ops were flown by a mixture of ten other pilots, including one by Pilot Officer J D Bisdee (qv). Its pilots were credited with a total of five German aircraft destroyed or shared destroyed, two more probably destroyed and four damaged. It had

R6915. Artist Barry Weekley produced this image of the Spitfire as it would have looked in 1940.

been damaged twice in combat, both times with Agazarian, on 7 September and on 30 September, by return fire from a He111.

The Spitfire left 609 on 7 December, sent to 12 MU, and having had a refit, went to No. 602 Squadron, being on its strength from January to July 1941. It then went to No. 61 Operational Training Unit before going into storage in October. In April it was sent to No. 1 CRU, then to 6 MU, before flying once more with 61 and 57 OTUs until June 1943.

From the end of 1943 until August 1944 it was with Nos 39, 82 and 52 MUs until finally Struck Off Charge (SOC) on 21 June 1947. Fortunately it was one of the wartime aircraft saved from being reduced to produce; it was preserved for display purposes, ending up in the Imperial War Museum in London.

For many years it has hung in the main gallery of the Museum, its only 1940 references being in its serial number and a duck-egg blue spinner. It has no code letter markings; the national markings are of a later date than 1940 and it retains the pale blue combat strip around the tail, which would have been applied to RAF fighters from December 1940. I know that several people, including me (twice), have written to the museum to try and persuade them to have it re-painted in its 1940 wartime colours, but so far to no avail. I first saw it in the mid-1950s and never miss a chance to look at it if I am in the area.

R6915 in 2014.

Chapter 2

Air Commodore R Berry CBE DSO DFC & Bar

Wing Commander Ronald Berry DSO DFC.

One is often amused at the nicknames RAF pilots gave to their fellow mates, and Ronald Berry became known as 'Ras' or 'Razz' throughout his RAF life. He was born in Hull on 3 May 1917, the son of Mr & Mrs W Berry of Kelvin Street. He attended the local Riley High School, and then, aged 11, went to Hull Technical College. Prior to joining the Royal Air Force Volunteer Reserve in July 1937 he had a job as a clerk with the St Andrews Engineering Company in Hull dockyard, and later with the Hull Corporation Treasurer's Department. Deciding to try for the RAFVR in 1937, he was accepted and trained at No. 4 E&RFTS at Brough, and spent some time with 66 Squadron at RAF Duxford. With the coming of the war, he was called up for full time service in November 1939 and sent to No. 603 Squadron of the Auxiliary Air Force, based at RAF Turnhouse. At this stage he was a sergeant pilot. Although he had been notified in July 1939 that he would receive a commission, the paperwork was lost and it took until December before he became an officer. He joined 603 on 17 October, and as an NCO was not treated too well by some of the officers, but finally he was commissioned on 1 December, with seniority back dated to 29 April.

Some of the early war actions took place over Scotland and the North of England; 603 and 602 Squadrons both saw occasional combat there and both scored a few victories, as did 43 Squadron RAF. 603 shot down a Heinkel bomber on 16 October which was raiding Royal Naval vessels in the Firth of Forth, and a week later both units shared another Heinkel – which was the first German aircraft to fall on British soil in the Second World War. Berry got his chance on 7 December, whilst operating from Montrose, but could only claim the Heinkel as damaged. The feature of this action was that it was the first time the squadron encountered a formation of hostiles, even if only three in number. Up till now only single raiders had been engaged. These came from I/KG26 who lost two of their number, but as 72 Squadron were also engaged with them, it is unclear who may have caused the fatal damage. In the event, the squadrons could only claim the three as damaged.

Berry and 603 continued sporadic actions in the north as Dunkirk came and went, and the Battle of Britain began. He had a narrow escape on 15 April, flying in cloud whilst descending towards Drem airfield. As he gingerly lost height he suddenly spotted the Lammamuir Hills through the gloom. Pulling hard back on the stick he just cleared them, but bent the wings in doing so. On 30 June he damaged a Ju88, and on 3 July he shared another destroyed south-east of Aberdeen (an aircraft from 8/KG30) with Flying Officer Brian Carbury and Pilot Officer Gerald Stapleton. Before the month was out, he had shared two more raiders shot down, a Dornier 17P on the 23rd (with Flight Lieutenant Rusty Rushmer and Pilot Officer Noel Benson), and a He111 on the 30th (with Rushmer and Pilot Officer Peter Pease), this one again from 8/KG26.

Richard Hillary was a brother pilot in 603 and in his famous book *The Last Enemy*, described Berry thus: 'He was short and stocky, with a ruddy complexion and a mouth that was always grinning or coming out with some broad Yorkshire witticism impossible to answer. Above his mouth, surprisingly, sprouted a heavy black moustache, which induced me to call him the organ-grinder. His reply to this was always unprintable but very much to the point. Even on the blackest days he radiated an infectious good-humour. His aggressive spirit chafed at the squadron's present inactivity and he was always the first to hear any rumour of our moving south.'

That move finally came on 17 August with the arrival of orders to prepare to leave Turnhouse, although this took some time. Not until the 27th did the pilots fly down to RAF Hornchurch to replace 65 Squadron that were down

to five aircraft and 12 tired pilots. 603 were soon in action, Berry claiming a
Me109 probably destroyed and another damaged on the 28th over Kent, but
both men with him were shot down. He was later to recall:

'We were off on patrol at 30,000 in the Dover area, and it was first
encounter. Unfortunately for me the chaps on either side of me got
shot down in flames, and that was typical. We were in these vic-three
formations and out they came, down out of the sun and that was when
we started to learn our fighter combat from then on. These two just got
shot down as quick as that and I turned round and got into a dogfight.
I thought I got one Me109, I definitely got another but credited with
only a probable.'

He made it two destroyed over Canterbury, and another destroyed over
Hornchurch on the 31st. These were fighters of JG77. His combat report
noted:

Ras Berry (right) with Wing Commander J G Sanders (qv) back in England at a conference
in 1944.

'Patrolling with the squadron at 28,000 over Biggin Hill, I saw a protective formation above bomber squadron. They formed a circle and soon split into combat. I stuck on the tail of a Me109 and closed in and fired two bursts of four seconds and the enemy aircraft broke up. I then caught up with another 109 and closed in and fired at close range. Pieces fell off the 109 and it sank out of control and broke up.'

The third 109 claimed this day began with Razz having oxygen problems which forced him to leave the other Spitfires at 22,000 feet, so he circled below hoping some straggling enemy aircraft might come along. Spotting a fast flying 109 he went after it, caught it up by using his emergency boost, then fired all his ammunition at it. Smoke streamed from the fighter and it crunched onto the mud at Shoeburyness. The pilot had been Oberleutnant Helmut Rau, Staffelkapitän of 3./JG3, who was taken prisoner. The 109 was later put on public display. It had a large yellow 4 on the fuselage and a yellow dragon/snake insignia on the cowling. Three victory stripes were painted on the tail, scored by Rau during the French campaign.

The next day he shared another 109 with Flying Officer J G E Haig, and then damaged another on the 2nd. In the early part of September, fighting was intense and dangerous and Berry only gained one confirmed kill; but he damaged, and probably destroyed, several: a He111 damaged on the 9th, a Me110 damaged on the 11th, two 109s probably destroyed (although one appears to have gone into the sea) on the 15th, and on this day one certain kill. Again they were fighting above Kent and several pilots were attacking a Dornier. They had been patrolling over Rochford at 22,000 feet and found 109s and He111s coming in. The 109 he engaged went into cloud leaving a smoke trail but then he spotted a Dornier 17 heading for home. His attack produced smoke from its starboard engine, but Berry had to break as oil was starting to cover his windscreen. However, the bomber was finished and ended up crash-landing in a field on the Isle of Sheppey. This appears to have been a Dornier from 4./KG3, although it came down on the Isle of Grain rather than Sheppey across the estuary. Three of the four-man crew had been wounded and the bomber burnt out after coming down.

On the 17th Berry shared a probable 109 with Pilot Officer J C Boulter, and on the 27th he shared two more with the CO, Squadron Leader George

L Denholm, then claimed another as a probable. On the 29th he claimed a 109 probable and another damaged, but on the 30th, two certain 109s in the Biggin Hill area.

At this time Ronald Berry was rewarded for his recent actions with the Distinguished Flying Cross. It was promulgated in the *London Gazette* on 25 October:

> *Pilot Officer Berry has personally destroyed six enemy aircraft, and assisted in the destruction of several others. Through innumerable engagements with the enemy he has shown the greatest gallantry and determination in pressing home his attacks at close range. The skill and dash with which this officer has led his section have done much to assure their success.*

He and his good friend and squadron comrade, Flying Officer Gerald 'Stapme' Stapleton, both received their DFC awards from the King at Buckingham Palace. Both men travelled down to London together in order to receive their awards from His Majesty. Stapleton recalled with a smile that in the queue was an Indian wearing a turban. On approaching the King, he gave such a wonderfully smart and enthusiastic salute that he struck himself on the turban, losing his balance for a moment, and then tottering as he regained his footing.

It was almost a month before his next combat success. In an engagement with JG27 on 27 October he damaged a 109 flying a Spitfire IIa, which the squadron had recently begun to receive in place of their old Mark Is. Then it was November, with the Battle all but over, except that now the 109s were carrying bombs while the bombers stayed home. On the 7th he shared a Me110 destroyed north-east of Rochford with several other pilots. It was a lone machine which they found at 10,000 feet and literally shot it to pieces before it plunged into the sea. This had been a reconnaissance machine from 3(F)/11 flown by Oberleutnant H Kopetsch, who died with his gunner. The next day Berry damaged what he thought was a Heinkel 113 fighter east of Dover. No end of He113s were reported by RAF pilots during the Battle of Britain, but they were all Me109s. The He113 was a real machine, well publicised before the war, but it took no part on operational flying.

On the 17th he knocked down another 109 north of the Thames estuary. Me109s were flying a fighter sweep across the area and 603, in company with 41 Squadron, became engaged. 603 claimed three destroyed; 41 Squadron also made claims, to make a total of nine 109s shot down. Sadly the Germans only lost two.

Germany's relatively recent ally, Italy, had begun to take part in the latter stages of the Battle of Britain. Mussolini was no doubt keen to share in the spoils of victory he believed were not far distant. Their first rather tentative raids began in late October but they did not fare too well against experienced RAF fighter pilots, especially with their almost antiquated aircraft. The first big encounter came on Armistice Day anniversary, 11 November, with nine Fiat BR20 bombers escorted by 40 Fiat CR42 biplane fighters, heading in over the Suffolk coast. Hurricanes of 257 and 46 Squadrons tore into the Italian force and the Italians lost three bombers and three fighters.

On 23 November, 603 had their chance against Italian raiders. Twenty-nine CR42s had been sent on a sweep over Margate to Dungeness, covered by 24 Fiat G50 monoplane fighters. Twelve Spitfires of 603 found the biplanes, attacked, and claimed more than were actually lost, but it was fun. 41 Squadron were nearby so when 603 radioed that they were seeing Italians, 41 wanted to know where they were. In one of the more famous recordings of events, 603's CO initially called out:

'Wops ahead.'
'Where are they?' asked 41.
'Shan't tell you,' said the CO, 'We're only outnumbered three to one.'

Several Italian fighters were claimed but only two were actually lost, while three more returned to their base badly damaged and crash-landed. Berry claimed one destroyed and another as probably so. These two claims by Berry were his last during 1940. He was among the most successful pilots in the squadron, for by this time his tally was eight destroyed, eight shared destroyed, six probably destroyed and nine damaged.

* * *

Ron Berry had also achieved another victory during the Battle, the winning of a bride, Nancy Watson. They would have a daughter. He remained with 603 until the spring of 1941, by which time he had become a flight commander. His rest period was as a fighter controller at Turnhouse. While so engaged, he had the opportunity to fly on a few scrambles in a Hurricane, but had no luck in finding elusive raiders. He became a squadron leader in December and in the new year, was given command of No. 81 Squadron at Turnhouse. In May the squadron moved south to Hornchcurch and began flying operations over France, but by the autumn he was told his unit would be going overseas.

Operation Torch was being planned – the invasion of North Africa – and 81 was moved by sea to Gibraltar, from where, once the landings in Algiers had been successful on 8 November, it flew its Spitfires to Maison Blanche in French North Africa, then later to Bone. Berry was heavily involved in air actions from the start, initially over Oran. In the late afternoon of the 9th,

Squadron Leader R Berry whilst CO of 81 Squadron in Tunisia. On the left is Wing Commander P H 'Dutch' Hugo, the wing leader of 322 Wing.

two US B17s were due to arrive from Gibraltar, escorted by 242 Squadron. As they approached, a large force of Ju88s and He111s came in to bomb the harbour and airfield. 81 and 43 Squadrons were scrambled and intercepted them. Berry, with two of his men, chased one across the airfield, firing at it despite AA fire from the ground, as well as fire from gunners on the B17s that had just touched down. The 88 crashed two miles inland from the airfield. Berry then shot down another 88 and shared a He111. After the raid, 81 had claimed three plus a probable, while 242 also claimed three with others damaged. 43 claimed a Heinkel and an 88.

Two days later, on the 11th, enemy bombers attacked the harbour at Bougie. Berry was leading a defensive patrol and managed to damage a Ju88. On the 14th, in a scrap with Italian fighters, he damaged a MC200 over Bone, and on the 26th damaged two Me109s over the same location.

Another raid on Bone after dark on the 28th wounded the OC of 322 Wing, Group Captain C Appleton, so his place was taken by Wing Commander P H 'Dutch' Hugo DFC, sharing the job with Ron Berry. Earlier this same day, Berry and Appleton had led a sweep to the Tebourba area, meeting some fifteen Me109s. In the scrap which followed, Berry shared one of them.

Berry saw his first FW190 fighter on 3 December. 81 Squadron were flying a sweep mid-afternoon in company with Spitfires of the US 2nd Fighter Squadron. They spotted three Focke-Wulfs, attacked, and Berry claimed one, shared with Flight Sergeant LeHardy of 81, and Captain A E Vinson of the 2nd. It was probably a machine from II/JG2 who had two pilots wounded on this day (the other by 72 Squadron). Three days later he had his second encounter with 190s. Again it was an afternoon encounter, during a sweep to Tebourba. Berry led a 'bounce' and shot down one fighter, while Sergeant Monston got another. Berry ended the year with a Savoia S79 bomber destroyed on the 10th. Four days later, whilst closing in on another enemy aircraft, he took his eye off the ball and was bounced by fighters, but fortunately they missed him and overshot, allowing him to break away and escape.

The squadron had been flying Spitfire Vs since arriving in North Africa, but now Spitfire IXs became available. Berry was ordered to get his old Spits to Gibraltar and pick up the IXs. While there, Squadron Leader Colin Gray DFC arrived from England pending a job as tactics officer. Gray had known

Ras at both Drem and Hornchurch, although with different squadrons. He came from New Zealand and had had much success during the Battle of Britain with 54 Squadron.

On 22 January 1943, Dutch Hugo was promoted to Group Captain, and Berry became Wing Commander Flying of the Wing, although he was still at Gib. With the CO's position vacant, Colin Gray got the job, as he had experience on Spit IXs, and on the 27th, Gray led nineteen of them from the Rock and headed back to Tunisia. Gray made his first sortie from there on the 29th.

On the last day of January, 81 Squadron made its first scramble of the year at 15.20 pm, Berry leading five Spitfires off to intercept, including Squadron Leader Gray. Near Bone they spotted eight Me109G fighters, east of Cap Rosa. Four began to dive towards Bone harbour while the other four circled above. Berry told Gray to take these on while he went for the bomb-carrying 109s. Berry shot down one fighter while Gray mixed it with the four above. Gray fired into one which promptly began to spin down inverted. He had told his No. 2 to go after one of the other 109s, but to his surprise this pilot continued down firing like mad into Gray's victim which eventually crashed. Gray, upon landing, asked why he had done this rather than go for another 109, but he said he had! Gray was not convinced but as the other pilot had yet to open his score in North Africa he allowed him to take credit. Two FW190s from I/JG53 were lost, one pilot being seen to bale out.

Berry's next success was to be his last confirmed victory. It came on 25 February, he and Gray again being airborne to intercept raiders – twelve 109s of JG53, escorting a reconnaissance aeroplane. Spitfires of 232 Squadron made the first encounter but while one pilot claimed hits on two, another pilot was lost to Hauptmann Wolfgang Tonne, this being the German's 111th victory. Berry and Gray waded in, Ras shooting down Flieger Josef Thaler over Bone, who became a prisoner of war. Gray damaged another.

While this was Berry's last confirmed victory, it was not his last claim. Between March and April 1943 he got two 109s as probables, two more and a 190 damaged, and also damaged a Ju87. These brought his combat successes to fourteen destroyed, ten shared destroyed, nine probables, and seventeen damaged. His reward was a Bar to his DFC. The recommendation read:

Squadron Leader Berry has been on operational flying since the beginning of the war, and at all times has shown himself to be a keen, courageous and resourceful pilot. At Hornchurch and again in North Africa he has acted as deputy Wing Commander flying in an exemplary manner. He has destroyed 15 aircraft, probably destroyed nine and damaged many others.

This recommendation was given to the AOC No. 242 Group, who added:

Wing Commander Berry took over the Wing leadership of 322 Wing whilst commanding a Squadron and has led Squadrons successfully on numerous sorties. He has shown great determination and courage over a long period both as a Squadron Commander and Wing Leader. Strongly recommended for the award of a Bar to the Distinguished Flying Cross.

In mid-March Ras Berry took over command of the Wing from Dutch Hugo. He continued to lead from the air, however, and although his air-to-air kills had come to an end, he still managed to destroy enemy aircraft. During two ground attack sorties on 6 and 7 May 1943, he recorded the loss to the Germans of one Ju52 transport plane and six Me109s. This led to the award of the Distinguished Service Order, gazetted on 1 June:

Out of a total of 412 operational sorties this Officer has carried out 45 Sweeps over France and no less than 85 Sweeps since coming to North Africa six months ago. The work carried out by Fighter Squadrons at Bone under his leadership during the first few months on the campaign was largely responsible for the sea supply lines being kept open. Later as Wing Commander Flying 322 Wing and then as OC 322 Wing his organising and directive ability coupled with sound leadership both in the air and on the ground have greatly contributed to the success of the Wing. He had personally been responsible for the destruction of 17 E/A, and the probable destruction of 8 others. In addition he has damaged a further 12 E/A. His gallantry and determination to engage the enemy at all times are outstanding and I strongly recommend him for this award.

With victory in Tunisia, Berry led his three squadrons in a celebratory fly-past over Tunis on 20 May 1943. Posted home to Britain he was given the job of Wing Commander Flying at No. 53 Spitfire OTU at Kirton-in-Lindsay before attending the Army Staff College, after which he attended the RAF Fighter Leaders' School, where he saw out the war. With the coming of peace he went to RAF Tangmere to form the Central Fighter Establishment, before taking command of RAF Acklington. He was made an OBE in 1946. After a period at 12 Group HQ as Wing Commander Operations, he commanded, in 1947, the Air Fighting Development Unit at West Raynham until the early 1950s.

Berry then went to America on exchange with the USAF, flying many different aircraft types at the Air Proving Ground, in Florida. Back in England he became Wing Commander Plans at Fighter Command and in 1954 he attended the Joint Services Staff College. Despite his background as a fighter pilot, his next task was to fly bombers, prior to becoming WingCo Flying at Wittering, equipped with Vickers Valiant bombers. He then took command of No. 543 Squadron at Wittering till 1959 at which time he became Director of Operations at Bomber Command. Station Commander at RAF Lindholme, responsible for Air Traffic Organisations for Northern Region, followed prior to his promotion to Air Commodore, becoming Director of National Air Traffic Control Services until he retired from the Service in 1969. He became a CBE in 1965.

In 1965 he was one of thirteen serving group captains and one air commodore who had fought during the Battle of Britain, chosen to march at the head of Sir Winston Churchill's funeral procession to Westminster Abbey.

His wife was now suffering from multiple sclerosis so they lived quietly at Hornsea on the Yorkshire/ Humberside coast, and later in Beverley, where he

Group Captain Berry at the time of Winston Churchill's funeral, Berry being one of the Battle of Britain veterans who attended.

Ronald Berry's Spitfire IX (EN199) showing the wing commander's prerogative of having his initials as code letters. It now resides in the Malta Aviation Museum at Takali.

devoted his time caring for her until her death in 1991. Air Commodore Ronald Berry died on 13 August 2000, aged 83. His daughter presented one of his uniforms to the Malta Aviation Museum at Ta'Qali. Also on display at this museum is his former Spitfire IX (EN199), fully restored, which had been one of those he used during the Tunisian campaign, with his wing commander marking of R●B on the fuselage sides.

Chapter 3

Group Captain J D Bisdee OBE DFC

Two things immediately struck me when I first met John Bisdee. As I pulled up into a large driveway in front of his house, I spotted him coming out of his front doorway and my thought was, that is Oliver Hardy! This is in no way meant to be rude, he just looked like him. The second, and more immediate thing, was that two quite large (to me at any rate) dogs were heading my way. I'm not good with animals and although I felt fairly confident they were not about to tear me apart, I decided to remain seated in my car. With some relief I heard my host call to the dogs whilst also assuring me I was quite safe. So there I was, about to meet a hero of mine and the first thing I had displayed was cowardice!

John Derek Bisdee came from Weston-super-Mare, Somerset, having been born on 20 November 1915. As a youngster he had attended Marlborough College, followed by Corpus Christi College, Cambridge. He also went to Spain in order to learn the language, but had to be evacuated at the start of the Spanish Civil War. With his schooling over he became a trainee with the Unilever Company but, like so many of his contemporaries, joined the RAFVR, in 1937, feeling certain war was not far off.

Once the arrival of this inevitable nightmare became reality, he was called to service, joining No. 609 Squadron the day after Christmas, December 1939. This was an auxiliary squadron, known as the White Rose Squadron, or more formally, the West Riding of Yorkshire Squadron, having been formed at Yeadon in 1936. 609 had only recently received Spitfires, having exchanged them with old Hawker Hart and Hind biplanes. Perhaps appropriately considering its future, its badge motto was *Tally Ho.*

The squadron's first war stations were in the north – Catterick, Acklington, Drem, Kinloss – before it finally moved south to RAF Northolt in May 1940, as things began to look serious across in Northern France. Despite bad winter weather, the pilots had been able to gain much experience on

Bisdee climbing out of his Spitfire following a 'show' over France 1941.

their new Spitfires. Convoy patrols had been the only real operational 'fare' up north, but they had bagged a Heinkel 111 off St Abbs Head in February.

By the time they got to Northolt, the Dunkirk evacuation was in full swing, but they were in time to get in on the tail-end of it. On 31 May its pilots were in action, claiming several victories, but overall the evacuation period cost 609 five pilots. The squadron remained at Northolt until July but then moved to Middle Wallop. The Battle of Britain was about to begin.

John Bisdee got his name on the score sheet on 18 July, sharing a He111 damaged. On 11 August he shot down one of four Me110s claimed by the squadron off Portland Bill and Swanage. These Messerschmitts came from ZG2 and ZG26 which lost seven of their crews and had a further seven return with varying degrees of damage. He followed this by damaging another 110 on the 25th, and on 7 September got a 110 destroyed during the Luftwaffe's first daylight raid upon London, and one more damaged. In a scrap on 26 September he probably destroyed a Heinkel bomber, while on the 27th shared yet another 110 destroyed, with Pilot Officer D M Crook – another loss suffered by ZG26. Damage to a Me109 on the 30th somewhere

A group of 609 Squadron pilots in 1941. From left to right: Keith Oglivie, Count Rodolphe de Grunne, John Bisdee, Willi van Lierde, S/Ldr M L Robinson, Roger Malengreau and Bob Wilmet.

west of the Needles was followed on 7 October by the destruction of yet a further Me110, north of Portland, again from ZG26, which lost seven aircraft in this late afternoon air fight with 609, 601 and 238 Squadrons.

Bisdee's contribution to the Battle was three and one shared confirmed victories, plus two probables and two more damaged.

* * *

As 1941 began he was still with 609, which had moved to Warmwell in November, remaining there till it moved to Biggin Hill in February. Here it became part of the Wing operating from there until July and then from Gravesend till September when it returned to Biggin. RAF fighter squadrons were now operating in Wings, and starting to take the air war to the enemy, with fighter sweeps and Circus Operations during the summer of 1941. Bisdee became a flight commander and was awarded the Distinguished Flying Cross, the citation appearing in the *London Gazette* on 11 July:

John Bisdee talking to 609 Squadron's intelligence officer after a sweep over France in 1941.

This officer has led flight and section with great skill and determination. He has participated in a large number of operational flights against the enemy, and has destroyed at least six of their aircraft besides damaging many others. He has set a fine example.

He had increased his score, as will be noticed in this citation, during operations over France or the Channel. This started with a 109 shared destroyed off Deal on 21 May, in company with Belgian pilot, Pilot Officer V M Ortmans (qv). Bisdee had a bad experience during this action. Having ordered an attack on 109s he saw below he led his section down, but checking his rear-view mirror during the dive, saw a mass of debris behind him, which turned out to be the Spitfire of one of his section disintegrating. John believed the Spitfire suffered wing failure during their dive. John told me that one of this pilot's last actions before takeoff was to rush back to the Intelligence Officer to retrieve his miniature lucky horse-shoe which he kept in his wallet.

The pilot had been another of the Belgians with 609, Pilot Officer Count Rodolphe Ghislain Charles De Hemricourt de Grunne, aged 29. He was a very experienced pilot having learnt to fly as a civilian, but who had volunteered to fight for the Nationalists in the Spanish Civil War. He was wounded in ground fighting, and in hospital, once it was known he held a pilot's licence, was persuaded to join the air force. Flying Italian CR32 biplane fighters, he shot down ten Republican aircraft in 1938. When the Second World War began he was again in uniform, eventually turning up in England, and flew with 32 Squadron in August 1940 before being wounded. He had been posted to 609 in April 1941.

* * *

On the evening of 17 June, 609 Squadron was part of Circus No. 13 against the Kuhlmann Chemical Works, and the power station at Choques, west of Béthune. As the Spitfires returned towards the French coast on their way back, several pairs of Me109s were spotted and attacked. 609 claimed three shot down, one by Bisdee, near Le Touquet. By now the squadron was flying the Spitfire Vb, armed with two 20 mm cannon and four .303 machine guns.

Five days later, the 22nd, Bisdee shot down another 109, this time of the 'F' variety. This was on Circus 18, directed against the marshalling yards at Hazebrouck. The Wing was escorting a dozen Blenheim bombers to this target this afternoon. 609 were part of the three forward support squadrons, along with 92 and 74 which made up the Biggin Hill Wing. They were acting as a form of fighter sweep ahead of the raid, in the hope of taking on any early 109s arriving on the scene. They patrolled Gravelines to Berques, ranging from 16,000 to 20,000 feet. Following an initial skirmish by 74 Squadron, the three squadrons split up into independent units. More 109s joined in and 609 became engaged. Bisdee shot down one and Sergeant T C Rigler claimed an amazing three! They were in action against JG26, which lost one pilot, and JG2 which lost two.

It has to be said that there was a great amount of over-claiming by pilots on both sides, not only in 1941, but throughout the war. The RAF this day claimed 29 enemy fighters shot down! JG26 claimed four Spitfires, while JG2 claimed five Spitfires and two Blenheims. RAF losses amounted to one pilot missing and one wounded. Unknown to the British pilots was that on this day Germany launched its attack upon Russia.

On 24 June Bisdee claimed a probable 109F on Circus 21, and his final claim came on 9 July: another 109F over the Le Touquet area – this was during Circus 41 while escorting three four-engined Short Stirling bombers. Blenheim bombers did not always tempt the German pilots into battle, so the RAF decided to employ larger bombers, but only in small numbers. Biggin's 91 and 609 Squadrons provided part of the Target Support Wing, along with squadrons from Hornchurch and Northolt. Over the target the Spitfires circled, watching the Stirlings on their bombing run, but 109s were about and some scraps developed as everyone headed for the coast. John and his Blue Section spotted a couple of 109s which appeared to be patrolling over two small boats off Le Touquet, 2,000 feet below. Covered by the others, Bisdee and Pilot Officer Jean Offenberg (another Belgian in the squadron) dived. The 109 pilots saw them and started to turn but the one Bisdee latched on to evidently lost his bearings due to some thick haze which blotted out his horizon. In any event, Bisdee had no problem holding him and after a few short bursts, the 109 began to trail thick smoke, falling upside down into Le Touquet Plage where it crashed.

In this engagement it was once again JG26 and JG2 versus the RAF raid. JG26 claimed three but lost one pilot, JG2 claimed ten Spitfires and also lost two pilots. RAF losses were two pilots missing and one wounded. They claimed twelve 109s plus another ten probably destroyed or damaged.

In the squadron at this time was Flight Lieutenant Paul Richey DFC, author of the book *Fighter Pilot*. First published in 1942, and covering his experiences during the Battle of France in 1940, Paul's book has never been out of print. His brother-in-law was Michael Robinson, who also happened to be 609's CO. Richey was posted to 609 in April 1941. That same year Richey recorded some interesting facts about John Bisdee:

'The Bishop – Flying Officer John Bisdee – had been running the Flight pending my arrival and showed me round. He was a big, tall, heavily-built man with straight blond hair, big blue eyes that slanted slightly downwards, a full mouth, rather a heavy jaw and the general air of a benevolent bloodhound. His slow, somewhat ponderous way of speaking sometimes caused his youngsters to refer to him as "The Pompous Bish". Bish was young himself but he had an old and wise manner. He was in fact, level-headed, steady and shrewd.'

I met Paul Richey on several occasions and, having failed to inspire him to write a second book about his post-France experiences, wrote it myself, after his death. *Fighter Pilot's Summer* was published by Grub Street in 1993. On one of my meetings with John Bisdee he told me about the tactics 609 employed during these 1941 operations:

'We soon invented a special flying style for Circus operations. We flew in three sections of four aircraft, led by the CO and two flight commanders (or their deputies). On the way over to France, each section flew in a round line abreast, stepped down from the leading flight. Once over enemy territory, each section went into line astern [stepped down so a pilot always had sight of the aircraft he was following] and weaved so that there were eyes looking everywhere. I don't believe we were ever "bounced" while in this formation.

'I don't know if any other squadrons used this manoeuvre, but I took it to Malta in 1942, although other squadron commanders asked me not to do it, as we scared them into thinking we were Messerschmitts.'

Another item of interest John recalled was during the funeral of a pilot:

'At his funeral, as the party was moving to the cemetery, it had been arranged for two Spitfires to fly over low, in salute. Two aircraft duly arrived but they turned out to be Me 109s. Everyone scattered, leaving the coffin in the middle of the road.'

* * *

John became tour-expired at the end of July, his place taken by Jean Offenberg, who had been the first Belgian pilot to receive the British DFC. John was posted to No. 61 OTU as an instructor, what was often referred to as a rest tour! Seeing out the year, in March 1942 he was finally moved back to operations, being posted overseas. He was given command of No. 601 Squadron at RAF Digby, that was about to leave for the island of Malta. This was another auxiliary squadron, often referred to as the millionaires' or even the playboy squadron in the early days, as most of the pilots were either well to do, from wealthy families, or both. Now, however, the early war years had turned it into an 'ordinary' squadron.

The island of Malta was under siege and needed reinforcements in both men and machines. In the early days it had survived against the Italians with a handful of Gloster Gladiator biplanes until Hurricanes began to arrive. Now, in 1942, Spitfires were desperately needed since the Luftwaffe had been forced to take over the battle for the island.

The squadron would be taken into the Mediterranean by aircraft carrier, in this case, the American USS *Wasp*. The carrier and her escorts sailed from the Clyde on 14 April, having taken aboard 50 Spitfires, while its resident American Grumman F4F Wildcats were parked on the deck. The convoy headed for Gibraltar then passing into the Mediterranean. By the 20th it was time to fly off the Spitfires, and while the Wildcats flew off to provide air cover, 47 serviceable Spitfires that constituted 601 and 603 Squadrons, began to head off for Malta, led by Squadron Leader E J Gracie DFC, who had flown to Gib, from Malta, in order to lead the force to the island. All landed safely, the first arriving about 10 am. One comment made by Bisdee, as German aircraft began to raid the island, was: 'Oh, the Battle of Brit all over again!'

Bisdee was in action the following day, the 21st. It was his first sortie from Malta, in company with Jumbo Gracie and one of John's flight commanders, Denis Barnham. They attacked a formation of Ju88s escorted by Me109s. Barnham probably destroyed one and damaged a 109 but he was badly shot-up by other 109s and was lucky to make a reasonable crash-landing. Bisdee attacked an 88, damaging its starboard engine and it was later seen to crash by an AA gun crew. However, he failed to spot a 109 coming down on him. Fire from the Messerschmitt smashed into the Spitfire (BP954); it was quickly evident that his fighter was done for, and he baled out. He had been shot down by Leutnant Walter Zellot of I/JG53, the German's 13th victory. As Bisdee's parachute snapped open it tore the webbing harness from his shoulders, and it was only by hooking one leg around one of the loops that he saved himself from falling to his death. He splashed down into the sea head first, got into his dinghy, and waited for rescue. Although searches were made he was not found, but in typical style, John paddled the four or so miles to the island, which took him six hours. Once reaching the rocky shore he had problems getting out of the water until helped by a navy seaman who pulled him out. Even then a Ju88 dropped a bomb near them, showering both with rocks and dirt.

John was taken to the pilots' rest camp at St Paul's Bay to recover from his ordeal and was back with his squadron at the end of the month; he was again in a Spitfire on 2 May, leading a dawn patrol. More action followed but the danger on the ground was just as deadly as in the air. On the 8th, during a dive-bombing attack on their airfield, Bisdee and others were in a slit trench as Ju87s swept in, bombing and machine-gunning. A bullet went right through his hat, fortunately without touching him. Two days later, in a fight against an evening raid by Cant Z1007bis bombers from 50° Gruppo BT, escorted by Macchi MC202s of 4° Stormo CT plus ten Re2001s of 2° Gruppo, the British pilots were heavily engaged. Ju87s followed with their escort of Me109s.

Bisdee singled out a Z1007 flown by Tenenti Domenico Robillotta of 211ª Squadriglia, which blew up, shedding wreckage into a field near Kalkara. Three of the five-man crew were killed, one injured, while the fifth baled out but his parachute failed and he plunged into Grand Harbour. On my visit to John's house, he showed me a colourful insignia which was cut from this bomber, given to him as a souvenir.

On the 11th, Spitfires were in action with Me109s that were escorting three Ju88s attacking airfields. Bisdee went after a 109 and left it spewing out smoke but could only claim a probable kill.

John now went down with 'Malta Dog', a dysentery ailment most people contracted during Malta's siege, due to lack of a proper diet, so he was only able to command from the ground. One unusual action by Denis Barnham was to have white spots painted on the wings of his Spitfire so that his men could easily and quickly identify him when reforming. He also had his cockpit canopy removed for clearer vision. However, Barnham soon realised that the spots attracted too much attention from 109 pilots, and when Bisdee arrived on the airfield, quickly ordered it to be repainted and the cockpit canopy replaced.

Back in the air towards the end of May, he had a lucky escape, or an interesting experience, on the 23rd. Flying a Spitfire usually flown by another pilot, he led a section in an attack on some Italian fighters, but when he opened fire, one of his cannons jammed and he had difficulty in controlling the machine. He was then engaged by a Re2001, which he found difficult to evade, but then the Italian pilot flew up alongside him, waved, then broke off and headed away. He was either a very gallant Italian – or out of ammunition.

In June, 601 was pulled out of Malta and sent off to Egypt, taking residence at Mariut. Heavy fighting in the Western Desert needed lots of support, especially in ground attack operations, and 601 found themselves flying scores of this type of sortie over the desert. The squadron moved into the desert, operating from LG (Landing Ground) 154 in July, then to LG173 and finally to LG85 as the desert war moved about. Air combat was less intense than over Malta, but John did find a Me210 reconnaissance machine near Aboukir on 5 July which he claimed as damaged.

His time as CO of 601 came to an end on 21 August, with a posting to HQ Middle East as Squadron Leader Fighter Training, which he continued till March 1943. He was then sent to the Tunisian Front as Wing Commander Day Fighters, where he helped to organise and write the cover plan for anti-submarine and shipping support operations for the invasion of Sicily. In July, after the fall of the island of Lampedusa, midway between Tunisia and Malta, he was appointed the island's Governor until after the Sicily invasion.

Returning to North Africa he helped train French pilots to an operational standard at Bone, and then moved to Ajaccio, on Corsica. His next move was to command 323 Wing at Bone before taking it to Foggia, in southern Italy. He had quite a large command, consisting of three Spitfire squadrons, a Wellington anti-shipping squadron, a rocket-firing Beaufighter squadron, a night-fighter squadron, plus Air Sea Rescue units, both RAF and American, as well as ASR launches, while also having some Italian floatplane units on a lake near Gargano. As well as operational commitments, his ASR elements were responsible for saving over 500 airmen from the Adriatic.

At the war's end he became a group captain, was made an OBE, and married a WAAF officer he had met in Cairo on the Yugoslavian/Balkan liaison team. She was Pamela Harden Jones. She believed that Yugoslav pilots should be trained on Spitfires, but John did not agree. However Pamela was not to be deflected and arranged for John to meet some of these pilots, whereupon he changed his mind. He left the RAF in 1945 and returned to Unilever, becoming chairman of one of its companies, and in 1951 became sales director of D & W Gibbs (toothpaste), later becoming chairman. He went on to chair the Thibaud Gibbs Company in France, but returned to run the newly formed Elida Gibbs, later Elida Faberge, that produced all Unilever toiletries.

He retired from the business world in 1976 and lived in Sussex. He died in Colchester on 21 October 2000, at the age of 84.

Wing Commander J D Bisdee DFC; a picture taken in Rome in 1944.

Chapter 4

Wing Commander M V Blake DSO DFC

When I was writing a book about the RAF's mammoth air action over the Dieppe Raid which occurred on 19 August 1942, I endeavoured to make contact with as many RAF airmen who had taken part in that momentous day, and Wing Commander Blake was one of them. Generally when they respond to my request for information, I will receive a letter back in reply, and from then on, we will either correspond with a few letters, or, if they live in a location that might be visited, one of us would suggest it. On a bright sunny Sunday morning, having just finished breakfast, I was about to entertain my two young sons, when the telephone rang. It was the Wing Commander. 'If you'd like to come and see me, I will be happy to talk to you,' said the Wing Co. I replied that I would be happy to, remembering he lived in Surrey, and not more than an hour from me. 'Fine,' he said, 'how about this morning?' I didn't have the courage to say no, and said I would be with him as soon as I could drive to his house. My wife was not best pleased to have her July Sunday suddenly reorganised, but I did not think I should say anything but yes.

After a rapid shave and collecting what papers I thought I ought to take concerning Dieppe, I was off. I suppose being a Sunday, the roads were pretty clear and I was amazed how quickly I arrived. He was in his garden, dressed in slacks and shirt, and swinging what I assumed to be a golf club. As that remark will suggest, I am no golfer. After the initial introductions and the production of a very welcome cup of coffee, and being still in his garden, he showed me the club. He asked what I thought of it, and seeing my indecision, asked if I played golf. Once I admitted I didn't, he went on to explain that he did, and was experimenting with a 'practice club'. I tried to look interested as he began to explain that he had an engineering background and had developed this practice club, which – as I recall it – meant that a golfer could practise his swing without the need for a ball, and therefore, the need to wander off and collect it afterwards. It seemed that as the swing was made and the club head reached what should have been a ball, some sort of weight within the head, clicked and it gave the feeling of striking a ball. I tried to look amazed and credulous but I am not sure I succeeded. Anyway, at this stage we went into his front room, where my interview took place.

Minden Vaughan Blake was originally from New Zealand, born in Newman, Eketahuna, south-east of Palmerston North, on 13 February 1913. He was the eldest of three boys, and received his secondary education at Southland Boys High School between 1926 and 1929. His father was a schoolmaster, but then decided to buy and run a chicken farm, where his sons could work and earn money while studying for a degree at Canterbury University. Early in our conversation, the Wing Commander brought up the subject of his two forenames. Apparently the family had two maiden aunts, the Miss Minden and the Miss Vaughan, both of whom were seemingly well off. His parents decided that giving their son their names would, in time produce some money for him. In the event it did not, so, as he remarked, he was stuck with these two names for life; he was eventually more intimately known as just 'Mindy'.

Blake did well at university graduating in 1934 with a M.Sc., with Honours, in mathematics. His inventiveness began to show itself by producing a machine which graded the family's farm eggs by weight. This he also marketed and it remained in general use in New Zealand for several years. In 1935, aged 22, he became a lecturer in physics at the university for a year. Twice he narrowly missed becoming a Rhodes Scholar, two years in a row, but, with a growing interest in aviation, he applied for entry into the Royal Air Force as a university entrant. He saw this as a means to an end, for he deduced that once he had learnt to fly he would be able to continue his studies in England in his chosen field of engineering. There were few RAF university entrant places available each year, but having become an outstanding athlete must have helped sway the balance – he had been the New Zealand universities' gymnastics champion for 1934 and again in 1936, while also holding the NZU and National titles for pole vaulting (later he held the RAF titles).

Once he was accepted into the RAF, he quickly sailed for England, in November 1936, and after pilot training went on to Hawker Fury fighters.

When fully trained, he was posted to No. 17 Squadron which had Gloster Gauntlets. He progressed well and was a flight commander before the war began. No sooner had the war started than he suffered a night crash. He had been on an exercise over London on 8 September, soon after the squadron had moved to Croydon. Coming down to land the lights all went out and then his engine stopped. His Hurricane hit the chimney of a nurse's home, turned over and crunched into the foundations of the new Purley Hospital. Mindy suffered a cut forehead that needed eighteen stitches, but he survived. It seems that the fighter's air intake had ingested some hay whilst out on the open airfield the previous day, causing the stoppage.

Just a month before the 'balloon went up' in France, Blake was posted away to be an instructor at Ternhill, which he endured for four months. With the Dunkirk evacuation over and the Battle of Britain started, he was keen to get into the action. However, his posting to an operational unit, 238 Squadron, sent him down to Cornwall, not exactly in the front line. Nevertheless, on 21 August he shot down a German raider, a Ju88 which he found over Trevose Head during the afternoon. The bomber came from Kampfgruppe 806, one of two this unit lost to 238 Squadron, the other going to Flying Officer J D Urwin-Mann (qv).

Within a week, Blake had a second victory, a Dornier 17 which he shared with Pilot Officer B B Considine on the 27th. This was a reconnaissance machine from 3(F)/31, which crashed at Hurdwick Farm, Tavistock at 10.13 am. The pilot had made a reasonable belly landing, and Blake and Considine later visited the site and had their picture taken in front of it. The Dornier was a 'P' variant so was quickly whisked off to the Royal Aircraft Establishment, Farnborough, for the boffins to take a look at. Later it was put on display in the towns of Salisbury and Bournemouth. It was coded 5D+JL, and Leutnant Walter Haffan and his two crewmen had been captured.

Minden Blake, 238 Squadron in 1940.

Pilot Officer B B Considine and Mindy Blake inspect a Dornier they brought down on 27 August 1940.

The squadron was moved on 10 September, going to Middle Wallop, which put them in the main arena. On the 14th Mindy claimed a Ju88 over Brooklands and the next day he downed a He111 at 3 pm over West Malling airfield itself. The Heinkel came from II/KG53 that had been raiding the London docks. Two of the crew were killed, three captured, two of whom had been wounded. The aircraft, code A1-AN, was piloted by Feldwebel Kurt Behrendt who made a good belly landing. However, one of its gunners, or perhaps one from the enemy formation, also scored hits on Blake's Hurricane, forcing him to make a quick landing on the airfield.

Mindy Blake was promoted to acting squadron leader on the 22nd, and posted back to St Eval, Cornwall, to take command of 234 Squadron. He also moved to a different aeroplane, as 234 were equipped with Spitfires. Before the year was out, Mindy had several encounters with Dornier bombers, the first being on 24 November, between St Eval and Falmouth.

Around mid-day, Mindy and Pilot Officer E B Mortimer-Rose took off on a patrol along the Cornish coast and were vectored onto a German raider.

They located a lone Dornier 215 (VB+KR) of Aufkläungsgruppe Ob.d.L near St Eval, chasing it southwards across Somerset and out across the coast at Falmouth. The Dornier was returning from a reconnaissance over the Irish Sea and the two Spitfire pilots finally shot it down into the sea about half a mile off Kynance Cove. Unteroffizier F Redmann and his two companions did not survive.

Edward Mortimer-Rose had had a successful summer with 234 Squadron and had already scored three confirmed victories, four probables and now this shared kill. He would go on to score more than a dozen victories, plus several probables and damaged and receive the DFC and Bar. He was also successful over Malta. Sadly he was killed in a collision during the Tunisian campaign in January 1943, still only 22 years of age.

Mindy's next encounters came five days after downing the Dornier 215, on the 29th. The Luftwaffe were fairly active this day, and Blake led a three-man patrol out on a convoy patrol off the Cornish coast, finding a Dornier 17 – claimed as a 215 – which he reported had crashed into the sea. In fact he was credited with two Dorniers on the 29th but German losses do not support these claims. The second Dornier was during an afternoon sortie, several bombers being engaged.

These actions were a little more important than merely a convoy patrol, as the fighters were covering the return of a damaged Royal Navy destroyer into Plymouth, HMS *Javelin*, commanded by Lord Louis Mountbatten. Later Blake dined with Mountbatten who thanked him for his part in the defence of his ship.

Squadron Leader Blake was awarded the Distinguished Flying Cross in December, the citation being gazetted on 7 January 1941, with a rather small account of his recent actions:

Squadron Leader Blake has displayed fine qualities of leadership and has personally destroyed five enemy aircraft. By his splendid example he has set a high standard to his fellow pilots.

By the time his award was gazetted he had been in action with another Dornier, this one on 20 December, twelve miles south of Land's End. Once again he was flying in company with Mortimer-Rose on patrol and, being vectored onto a hostile plot, located another reconnaissance Dornier 17P from 3(F)/31 at 10.30 am. Both men attacked and claimed damaging hits, but the bandit escaped, returning to its base severely damaged.

Early in 1941 his squadron moved to Warmwell, Dorset and took on Spitfire Mark IIa machines. They were soon involved in cross-Channel operations over France, one particular target being German radar sites. They still went up after enemy raiders, and on 11 March he and his section shared the destruction of a Me110 twenty miles south-west of Portland. Forty miles south of this same location, on 8 May, he shot down a Ju88, and three days later bagged a Me109 ten miles south of Swanage.

The tenth of July turned out to be quite a day for Mindy Blake. His Squadron was part of an escort for Blenheim bombers attacking ships in Cherbourg harbour. As the force began to turn for home, it was attacked by Me109s from 1 Erg./JG2. This was JG2's *Ergänzungsgruppe*, a sort of pool of pilots completing their training before moving to replace losses within the main JG2 staffeln. There was some confused fighting between 234 and 501 Squadrons, and several 109s were claimed as shot down, Blake being credited with two. However, the 109s scored as well, shooting down Sergeant I E Pearce of 234, who was killed, wounding Sergeant H A Newman, although he managed to return to base, and Mindy Blake. One of the Blenheims was also lost, its crew taken prisoner. The Me109 pilots claimed one Blenheim and three Spitfires.

Mindy knew he had been badly hit and headed for the water. It was well known that ditching a Spitfire was no simple task and the danger was immense. With his engine rapidly over-heating, he called his wingman, saying he was going to ditch. He had already worked out the best way if ever this happened: as he was about to hit the sea, he tilted one wing-tip into the water, which caused the Spitfire to cartwheel, and in so doing reduced the G-force. The Spitfire, nevertheless, went under the water immediately, but within seconds he had undone his straps, radio lead and oxygen tube and struggled out. RAF fighter pilots had only recently been equipped with a dinghy pack, which was attached to his harness. They had only been supplied to Fighter Command during June. Bobbing to the surface, the dinghy inflated and within moments he was sitting in it, safe and alive. He estimated he was about seven miles off the enemy coast, and that it was about 1 pm. He found that what breeze there was was taking him further out to sea, but as the afternoon was calm, and search aircraft were likely to find him, he let himself drift. But search aircraft did not find him, and he began to paddle towards England. He carried on with this all through the afternoon and evening. After he had been paddling for twelve hours a launch finally motored up to him; he was about two miles off the Isle of Wight. It was already past midnight so it had been some paddling! Obviously there was either enough light still to find him or perhaps he had been spotted earlier and his position noted and reported.

The story soon found its way into local newspapers back home in New Zealand, one running in the *Bay of Plenty Beacon* on 19 November. The article gave a glowing report about the Air Sea Rescue Service, and quoted Mindy:

> 'My Squadron was escorting Blenheim bombers across the English Channel. Glancing round I saw three 109s about to attack one of my rear sections. I broke away quickly and intercepting the first of the enemy planes, gave it a short burst of fire, but without effect. Then another 109 came for me and, pulling round quickly, I shot him down and started for home again. But the third 109 attacked, I pulled up, got on his tail and gave him a burst. Before I could attack again the pilot baled out and his machine went crashing into the sea.
>
> 'Starting home again I found smoke coming into the cockpit. Nursing the aircraft as far as possible, I called up and gave my position as 14 miles due north from Cherbourg. The engine stopped, and as soon as my plane landed on the sea it sank straight to the bottom. I got out and came to the surface, where I inflated my dinghy and climbed in. My position was then about 25 miles south of the English coast.'

The article continued:

> 'As the squadron leader was drying his clothes he could hear motor boats, and aircraft, searching all over the horizon. During the rest of that day eight aircraft passed over without spotting the tiny speck far below. It was not until late in the evening that the airman was seen.'

Blake continued:

> 'When one spotted me, all the others came over and soon there were eight Spitfires, a Lysander, a Wellington and several Hurricanes milling about overhead. Then motor boats appeared on the horizon. They were a very welcome sight, for I had been in the dinghy nearly ten hours and had drifted and paddled about 13 miles. Every aircraft of the squadron had been out searching for me.'

The article differs slightly from the official report, so perhaps the Intelligence people did not want to give too much away, but Mindy Blake certainly told me he had paddled an awfully long way and had been determined to make it.

* * *

Two weeks after his rescue Mindy was appointed leader of the Polish Wing at RAF Exeter, but on 21 September became wing leader of the Portreath Wing. Mindy had rarely drifted too far away from his engineering inventiveness and now he began working on a gyro gun-sight. He took the basic fighter gun-sight, and combined the features that were already in use with the gyroscopic bomb sight. Over many months, in between operations, he worked on this, and in the meantime was awarded the Distinguished Service Order, in July 1942, gazetted 11 May.

On 19 August 1942 came the Dieppe Raid, a combined operations assault on the harbour town. Russia had been pressing Winston Churchill to open a second front so as to take some of the heat off his forces on the Eastern Front, but there was no way this could happen at this stage of the war, with things still going badly in the Middle

Wing Commander M V Blake DFC in 1942.

East and in the Atlantic. However, the planners for a future invasion of France needed to know if it would be better to capture a port on the French coast, or, as happened in June 1944, land in Normandy and take their own port with them.

By this time Mindy had almost perfected his gyro gun-sight and was eager to try it out in combat. But then suddenly he was notified of a further promotion to group captain and a posting to Fighter Command operations. He need not have taken part in Operation Jubilee, but seeing that this was possibly the last chance he had to try out his gun-sight, he decided to lead his Wing. A vast array of fighter squadrons moved from various parts of the country down to the south-east, the Portreath Wing moving along to RAF Thorney Island, Hampshire. There it made a composite Wing made up of 130 and 131 Squadrons, plus the American 309th Fighter Squadron.

On the day, Mindy flew with 130 Squadron, as number two to 130's CO, Squadron Leader P J Simpson DFC, another Battle of Britain veteran. Off the French coast the Wing engaged several FW190s. Blake told me:

'I had been advised of a pending promotion to group captain ops, but having been working on a gyro gun-sight, wanted to try it out. I flew as wingman to Pete Simpson and over Dieppe saw several FW190s above the ships. I dived down and using the new sight shot down one of them. However, my moment of triumph was short-lived, as I was immediately engaged by three others and round and round we went, getting lower and lower with each turn. Suddenly a 190 came at me from head-on, seeing its engine cowling as large as a house right in front of me. My Spitfire was hit and the canopy shattered, but having flown with my goggles pushed up onto my head, Perspex splinters went into my eyes and for several moments I couldn't see a thing. Having religiously practised a 'blind' bale out, I found it easy to get out, undoing my straps and then I simply jettisoned the hood, kicked the stick forwards and shot out. Shortly afterwards I splashed down into the sea.'

He had engaged 190s from the 4th Staffel of JG26. Sergeant A W Utting had also been shot down, but did not survive, while Flight Sergeant Cane

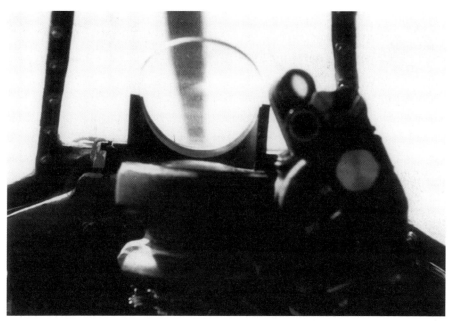

Blake's gyro gunsight which he invented and installed in W3561. It was while testing this over Dieppe that he was shot down and became a prisoner of war.

was wounded but managed to get his damaged Spitfire back to England. Blake was shot down by either the Staffel leader, Oberleutnant Kurt Ebersberger, Feldwebel Adolf Glunz or Feldwebel H Meyer. 131 Squadron also had two Spitfires damaged, while the 309th lost three, with two pilots killed.

'Clambering into my dinghy my eyes began to clear slightly but still badly impaired. Looking about I found that I was near another dinghy and calling out, discovered this was Lieutenant Robert D 'Buck' Ingrams of the 309th Fighter Squadron. Having formally introduced ourselves, Ingrams asked what we should do. We were only a few miles off the French coast, but north of the ships and the tide was taking us towards shore.

'Ingrams told me this was his first mission and was then somewhat surprised when I said I intended to paddle back to England. I told him I had done it before and intended to repeat the performance. Together,

Blake's Spitfire V W3561 in which he was shot down during the Dieppe show on 19 August 1942.

in our respective dinghies we began paddling, hoping the wind would change in our favour. I remember hearing the terrific noise of battle coming from the shore to the south of us.

'We struggled on for the rest of the day and into the night. I was well clothed but the American was only dressed in slacks and shirt sleeves and was soon affected by the cold, despite it being August. Finally he had to give up and saying our goodbyes, he allowed himself to drift ashore where he was captured.

'The wind did change and I finally began to make headway and for a while it looked as if I might make it but opposite Cap Gris Nez, late on the afternoon of the 20th, being only about five miles from the cliffs of Dover, my luck ran out and I was picked up by a German motorboat and became a prisoner. I was taken to a Paris hospital where a German doctor operated on my eyes and I was then questioned daily about the undamaged FW190 which a German pilot had landed at

RAF Pembrey, in south Wales, by mistake.[1] The Germans thought I had been the wing commander who had test-flown it. This continued for several weeks until they finally gave up and sent me off to a prison camp.

'On the journey I managed to smash a toilet window and climbing out, dropped from the moving train, but injured my face and left arm. I managed to evade for several days before being recaptured and eventually sent to Stalag Luft III [PoW No.759], where I was to remain for the rest of the war.'

Blake was released from captivity in May 1945, returning to New Zealand for an extended leave. He resumed his RAF career in 1946 at Fighter Command HQ, and then attended the RAF Staff College, finally being given a job with Transport Command. With the coming of the 1948 Olympic Games, having regained RAF champion in the pole vault for 1946, he was considered but not chosen. However, he retained the championship again in 1948 and 1949. He also returned to golfing.

He was at Bomber Command in 1950 and two years later was appointed Inspector-General, Northern Command NATO, in Oslo. It was in September 1952 that he won the amateur open golf tournament in Oslo, beating Denmark's Joergen Schnack, by 5 and 3. When residing in England he was a member of the Wentworth Golf Club. Between 1954 and 1958 he was at Air Ministry in London, but then decided to retire from the service.

Once in civvy-street he ran a factory which made car wax until 1960, at which time he worked for a textile company in Swansea, but later returned to his Surrey home, joining an electronics company. His lasting desire was to have his own workshop in his garden, where he could spend his time inventing. It was here he came up with the idea of the swing simulator he was testing when I first met him. It became a success and was developed further. He also found time to write two books on golf.

Mindy Blake died on 30 November 1981, aged only 68.

---

1. This FW190A-3 pilot, from III/JG2, had mistaken the Bristol Channel for the English Channel and thought he was landing on a French aerodrome, on 23 June. His surprise can be imagined, but the RAF were happy to have an undamaged 190 gifted to them.

Chapter 5

Squadron Leader T P M Cooper-Slipper DFC

W hen I was helping the late Wing Commander Bob Foster write his biography (*Tally Ho!*, Grub Street, 2008) this name came up several times, as Cooper-Slipper flew alongside Bob in 1940 with 605 Squadron. He sounded a very interesting character, and as Bob put it: 'Mike was a character in those days – quite mad – but he quietened down a lot in later life.'

Thomas Paul Michael Cooper-Slipper, known by the name of 'Mike', or sometimes as 'Slips', had been born at Kinver, near Stourbridge, Staffordshire, on 11 January 1921, the son of a vicar. He was educated at King Edward VI Grammar School in Stourbridge, and his first love, involving speed, was his enthusiasm to race motor-cycles. He joined the Royal Air Force in 1938, aged just 17½, directly from school.

Like many young men he joined via the short service commission route. He became a pilot via 12 E&RFTS at Prestwick, took the usual disciplinary course at Uxbridge, trained at 9 FTS at Hullavington, and joined 74 Squadron in July 1939. Moving on to Hurricane fighters he had brief stays at Fighter Command's Ferry Pool and then 11 Group's Pilot Pool at St Athan. Shortly after war began he started to increase his flying hours on the Hurricane, in order to join No. 605 (County of Warwick) Squadron in December 1939, at RAF Tangmere. Soon after he joined it, the squadron moved north to RAF Wick, in Scotland, the pilots being billeted in a local hotel, of which he wrote home: 'We live in a hotel run by two elderly sisters who were not completely up-to-date on the somewhat irregular behaviour of the modern fighter pilot.'

They remained in Scotland, chasing a few elusive 'bandits' during the winter, until the 'balloon went up' in France and once the British ground troops were retreating towards Dunkirk, several squadrons were moved south to join in the air cover operation, including 605, who moved to Hawkinge on 21 May. Although Operation Dynamo was not to start until the 26th, several squadrons had engagements with enemy aircraft north and east of Dunkirk, and Mike was in action on day two, as he later recalled:

Flight Lieutenant Mike Cooper-Slipper DFC, 605 Squadron, 1940.

'The Squadron carried out a patrol in to France behind Calais and Boulogne without seeing any other aircraft; it was the last time that we had that pleasure during our stay at Hawkinge! We took off again about 11.00 hours and the two flights got separated over France. 'A' Flight was jumped by 109s and lost a couple of pilots. 'B' Flight got itself split into two sections in cloud. My Section, in which I was Number Three, came across two He111s at about 5,000 feet, about 500 feet below us. The Section Leader saw them but did not attack; No.2 and myself took one each and set them on fire. I was excited and went alongside, whereupon the front gunner gave me a burst, including two through the canopy. I then dropped back and shot a couple of crew members getting out of the top of their canopy. The 111 went down in a spin and crashed in a field. On getting back to Hawkinge, I got an enormous strip torn off for leaving the Section Leader.'

The bombers were from KG27, with an escort of 109s from JG3, and 605 did indeed suffer losses. One pilot was killed and three others force-landed, two pilots being wounded. KG27 had three of their aircraft shot down, one being flown by the *Gruppenkommandeur*, Hauptmann Ulrich Schirmer, who was killed.

On the 25th, again over France, Mike shot down a Ju87 dive-bomber, no doubt one of several lost by StG2 found attacking refugee columns. The following afternoon, several Ju88s were encountered, 605 claiming three.

Mike shot down one from 7./KG4 over Dunkirk, that went down and crashed into the sea. None of the four-man crew survived. One of these was Hauptmann Rabe, a senior officer in KG4.

However, 605 had suffered a number of casualties which resulted in the squadron being withdrawn from the fighting on the 28th and sent back north, to RAF Drem, Scotland. Mike later wrote:

'The squadron was withdrawn. We had lost half our pilots either dead or missing; our aircraft were all shot up and in bad shape. I had about 75 bullet holes through my Hurricane! There was quite a collection of shot up aircraft that made it back to Hawkinge.

'The batmen were full of news when they woke us in the morning with a cup of tea and a biscuit or two. One prize bit of news was that the Germans had landed during the night, and were fighting down in Folkestone at that moment!'

Despite some delay in moving north, due to a shortage of petrol, 605 eventually headed back to Scotland where it rebuilt its strength with new pilots and aircraft, also taking time to teach the newcomers how things should be done. Gerry Edge, who had been one of the flight commanders, was promoted to lead the squadron at this time, and he recalls Mike helping in the training. Teaching the pilots to fly in close formation, Mike thought on a few occasions his flight commander needed waking up so would edge in and tap his leader's wing tip with his and then pull away quickly, pretending not to be the culprit. Edge later remarked that Slips was a very good pilot – and very young – and had been the only pilot to have been on every patrol flown from Hawkinge.

The squadron remained at Drem until the start of September, moving south once more on the 7th. As they began to arrive at Croydon, they could see London had been attacked that same day for the first time. Smoke and flame coloured the late afternoon sky. It was a sobering arrival back into the main combat arena. Bob Foster wrote:

'As we headed in we could see all this smoke while still some 30 miles away, and as Croydon hove into view we could not fail to notice a huge pall of smoke that continued to hang over the city to the north of us. As daylight gave way to darkness further bombing stoked up the fires and created more, so that we could see this red sky in the distance. It was like Dante's Inferno.'

* * *

At Croydon the squadron found themselves in an unusual if not unique situation. Alongside the southern edge of the aerodrome ran Forester's Drive, most of which had been evacuated by the locals, and the houses became the homes of officers and other ranks. One side of the road was for the airmen, the airfield side for officers and pilots. So here they were, living in fairly modern semi-detached houses, in upstairs bedrooms, with bathrooms and kitchens, just like being at home, but walking out into the back garden, their Hurricanes were at dispersal the other side of the rear fences. And of course, London, for some relaxation was just a short train journey away.

The day after their arrival they were in action. Scrambled to intercept a raid, they met a large formation of bombers with escorting fighters, and waded in. The two flights were led by Flight Lieutenants C F 'Bunny' Currant and A A McKeller, and no sooner had they made the interception than the enemy force began to turn back south without bombing. A couple of Dorniers were hit and two 109s claimed damaged, but Mike Cooper-Slipper claimed a kill, as his combat report indicates:

'I was Yellow 2 in 605 Squadron ordered to take off at 1150. Yellow Section was the rear section of the formation which climbed to 17,000 feet. A large formation of enemy aircraft heading west was sighted about ten miles to the north. As the leading section approached the enemy bombers the enemy aircraft turned to meet them. At this time about 15 Me109s came through a slight haze and attacked Yellow Section. Yellow 3 was shot down in flames and I turned to meet the next wave of enemy fighters, one of which passed me on my right side and then turned to the left. I turned inside and slightly below him getting in a 2-3 second burst at about 100 yards. The enemy aircraft slid away on its back and I did not see it again. P/O Ingle saw this aircraft going down in a steep spiral with large volumes of black smoke pouring from it. I broke away from the fight and after diving 10,000 feet found myself above and on the port beam of three Do215s. I did a beam attack on the port enemy aircraft, closing to 50 yards with a 4–5 second burst. The E/A appeared to lag behind the other two, then I went into some cloud and did not see them again. I returned to Croydon and landed at 12.50.'

Yellow 3 was Pilot Officer Jack Fleming who baled out, badly burned, but he survived. The 109s were from JG53, the Dorniers from KG2.

On the 11th Mike damaged a He111, and on the 12th shared a Ju88 with Bunny Currant and Sergeant E W 'Ricky' Wright over the Channel. This was a machine of 1(F)122 on a long range reconnaissance mission during cloudy conditions. There were no survivors. At the time it was thought this German machine was a Dornier.

It was definitely a Dornier on the 15th, south of Dungeness, and claimed in spectacular fashion. The squadron had already been in action late morning, claiming a number of enemy aircraft shot down, and after lunch they were scrambled again, this time finding three waves of bombers and fighters between Maidstone and Folkestone. Once again several of the raiders were claimed shot down, but 'Slips', having used up all his ammunition, found himself behind a Dornier from 5./KG3. His Hurricane had already been damaged and his lateral control made useless; he was only able to move his control column about three inches forward and back. He then collided with the bomber, although the story was told that he deliberately rammed the German. It was a good story, but Mike said later that he had no way of avoiding it. Hitting the Dornier, one wing of the bomber was ripped away, so too was the Hurricane's port wing. Some years later, Bunny Currant said of this incident:

'Now Cooper-Slipper, he was a lucky chap. We attacked a formation of German bombers. I was leading the squadron at the time, and I got there with plenty of height on the port side of the German aircraft which were coming this way, and we did a beam attack from above; I led with Cooper-Slipper being my number two.

'I took the first Vic of bombers, fired at them, broke straight down beneath then, looked up, and when I looked up there was one Dornier going round slowly with one wing off, and alongside it a Hurricane going round very, very much quicker, because it was a little aeroplane, also with one wing off; then a parachute suddenly appeared.

'When we got back Cooper-Slipper was missing. He was only 19 at the time and later he rang up to say he was all right and was down in Kent somewhere, and he came back and brought me a German Mae West. What happened was, he actually dived and hit the wing-root of the Dornier, glanced off it upside down, into an inverted spin with one wing off. All he had to do was to open his hood, undo his straps, and he shot out because of the inverted spin, like a cork out of a bottle, quite unhurt. He was very lucky.'

According to the squadron diary, he brought back two German life vests and a rubber dinghy that had been presented to him by the Maidstone police. He had landed in a field at March Farm, near Marden, and the Dornier went in on Skinner's Farm, Beltring, east of Tonbridge. One of the crew, pilot Oberfeldwebel Erich Rilling, was killed, baling out too low, but the other three landed safely. Mike's Hurricane (L2012) crashed at 'The Leas', Yalding, south-west of Maidstone.

Mike had been slightly injured in this action but was soon back flying, damaging a Me109 on 27 September in a scrap above Sittingbourne. It was to be his last successful combat with 605, although he remained active during the last weeks of 1940. His reward was the Distinguished Flying Cross, gazetted on 26 November, and the 'ramming' incident was perpetuated in the citation:

Flying Officer Cooper-Slipper has displayed great skill and daring in air combat. On one occasion he deliberately rammed and destroyed a hostile aircraft after his own controls had been practically shot away. He has destroyed seven enemy aircraft and damaged three others.

Like most pilots after a long period of action, he was sent on rest, although the 'rest' was actually to become a flying instructor with all its responsibilities, sometimes even having one's life in the hands of some embryo pilot. In September 1941 he was sent to join 96 Squadron at Cranage as a flight commander, then to 74 Squadron, and finally to join a new squadron, No. 135, formed at RAF Baginton in August 1941 under one of Britain's most successful fighter pilots of the time, Squadron Leader F R Carey DFC DFM. This squadron, along with others, were slated for overseas duty, probably the Middle East, sailing in November towards Africa. While twenty pilots made their way by air, the rest, and the ground personnel, embarked on HMT (His Majesty's Troopship) A6 – *Duchess of Bedford,* Cooper-Slipper being officer in charge. However, the Japanese attack on Pearl Harbor on 7 December changed everything, and the destination was changed to India.

Over the next few weeks the pilots made their way piecemeal across Africa ending up in Burma, their ground crews taking the long sea route via Durban. By January 1942, pilots had arrived at Mingaladon, Burma, knowing that the big British base at Singapore was under serious threat. Meantime, Mike and twenty-three other pilots of 232, 17, 135 and 136 Squadrons arrived at Singapore, along with fifty-one Hurricane IIBs in crates, in convoy DM-2, on 13 January. The immediate task was to un-crate and assemble the aeroplanes. The other main aircraft type at Singapore was Brewster Buffalo fighters with 243 and 488 Squadrons.

Japanese aircraft were often in the sky above Singapore and several combats occurred. The new arrivals were formed into one unit, becoming effectively 232 Squadron. Mike Cooper-Slipper's first positive engagement came on the 22nd, with bombers and fighters bombing Kallang airfield. Eight aircraft of 232 took off at 10.55 am, and then Mike's C Flight showed up as the other group were engaging a large formation of enemy bombers. As C Flight did so, one bomber was already going down on fire. Mike attacked another bomber – a Mitsubishi G3M, code named *Nell.* Its port engine caught fire and the bomber turned over and went down. Quickly turning in behind another Vic of bombers he set one on fire, but he was then hit by cross-fire from other bombers, his Hurricane being hit several times. Forced to break away, he got his damaged fighter safely down on Kallang. Sergeant S N Hackforth later reported seeing both bombers go down, one on fire, the other trailing smoke.

Mike had to spend a few days in hospital with a stomach complaint, and upon release was in action again. However, Singapore was lost and he had to lead survivors from the squadron to Palembang from where he led missions strafing barges loaded with Japanese soldiers, and in the air he is reported to have shot down three more bombers. Finally the Japanese captured Palembang and he was taken prisoner, but fortunately, in the confusion that followed, he was able to slip away and got himself to Java, but not before the truck he was in struck a land mine. He was badly wounded and evacuated to Ceylon in a hospital ship, spending the next six months in hospitals in India, South Africa. After being discharged he went to Egypt to take command of the Special Performance Flight there, becoming chief test pilot at No. 103 Maintenance Unit at Aboukir.

During this time he tested specially-equipped Spitfires that were able to reach the heights flown by high-flying German Ju88P and Ju188 photographic reconnaissance aircraft. He had two combats with these aircraft, damaging a Ju188 during one of them. However, he was now restricted to low level flying and began flying C47 Dakota aircraft with 267 Squadron, before he was posted home to England in 1944, where he became chief test pilot at RAF Lichfield for the rest of the war.

Mike left the RAF in 1946, emigrating to Canada the following year where he took a job with Avro Canada in Ontario, soon becoming a company test pilot in 1948. The next year he became head of development of the Avro Jet Liner, and in 1950 Captain of the *Orenda* Lancaster test bed. He then began flying the Orenda-engined F-86 Sabre fighter, before moving on to fly and test the Avro CF-100 *Canuck* jet fighter. In 1955 he became chief test pilot for Orenda Engines. This was followed in 1957, after completing the USAF

Test Pilot for Avro in Canada, Mike Cooper-Slipper.

commanders' course on B47s of the US Strategic Air Command (SAC), by flying several hundred hours of development work with the *Iroquois* engines, loaned to the Royal Canadian Air Force.

He finally retired from flying in 1959, and remained in Canada, working in aviation sales, starting with de Havilland, and later with Field Aviation. In his later years Mike worked for the Ontario Ministry of Industry and Trade, travelling extensively in order to advance Ontario's aviation manufacturing companies. In 1986 he retired to Victoria, British Columbia, where he spent his time pursuing photography and working on his Alpha Romeo car. In 2003 Mike was inducted into Canada's Aviation Hall of Fame.

He died in Vancouver on 23 February 2004, aged 83, with his wife Rita and adoring granddaughter Jessica by his side. He had married Rita in November 1941, just a few days before he sailed to the Far East. They had a son Christopher who also became a pilot, lived in Toronto and also worked for Field Aviation, becoming vice-president of marketing. In 2014 Chris was also inducted into Canada's Aviation Hall of Fame.

Chapter 6

Squadron Leader Count M M E R B Czernin
DSO MC DFC

Manfred Maria Edmund Ralph Beckett Czernin was the subject of my first book, which the publishers entitled *Double Mission, RAF Fighter Ace and SOE Agent*. I had no problem with this, and who am I do argue with my first publisher? After all, it did cover the amazing dual roles Czernin had handled during the Second World War.

It was quite by chance that I became involved with his story, after seeing a memoriam notice in a London newspaper, merely signed by 'M'. I deduced that an M Czernin might be living in London, and the telephone book confirmed this. A call to the number resulted in me meeting 'M' who, it turned out, had been his former wife Maud. It quickly emerged that Manfred Czernin had had an absolutely fascinating life and one that just had to be written down, hence the book.

Manfred had been born in Berlin on 18 January 1913, the fourth son of Count Otto Czernin von und zu Chudenitz of Dimokur, Austria. That made the baby's formal name very long! Otto was an Austrian diplomat (of Hungarian extraction) and he had met, courted and then married Lucille (Lucy) Katharine Beckett, the daughter of Ernest William Becket, 2nd Baron Grimthorpe (1856-1917). He had bought a villa just outside Ravello, on the southern Italian Amalfi Coast, and it was while the young Lucy

Flying Officer Count Manfred Czernin shortly before the war began.

was staying there that she met Otto, then a diplomat at the Austrian Embassy in Rome.

However, by the time Manfred came along the marriage was failing, and when the First World War began the following year, Otto returned to his homeland with three older sons, leaving Lucy to look after his newborn son in Italy. At the end of the First World War, with the Austro-Hungarian Empire in ruins, Otto decided that Lucy should keep Manfred, and take him to England to be educated. This she did, and once of school age, she put him into Oundle School. She later reverted to her maiden name and was known as Mrs Beckett. He was better known as just M B Czernin.

His mother re-married in 1926, to Captain Oliver Frost OBE MC, who had been a pilot in the First World War, so it was no doubt this influence which later led Manfred into the RAF, following a brief period working on a tobacco plantation in Umtali, Southern Rhodesia. Manfred eventually joined the RAF on a short service commission in 1935 and once successfully passing his flying training, became a bomber pilot with No. 83 Squadron, between December 1936 and June 1938, flying silver, two-seat biplane day bombers such as the Hawker Hind and Hawker Hart. Once his short service period ended, he became a member of the RAF Reserve and it was while attending summer camp in 1939 that war was declared, so Manfred was in uniform from day one. He also became a married man, having married Maud Hamilton on 4 November. They would have a daughter and a son.

Manfred was now almost 27 years of age, but he managed to get himself on to fighters and, via No. 12 Group's Fighter Pool, was posted to 504 Squadron at Debden, Essex. Next he moved to 213 Squadron at Wittering, and then to No. 85 Squadron in France on 9 May 1940, the day before the Germans invaded France and the Low Countries. Some people might have felt they were in the wrong place at the wrong time, but Manfred was thinking quite the reverse.

His Squadron was part of the Air Component, the other unit being 87 Squadron. They were both in action from dawn on 10 May. Of course, his new comrades were slightly taken aback by having someone named Count Manfred Czernin thrust upon them. He spoke perfect English of course, but was also fluent in Italian, French – and German. Was he on the right side? Just to confuse everyone, Manfred, who was always ready to take advantage of his background, informed everyone that he had previously been in the Luftwaffe and had flown Messerschmitt 109s!

On 16 May, he had his first real combat, but was bested by a German pilot, who damaged his Hurricane, forcing him to make a landing at the nearest airfield. In a fight with fighters from II/JG26, Leutnant Hillecke of the Stab Staffel got him. The time was 3.50 pm, although Hillecke claimed a French Hawk 75, but then another German pilot also claimed a Morane 406. With no French losses recorded, obviously the Germans' recognition skills were wanting.

Three days later it was Manfred's turn. In fighting, he claimed four German bombers shot down, and was credited with a He111 destroyed, another unconfirmed, and two Do17s destroyed. The Heinkels were from KG54 and several were either shot down or damaged. The Dorniers were from KG76. One of them Manfred spotted making a strafing attack on troop columns and he shot it down into some woods east of Valenciennes at 8 am. He claimed the second one he attacked but this may have only been damaged.

The following day, the 20th, he found and claimed a Henschal 126 observation machine. Again it was early morning, 7 am. A pilot of 3 Squadron had first attacked it, south-east of Arras, but Manfred then chased it and shot it down west of Cambrai. It was a machine from 3.(H)/41, its pilot being killed and observer wounded. On the afternoon of the 20th, his CO, Squadron Leader M F Peacock, along with Manfred, Pilot Officer R W Burton and Pilot Officer R W Shrewsbury, went out to strafe German troop columns east of Arras. All four dived to the attack, being met by much ground fire. As Manfred ended his run and pulled up he looked round to find himself alone. It was thought the other three had been hit and crashed. They had indeed been shot down, and killed, but apparently, unknown to Manfred, they had been caught by Me109s of JG3. One of the German pilots was Leutnant Franz von Werra, who later found fame as the only German pilot to escape captivity, but from Canada. His story is told in *The One That Got Away*, in both book and film.

Later that afternoon, Manfred and another pilot escorted two transport aircraft back to England taking back the squadron's ground personnel. All the RAF squadrons were now in retreat, falling back from airfield to airfield, while the main British army was pushed back to the Channel coast, evacuating from Dunkirk. 85 and 87 Squadrons headed west across the French countryside until they were flying patrols over Le Havre where further British troops were trying to get away by sea. Back in England, Manfred was sent to 17 Squadron. They had arrived back from France too but then returned to continue the fight in the west of France, on 8 June. On 12 June Manfred claimed a He111 destroyed, probably one from KG54 again, and on the 14th a Me109.

Once finally back in England, 17 Squadron were again at Debden by the 18th. This was in 12 Group, north of the Thames, but several times they were moved into 11 Group further south, operating from a forward base. It was during this period that Manfred opened his 'Battle of Britain account' by shooting down a Do17Z on 12 July, in company with 151 Squadron. This machine came from II/KG2 and went into the Channel at 09.30 am, and he assisted Flying Officer D H W Hanson in knocking down another. On 24 July he damaged a Ju88, and damaged another on 8 August off the Norfolk coast, the bomber jettisoning its bombs over the sea. On the 18th he damaged a Me109 although he had to chase it towards the French coast; but then two more 109s were spotted behind, forcing Manfred to break off and go home. There were several 109s that did not make it back or who returned wounded, or crash-landed in France.

Manfred still managed to pull the legs of his fellow pilots as he had done in his early days with 85 Squadron. They all knew, of course, that his background helped to ferment a number of stories that he gladly offered them. Newspaper journalists were always on the look-out for unusual things to print and somehow latched onto a story about Czernin. One story that appeared in the press amused the other pilots in the squadron:

IN FIVE FORCES

British-born count Manfred Czernin, a relative by marriage of Dr Schuschnigg, former Austrian Chancellor, is now a Flying Officer in the RAF, serving with a Hurricane squadron. Having recently brought down his eighth Nazi aircraft, Count Czernin is spending a week's leave in London. He walked in to dinner at the Mayfair last evening accompanied by his elkhound *Cairo* [actually its name was spelt *Kyro*] whose picture is painted on the side of his plane.

When meat was refused Cairo, Count Czernin shared his portion with the dog.

The airman's tunic has French, Belgium, Czech and Dutch buttons to show he has served with units of these forces.

Reading this, his pals in 17 Squadron decided to write to the paper's editor, with their version of 'the truth' and this too appeared in the paper:

BAGGED PLANES

The adjutant and members of the RAF squadron to which Count Czernin belongs wrote me a letter. They say: – 'In fairness to our fellow pilot we should tell you that his bag of Nazi planes to date is eighteen not eight. He is such a modest bloke we think it our duty to let you know this.'

Insult from Hitler.

Before the Anschluss Count Czernin owned the Czernin Palace at Vienna. Hitler wrote him and offered 30,000 RM for the Palace. The Count threw this insulting letter into the fire. An American had offered him £50,000 for a single picture from his gallery. Hitler has got the Czernin Palace now. It cost him nothing.

During a lull in the fighting, the pilots got one of the ground crew boys to fashion a large medal which was duly presented to him at dispersal by the CO on 20 August. It was referred to as 'The Line Shooter's Medal.'

However, Manfred's big day came on 25 August, the squadron having moved down to RAF Tangmere. Led by the CO, Squadron Leader C W Williams, the squadron went up against a large formation of Me110s that afternoon. In fact it was nearing tea-time when the call to scramble came and they climbed into the sky above Weymouth. Still climbing hard, they found the 110s above them, with Me109s higher still. The 110 pilots saw their approach and began to peel off and down, heading into the climbing Hurricanes. Manfred watched as Williams and one Me110 came towards each other head-on, both firing. At about 400 yards from each other both seemed to stop in mid-flight and flutter gently to pieces. Manfred saw the other 110s begin to form one of their famous defensive circles, designed to protect

Manfred Czernin being 'awarded' the Line-Shooter's Medal by his CO, S/Ldr C W Williams, at Tangmere on 20 August 1940. Williams was shot down and killed five days later. 'Kyro' is in the foreground.

each other with their rear gunners. Manfred saw a 110 start to break away, opened fire on it and set it on fire. Others watched as the 110 dived into the sea far below. Manfred half rolled, got behind another 110 and his fire set this one ablaze too and it fell towards the water. He was then attacked by a 'friendly' Spitfire and had to evade being shot down but having done so, clamped onto a third 110. His fire caused smoke to issue from it but then Spitfires of 609 Squadron were hammering at the German too. It finally went down to crash into a wood near Warmwell. The 110s came from ZG2, which had been escorting bombers of KG51. It was a very confused air fight, and 609 Squadron appear to have claimed the lion's share of the action. Nevertheless, Manfred was credited with three and Williams one. Other 110s limped away damaged. Williams was the only fatal loss, although Flight Lieutenant A W A Bayne had to bale out of his fighter, landing in the sea from where he was rescued. That evening Manfred flew his first night patrol – without seeing anything. His fuel began to run low and as luck would have it, he had to land back at Tangmere during an air raid! The squadron then spent a few days flying from RAF Northolt, but had no successes.

On the first anniversary of the war, 3 September, Manfred was in action once again. 17 Squadron had gone back to Debden the previous day, and this morning they sat around at readiness. This continued until 10.25, when the shrill ring of the dispersal hut telephone sent them running to their fighters.

Enemy aircraft were coming towards their area, and when they saw them it was an awe inspiring sight, something like 150-200 raiders.

Many were Dorniers and they were spotted over the River Crouch estuary. They came from II/KG2 and were heading for nearby RAF North Weald. Escorting Me110s were those from I/ZG2 and II/ZG26. Alfie Bayne led his section into the attack on a gaggle of Dorniers while Manfred led his section, Sergeant Desmond Fopp and Pilot Officer Geoff Pittman, into a head-on attack on some others, estimated to have been about forty. Escorting 110s were also in evidence but the attack had no visible effect on either types. However, one 110 turned after Manfred's Hurricane from the beam, forcing Manfred into a tight turn. Being able to turn tighter than the Messerschmitt, Manfred soon closed in on his antagonist, and opened up with two quick deflection bursts. His target hit, went straight down, burst into flames, hit the ground and exploded. Manfred was quickly behind another 110, which was also hit and dived vertically. He lost sight of it as he had to stop himself attacking three Blenheims that sailed into his vision. However, his second 110 was later confirmed, its wreckage located in a wood close to Malden. Probably the machine was from 6./ZG26. It came down along the Malden to Latchingdon Road, the captured crew being Leutnant Walther Manhart and Unteroffizier Werner Drews, the latter being severely wounded.

The two German Gruppen lost seven aircraft in this fight with 17 and 46 Squadrons, with others returning home damaged. 17 Squadron lost one pilot killed, and Fopp baled out badly burned. The new CO, Squadron Leader A G Miller force landed near North Weald but was unhurt. 46 Squadron also lost one pilot with two others having to bale out.

Two days later Manfred again scored multiple kills. North Weald was the target again for one raid, but although 17 Squadron were scrambled, they made no contact. In mid-afternoon they were sent off again, this time heading for the Thames Estuary, as He111s of 7/KG53 were going for the oil storage tanks at Thamshaven, escorted by 109s from III/JG54. Not far from Chatham, Manfred saw about fifteen Heinkels and some thirty Me109s heading in. Led by the CO, the Hurricanes intercepted near Gravesend, while the Polish pilots from 303 Squadron engaged the fighter escort.

Manfred had Sergeants Glyn Griffiths and C A Chew in his section. He and Cliff Chew closed in leaving Griffiths to keep a look-out behind. Fire from Manfred's fighter set one Heinkel's starboard engine ablaze. As it began to lose height, Pilot Officer Eric Lock of 41 Squadron continued to attack this bomber which finally ditched and sank just off the Nore. Meantime, Manfred and Chew closed in behind another bomber. Both attacked and the German crashed near Chatham, probably in the sea. Two of its crew managed to bale out but one of the parachutes failed to deploy. The pilot had been Feldwebel Anton Maier, who survived. The crew of the first Heinkel all died, and only one body was washed ashore one month later at Reculver.

Then the 109s got in on the act, coming down on the Hurricanes. One came behind Manfred, but he throttled back, turned and got in a position to attack. The 109 reared up when hit, and seemed to flop down and dive earthwards. Its pilot, Feldwebel Heinrich Dettmer of 9/JG54, baled out but his parachute too failed to open and he fell to his death on Pitsea Marshes, where his body remained undiscovered for twelve days. The Gruppen Kommandeur, Hauptmann Fritz Ultsch, was shot down by Alf Bayne. As his 109 disintegrated, Ultsch baled out but his parachute failed to open. The fighter crashed at Bowers Gifford. KG53 lost two bombers and had two more damaged, one making a belly-landing at Vendeville. JG54 lost two fighters, adding to losses it sustained during the morning.

On the 7th Manfred sat for Captain Cuthbert Orde, the war artist, employed by the Air Ministry to make charcoal sketches of a large number of RAF men and women over the initial war years.

Four days later, 17's day began with a convoy patrol and in the afternoon came the scramble to intercept hostile aircraft. They ran into about fifteen Me110s and in the resulting combat Manfred and Bayne each bagged one. They came from ZG26, which lost four aircraft, two by 17 Squadron, and the other two going to 73 Squadron. Manfred appears to have accounted for Oberleutnant Walter Henken, the Gruppe adjutant of the Stab Staffel of II Gruppe. His body was not recovered, but his gunner, Feldwebel Josef Radlmair, was washed ashore at Broadstairs on 23 October.

Manfred shot down a Ju88 on the 19th, but rather than a massive air assault by the enemy, this rainy day saw just isolated raids by single aircraft. Manfred led his section up, consisting of Griffiths and Sergeant L H Bartlett. Climbing above cloud, control vectored the three fighters towards their radar plot out to sea. A hostile aircraft was approaching a convoy in the

North Sea. They were still passing through some cloud at 14,000 feet but Manfred spotted the enemy machine, which turned out to be a Ju88 some ten miles away. They began to approach but the bomber was moving fast and it seemed unlikely they would reach it before being seen, at which time the enemy pilot was bound to nip into cloud cover. Then, without reason, the 88 suddenly turned, changing course, heading straight towards them. When the German crew finally saw the danger they rapidly started to dive but Manfred was allowed to make a beam attack from slightly underneath the bomber, giving its starboard port engine a three-second burst of .303 fire. Smoke began to trail from this engine which then promptly stopped. Griffiths then attacked, followed by Len Bartlett, leaving the 88 with both engines on fire. The Hurricanes continued to harry the bomber until it finally glided into the sea ten miles off the English coast. The Junkers came from 1/KGr.806 and none of the four crewmen survived.

In one of many air fights over the mid-September period that produced few real successes, Manfred managed to wing a Me109 on the 24th, losing sight of it as it began to descend off Margate. He was credited with a 'probable'. On the 27th more heavy raids on London occurred, mostly by bomb-carrying Me109 and Me110 fighters. The Luftwaffe had suffered serious casualties over recent weeks, so their tactics changed to that of nuisance raids by fighters carrying bombs.

These fighters were harried all the way from Dungeness to London, 17 Squadron being scrambled shortly after 9 am. Together with 73 Squadron they attacked about 30 Me110s over Redhill. After this scrap, 17 Squadron put in claims for five destroyed and two probably destroyed. The fighters were from V/LG1. Manfred claimed one destroyed that he saw crash and explode east of Redhill.

Manfred was now awarded the Distinguished Flying Cross. The citation appeared in the *London Gazette* dated 1 October 1940, and read:

This officer has displayed great keenness in his desire to engage the enemy, and has destroyed nine of their aircraft. In August 1940, he led his section in a head-on attack on large formations of enemy aircraft, destroying three of them.

In early October, 17 Squadron had moved its base to Martlesham Heath, Suffolk. The Battle of Britain seemed to have slackened somewhat, but night raiders were beginning to be reported. Long hours at readiness became a bore if nothing much happened, but Manfred and Pittman got a scramble shortly after 2 pm, in order to investigate an unidentified aircraft. In ten-tenths cloud they climbed in the direction specified and Manfred eventually spotted an aircraft flying west. He fired a warning burst across its nose as he could see RAF markings on it. The aircraft's crew fired off a Red-Red flare, which was not the colours of the day, but as far as Manfred could observe, it was a Blenheim.

Leaving this aircraft, the two pilots continued to fly through much broken cloud and found another aircraft, but this time one that carried black crosses on its wings. He attacked, his fire smashing into the starboard wing and engine. This began to flame and the aircraft dived into cloud. Pittman closed in before it did so and also opened fire, but finally had to break away as the enemy pilot, either with courage or ignorance, took his machine through the Harwich balloon barrage!

There were two Do17s damaged this day, one from 9/KG2, damaged by fighter attack over the Channel, which got home. Another was one from I/NJG2, out on an intruder sortie over England. It got home with three crewmen wounded, but the Dornier was a write-off.

One week later, the 24th, Manfred and his section of Sergeant R D Hogg and Pilot Officer F Fajtl, a Czechoslovakian pilot, were scrambled. A suspected German raider had flown towards the Midlands and the three Hurricanes were vectored to a spot where the Controller believed the hostile would be upon its return. The weather conditions were far from good, and unknown to him, the raider was being intercepted by Hurricanes from No.1 Squadron, who managed to inflict some damage on it. However, Manfred spotted the bomber – a Dornier 215 – on its own, and led the attack. All three pilots made firing passes at it and it began to trail smoke and flame, finally going down to crash near the Crown Inn, Eaton Socon, near St Neots, on the Bedfordshire/Huntingdonshire border. Leutnant Erwin Meyer of 3/ Aufkl.Gr.Ob.d.l had been on a photographic reconnaissance operation over Coventry and Birmingham. The crew baled out, but only one survived. This survivor, Gefrieter Max Dorr, the flight engineer, later confirmed it had been the attack by the last three Hurricanes that had brought them down.

Manfred's final contribution to the Battle came on 28 October, the day he attacked and damaged two Dorniers over the North Sea. This was followed by the probable destruction of a Me109 on the 30th. In a brief fight Manfred seemed to riddle a 109 and it began to fall earthwards into cloud. Wreckage later appeared to confirm its fall but pilots of 504 Squadron also claimed a 109 in the same location and time, so who actually got it, or perhaps they all did, is uncertain. It was a JG3 machine and a second 109 from this unit that was damaged, but managed to get home.

* * *

The squadron was still at Martlesham in November, and at the time the Italian Air Force was making a contribution against Britain. Mussolini's Italy had come into the war on what the dictator thought was the winning side – Germany's – in June 1940, and he was keen to show Hitler how well his airmen could perform.

Manfred missed the big Italian effort on 11 November, although his squadron saw some of the action, and on the 17th, Manfred was fooled during an interception over Suffolk. It was no doubt a case of the eye seeing what the heart wanted it to see. Considering the number of actions he had had against Me110s during the summer, for some strange reason he determined that a formation of 110s were Fiat BR20 bombers. The day had started early with 17, and 257 Squadron, also at Martlesham, being sent up to cover a convoy. No sooner had they got into position than the Controller was vectoring them onto a raid estimated at 50+. They found the hostiles at 10,000 feet near RAF Wattisham, but they began a turn so the interception did not take place until shortly after 9 am, over Ipswich. Rather than Italian bombers, the enemy consisted of two groups of bomb-carrying Me110s of EG210 (Erprobungs-Gruppe 210), escorted by yellow-nosed Me109s of JG26, led by the formidable Adolf Galland. The main engagement began to the east of Ipswich and Manfred curved in behind one 110 that he was convinced was a BR20. Later he was to recall seeing Italian markings on the aircraft, but whether he was deceiving himself, or whether the Germans were carrying such markings to swell the idea of Italy's involvement, is not known. Manfred opened fire and saw his bullets hit the tail, part of which came away, and one engine stop. As it began to trail smoke, Manfred, his attention having wavered, suddenly found himself under attack. A 109 was right behind him. The pilot was none other than Galland who, opening fire from 150 down to 50 metres, saw the Hurricane burst into flames and shed numerous pieces before falling away steeply, leaving a smoke trail. It was the German's 54th, and he would also knock down two of 257 Squadron's machines in this fight. As Galland pulled away after shooting down Czernin, he spotted the 110 his opponent had attacked, going down streaming smoke from both its engines. Although Manfred was only able to claim one 'Fiat damaged', the 110 eventually crashed into the sea. In the meantime, Manfred had exited his doomed fighter and was swinging gently below his parachute, landing near Bredfield. EG210 lost three aircraft in this action, one being credited to Alf Bayne, one to Sergeant Neil Cameron, and one shared between Flying Officer F K Kordula (Czech) and Pilot Officer P Niemiec (Polish). Oddly enough, pilots of 41 Squadron on the fringe of this scrap also reported seeing Italian aircraft, or at least, aircraft with Italian markings.

This effectively ended Manfred Czernin's RAF combat career. He had done well in combat both over France and during the Battle of Britain. As fellow pilot Neil Cameron later told me: 'I am sure there is no need to tell you that he was an extremely colourful character and though, in my estimation, his actual flying ability was not of the highest standard, he was undoubtedly one of the best shots in the business.' Cameron later became Marshal of the RAF, Baron Cameron of Balhousie KT GCB CBE DSO DFC AE.

Manfred remained with the squadron until early 1941. There was the odd skirmish with enemy aircraft but nothing of significance. He left the squadron at the end of May and was sent to be an instructor at No. 52 OTU, now established at Debden, but in July it moved to Aston Down. Completing six months as an instructor, Manfred was promoted to squadron leader and given command of 65 Squadron at Tangmere, flying Spitfires, but after a week this was changed to OC of 222 Squadron at North Weald. In 1942 he was attached to 41 Squadron, but at 29 he was thought to be a little old for front line fighter combat. He was now posted overseas, his last operational sortie from England being during the famous Channel Dash show on 12 February.

Manfred Czernin DFC while an instructor at No. 58 OTU in 1941. The significance of the goose is not known. Pilot Officer Viv Jacobs, third from left, later flew with 136 Squadron in Burma.

In March he was sent to India where he took command of No. 146 Squadron. His area of operations was Upper Assam and although Hurricanes were the main equipment, it also had Curtis Mohawks on strength, and even the odd Brewster Buffalo and Hawker Audax.

Spending most of 1942 flying all sorts of missions over the jungle, and other places, it was obvious that he was in need of a rest, so was sent to 224 Group HQ, but was on the sick list for some while. Eventually it was time to return to Britain.

He was hoping to be given command of another squadron but at 30 his chances were slim despite his past record. He was spotted one day moping around Air Ministry in London by an air marshal who had known him earlier. Czernin talked with him, and the AM told him to come and see him the next day. That meeting resulted in Manfred being recruited into SOE –

Special Operations Executive. With his languages and knowledge of Europe, especially Italy, his experience would be invaluable.

So, in due course, he became a trained SOE agent, and was twice parachuted into northern Italy to work with Italian partisans. In mid-1944 he went by US Liberator bomber to his first mission, one mainly of reconnaissance of the area on the Austro-Italian border. Here he worked with the local partisans. On at least three occasions they had to evade German troops, each time losing all their equipment, but each time they were able to evade and lose themselves in the vast Italian mountains of the Friuli region. It also seems that at one stage Manfred was arrested but the Germans were not fully convinced he was anything other than an Italian worker. However, when waiting to be interviewed, he discovered that in nearby Trieste there was a cousin he knew in the German SS; if he was ever sent there, the game would be up. Taking his chance he managed to effect an escape; his German guard did not survive.

Squadron Leader M B Czernin DSO MC DFC with the partisans in Italy in 1945, following the German garrison's surrender in the town of Bergamo.

Returning from this mission, Manfred was awarded the Military Cross, although of course the citation tells little of the mission itself. There followed another period of inactivity until March 1945 when Manfred, leading a group of four Italians, was again parachuted into Northern Italy. Their main objective was to help partisans infiltrate the German-occupied towns in the region and capture the garrisons. This they did at six towns until finally they took over the major town of Bergamo, north-east of Milan, again capturing the garrison. For this mission, working with local partisans, he received the Distinguished Service Order.

Returning to peacetime, Manfred found it difficult to find a niche in the world. He remained in the RAF for a brief period until released in September 1945, and within a couple of years he and Maud had divorced. An idea to start an air transport business in South Africa did not progress but then in 1948 Manfred became quite ill and it came to nothing. Getting over this he went into the motor car industry, eventually becoming sales manager for Fiats in England.

He was still very much the man-about-town, playing cards and being seen at all the right night spots in London. His charm and charisma never left him and he was always popular with the ladies. His final years were happy ones, but his wartime activities had left him a weakened man and he died in his sleep at his London flat on 6 October 1962, aged 49. His remains were buried at the Villa Cimbrone, Ravello, Italy. He had a daughter and a son, both born during the Second World War.

Chapter 7

Wing Commander R M B Duke-Woolley DSO DFC & Bar, DFC (US)

Raymond Myles Beecham Duke-Woolley was born in Manchester on 18 August 1916. His father was a surgeon and his mother was Emily Beecham, part of the family of of Sir Thomas Beecham, the famous conductor of the London Philharmonic and Hallé Orchestras. He was educated at Marlborough College and in 1935 decided to join the Royal Air Force. He attended the RAF College at Cranwell, graduating the following year, and was then posted to No. 23 Squadron before the year was out.

This, his first squadron, was equipped with Hawker Demon two-seat fighter biplanes, and based at RAF Northolt. He had two years flying Demons, Myles Duke-Woolley told me when I interviewed him in July 1990. They never used oxygen in the biplanes as nobody ever bothered to go high enough. However, they were allowed to do what was called a 'battle climb', during which they made a rapid climb to around 25,000 feet, although this happened only once a year. Otherwise their normal operating height never exceeded 10,000 feet.

Gradually, as war seemed to be approaching, the biplanes began to be phased out and the new Hurricanes and then Spitfires started to arrive. However, 23 Squadron, being a two-seat squadron, were among the first to receive the Bristol Blenheim. 114 Squadron was the first to get them, in March 1937; 23 Squadron began to receive theirs in December 1938. It was a massive change for the pilots, who suddenly had to convert from open cockpit biplanes to an enclosed cockpit, retractable undercarriage, and two engines! There was little help for the pilots as virtually all Staff members had little or no idea about flying twin-engined monoplanes, having themselves been brought up on single-engined biplanes from the First World War onwards.

Fortunately for 23, Myles and his flight commander, some time after getting the new aeroplanes, had flown down to the West Country, visited the

Bristol Works and managed to scrounge some pilot handling notes. They were dated June 1939, and the Blenheims had arrived in December 1938, by which time they had been flying them for six months, and even been flying them at night. This in itself was extraordinary, for RAF pilots just didn't fly at night before the war.

Britain's night defences were virtually non-existent. Searchlights and anti-aircraft guns of course were around in some numbers but the RAF had little in the way of an aircraft that might intercept night raiders; on nights that were not totally dark, or with something of a moon, a pilot or observer in the right area might have the good fortune to spot a raider, either by seeing it in the gloom, spotting any tell-tale signs, like a glowing exhaust, or, when the war began, some indication of where it might be by exploding AA shells. But the pilots did their best to acclimatise themselves for night operations now that war seemed almost inevitable. Myles told me:

'When the war started all the lights went out so we'd be flying over a totally blacked out countryside, except when there was some sort of moon. All we had on the airfield then were the shaded glim-lamps, which couldn't be seen until you were down to about 2,000 feet and pretty close (hopefully) to the airfield. That was why so many pilots were killed in the early part of the war. Fortunately, before this, some of us had started to think about these problems before the war started. My flight commander, "Spike" O'Brian[2] and I talked this over and had started to plan what we should do and how we might do it. We imagined we were somewhere over the Wash in a jet black sky and worked out course and distances to get us back to base.

'We hadn't, of course, the slightest idea how we were going to find a target. It wasn't until well into 1940 that Spike said to me that we had some electronics expert and new instrumentation to see and he volunteered me to fly it around. It was fitted into a Blenheim and it so happened that the "expert" had been at Marlborough with me, and

---

2. Flight Lieutenant J S O'Brien. Later Squadron Leader, DFC, killed in action leading 234 Squadron on 7 September 1940.

had been working on the first A.I. gear [Airborne Interception radar]. It was very heavy and I recall that no air gunner wanted to come with us!

'We took off and climbed to 6-7,000 feet and he got ready to switch the "gubbins" on. He said, OK, and switched it on. There was the biggest blue flash I'd ever seen which seemed to zip past me and shoot out in front. I said, "Wow! If there had been an aircraft in front of us we'd have burned him up!" He said he was awfully sorry but the thing had blown up! The insulation had broken down completely, but it was a spectacular flash – just like a ray gun.

'He reappeared about a month later with the Mark 2 version and we flew this about quite a lot, and we did in fact make an interception one night. It was very difficult as each time I turned, the enemy aircraft turned the other way and we lost it. Then we picked up another one and he said it was flying away from us, so I increased speed but still it was going away from us. Eventually I had to throttle back. Then it transpired that this early A.I. worked just as well backwards as forwards, so in fact, what we'd been doing, was not chasing a German, but running away from one. So the A.I. disappeared for the second time whilst they got it to work just forwards.'

* * *

Eventually Duke-Woolley shot down a night raider. This came on the night of 18/19 June 1940, six miles north-east of King's Lynn, by which time he had become a flight commander. Just thirty seconds earlier on this same night, Flight Lieutenant A G 'Sailor' Malan DFC of 74 Squadron had shot down a Heinkel 111 flying a Spitfire, so Myles' kill was the second night victory for the RAF, although he was in a Blenheim If.

In fact British defences claimed four raiders down this night, the luckless German unit being KG4 operating from Merville, France. Malan shot down the bomber piloted by Leutnant Erich Simon, the sole survivor of his four-man crew, and he himself had baled out wounded, as his aircraft crashed in Chelmsford, Essex. Myles' victim crashed at Cley-next-the-Sea, Norfolk. The pilot had to ditch just off shore and the crew swam ashore. Among

Oberleutnant Ulrich Jordan's crew was the Gruppenkommandeur, Major Dietrich Fr. Von Massenbach. RAF fighters downed three more He111s this night – a rare success for Fighter Command. Myles recalled the night for me:

Myles Duke-Woolley DFC, with that first cigarette after landing from a combat sortie.

'I have never been so frightened before in my life and was never so frightened again. I was on patrol off the East Coast, over the Wash, on a gin-clear night, and Control called up to say that some German aircraft had been raiding the Midlands and some of them were coming our way. I looked to the west and could see a number of searchlights criss-crossing about, and called back to say that it looked as if the searchlights had somebody and should I investigate? They said no, it's being dealt with so I just watched.

'Then, about 10-12 miles away I saw a very small yellow light going down, then it went out, then I thought I saw a parachute, and realised that one of our aircraft had intercepted it and it had been shot down. The yellow thing had indeed been a Blenheim on fire. I called Control again and said I was going to engage. After a short silence I was told to engage in my own time. I then realised we'd never had any real briefing on how to actually shoot down an aircraft. The only instruction we had had was by some chap who'd shot something down in 1918, and that the thing to do was to rush up behind the bomber, close to 100 yards and with our outstanding armament, blow it apart!

'So as I closed in I began to realise I should also soon be fired at myself, that I had no armour protection in front of me, my fuel tanks were not self-sealing, and the more I thought about it, the more I realised that I was going to live just long enough to get tangled with this German aircraft – in about four minutes. I had been married just over nine months (31 August 1939), and my wife had just given birth to our first child and I knew I was never going to see it. I was convinced of it, I just could not see any hope.

'I was thinking furiously on how I might attack and get away with it and then a plan occurred to me, which I then imparted to my gunner. Fear was growing inside me and it came up to my throat and I realised I wasn't able to talk. Then, an extraordinary thing, I began to hear my voice speak and it was absolutely calm. I told Control I was in touch with the bandit and would engage it shortly. Then, this same calm voice spoke to my gunner: "Have you got your parachute on?" He said no, so this voice then said: "They've still got a searchlight on him, and what we are going to do is this. I'm going to keep to port until the light goes out, then I'm going to come up in line astern of him at 100 yards, and open fire with a 5-second burst. If that doesn't work I'll come up under his wing and I shall want you to put bursts up into him. If that doesn't work, we'll have to go back and start again." So that's what we did.

'I flew alongside the bomber, about 500 yards away, until the last light flicked out, came up behind it, put the sight on it and counted out five seconds as I pressed the gun button. I then broke off and looking where I'd just been could see all these red flashes, which I later realised was return fire from the German gunners. I then went in again but after another long burst the bomber was still flying along. I then flew underneath it and let my gunner have a go but we still didn't appear to be doing any damage. All the time something kept nagging in my brain that I was doing something wrong. Then I suddenly realised that our guns were harmonised at 250 yards. This meant that at 100 yards, the range I'd been told to fire from, I was hardly hitting him at all, so I deduced I had to fly at least four feet higher for it to be more or less right.

'I slid in again, aimed high up on the German's tail-fin, fired and broke to port, but this time the return fire was less. I then pulled in again, fired once more with a 7-second burst and as we broke, we were hit. There was a smell of cordite, and a scream from my gunner. As I turned, the bomber disappeared. My gunner said he'd been hit.'

In the event, the air gunner had not been hit. A couple of bullets had come up under him and hit his chest-type parachute, which had knocked it upwards and it had hit his chin. Myles then asked the gunner if he could see the German, and he replied, "Oh, yes, he's on fire." Coming back over the coast, Myles' starboard engine stopped. A bullet had hit one tank and fuel had drained out. However, he got home and landed safely.

* * *

With his experience with the early development of airborne radar, one would have thought that his career would have continued as a night fighter, but he was keen to move south to the main battle area once the Battle of Britain started to warm up. It took two requests to transfer to day fighters but at last a posting came through to join 253 Squadron in September. 253 had been seriously depleted during the Battle, having lost two commanding officers, four flight commanders and several other pilots. It had been stood down from the front line and was in the process of rebuilding itself at RAF Kenley. The two COs had been Squadron Leaders Tom Gleave and Harry Starr, while its new Boss was Squadron Leader Gerry Edge.

Gerry Edge was 26, almost 27, and in his youth, while employed in the family metal business, had joined the Auxiliary Air Force in 1936, serving with 605 Squadron. With 605 from the start of the war he had seen action over Scotland, then over France in May 1940, and finally in the early stages of the Battle of Britain. By the time the squadron returned to Scotland on rest, he had shot down a number of German aircraft, but he remained in the south, being given command of 253. During the first weeks of September, Edge claimed ten hostile aircraft and damaged others, including four Ju88 bombers on the 9th and two He111s and a Me109 on the 11th. Duke-Woolley arrived on the 12th and both men were to score on the 15th, Edge a Dornier 17 and a Ju88, Myles a Dornier 17 damaged. However, it was Edge's last success, for he was shot down over the Channel on the 26th. He was rescued by a motor boat and admitted to Ashford Hospital. On 29 September, Captain Cuthbert Orde finished his drawing of Myles, and wrote of him:

'I drew him at Kenley when three or four Scrambles were the order of the day, and it was difficult for a Flight Commander to guarantee two free hours. I remember having to haunt his flight dispersal hut – a caravan with tent attached – and eventually grabbing him immediately after landing from a show. It sounds harsh, but I have no doubt that sitting still for two hours in those hectic days did him a power of good!

'He is one of those chaps who doesn't care a damn for anyone and to whom a really fast car is the thing that matters most. But he is a very intelligent person, and I found him interesting and clear in his descriptions of air-fighting.'

With the squadron's third CO out of the fight, Myles became the senior officer and took over leadership. One of the first things he did was to reorganise how the squadron flew.

'We soon went over to pairs and we really started to develop this. I was finally operating in pairs above 30,000 feet, which in Hurricanes was absolutely unheard of. But I got them up there and then dived them for 2,000 feet which put on 20 mph. Once you'd got the tail up and in a correct flying attitude, one could hold the speed and at 30,000 feet we were cruising at much the same speed as the Spitfires. We were able to bounce the odd German fighter formation from this height.'

However, when talking to Myles it became apparent he was not a supporter of Douglas Bader's Big Wing that operated from 12 Group's airfield at Duxford. The argument about this Wing has been aired many times, but as far as Myles was concerned, one event stood out. His squadron had gained height and found a formation of German aircraft some way below. This did not often happen and he was looking forward to a good bounce on them, but suddenly spotted a large formation of fighters off to the north; so many in fact, they just had to be Me109s. RAF fighters generally numbered only around a dozen. So he was forced to abort the pending attack and head away. Only later did he discover it was Bader's Wing heading down from the north, with some thirty-six fighters, so his perfect chance of a good bounce was lost.

Nevertheless, Myles managed to do some damage in the final weeks of the Battle. He shared a Dornier 17 of KG3 on 6 October between East Grinstead and Tunbridge Wells, with Pilot Officer L C Murch, damaged a Ju88 on the 21st, shot down a Ju88 of KG77 on 9 November, and on the 22nd he shared a Dornier from KG2 destroyed and shared another damaged. By this time he had reverted to flight commander status with the arrival of Squadron Leader P R Walker DFC. Myles received the DFC, promulgated in the *London Gazette* on 24 December.

This officer has commanded his squadron since September 1940, and his fine leadership and personal example have contributed to the many successes obtained. He has destroyed at least three enemy aircraft and damaged several more.

* * *

Myles was rested in January 1941 and sent to 12 Group HQ at RAF Digby. In May he was posted to Castletown in the Orkneys, to form 124 Squadron which he would lead until June 1942. 124 was equipped with Spitfires. Apart from coastal and convoy patrols, it also acted as a training unit for pupils coming from Operational Training Units for a final polish. In November the squadron moved to Biggin Hill, becoming part of the Wing operating from there. The following month, 17 December, Myles Duke-Woolley intercepted a Ju88 off the North Foreland during a convoy patrol and shot it down.

In early 1942 124 Squadron participated in a number of fighter sweeps and other operations over Northern France, but the major event occurred on 12 February, the famous Channel Dash, the day the German Navy sent three battleships along the Channel and North Sea from Brest to Norway. Despite the RAF and Royal Navy keeping a close watch on these ships, the *Gneisenau*, *Scharnhorst* and *Prinz Eugen,* managed the dash virtually unscathed despite belated assaults from RAF and Fleet Air Arm aircraft. Myles had vivid recollections of that day:

'We had been released because the weather was so bad and I said we would spend the morning in the Intelligence Section and catch up on the reading we hadn't done. I'd been chatting to the other squadron

Squadron Leader Myles Duke-Woolley DFC, 124 Squadron, 1942.

CO so he and his pilots were doing the same thing. The Station Commander and Wing Leader were off the Station, when the telephone rang. Nobody was about so I answered it and a panic-stricken voice yelled, "Scramble, scramble!" followed by a word I didn't understand, then click, he was gone.

'I thought I'd heard the word somewhere but could not place it. So I walked back into the Section's room and said to the boys that there seemed to be a panic on, and to get down to the dispersal hut, while someone phoned to get the aircraft ready. Meantime I would try to find out what it was all about. I rang back 11 Group HQ and the same squeaky voice came on. I tried to calm him down but all I got was "Scramble" and this code word again. He put down the 'phone but I just called him back and before he could say anything I asked, "Scramble where?" He replied, "North Foreland, 12.30." Then I remembered the word – Fuller – the code word that signalled that German battleships were out of Brest and, presumably, heading for the North Foreland. It was now ten minutes to mid-day.

'We were soon airborne and I quickly briefed the chaps over the radio – in clear – but said that apart from what "Fuller" stood for, I knew little else. In fact we were going to give cover to a handful of Swordfish torpedo bombers that would endeavour to attack the three warships at 12.30 and I'd only been in the office of the I.O. since about ten to twelve! As I recall we had taken off five or ten minutes past, which considering we had been released for the day, was pretty good going.

'I seem to recall we reached North Foreland about two minutes past the half hour. In between times, I had got hold of the second squadron at Redhill and they made rendezvous with us, seeing them arrive a couple of miles ahead of me. But by now, the Swordfish had gone on. I had no idea of where the ships were for nobody had bothered to tell me. Probably they didn't know.

'We headed out to sea, with visibility down to three or four miles, and cloud base down to about 1,200 feet. Then, some miles out, I suddenly saw off to my right, that the area between the cloud base and the sea was black with flak. In the middle was what I took to be the six Swordfish, amidst the biggest concentration of flak I'd ever seen in my life. I cut round the front of this lot, went up into the cloud, on the basis that we might be able to find the odd German aircraft scudding about above. There was certainly no future in going into the flak with my Spitfires. Coming out, we flew around, saw a couple of Me109s but they smartly disappeared when they saw us. Then, finally, I let down and breaking through, found myself slap on the top of the *Scharnhorst*! I quickly turned towards France thinking it safer to fly south, than north, at the moment. Soon afterwards we had to return home. I called the Controller, again in clear, and told him it was definitely the *Scharnhorst, Gneisenau* and *Prinz Eugen*.'

The ships got through and a number of RAF aircraft were shot down attempting to stop them. Among the losses were all six FAA Swordfish. Their leader, Commander Eugene Esmonde, was awarded the Victoria Cross for his sacrifice. Esmonde knew it was a suicide mission. Tom Gleave [ex 253 Squadron, having recuperated after his serious burns when shot down in the Battle of Britain] was the station commander at RAF Manston. Gleave once told me that he was out on the airfield as the order came for the six Swordfish to take off. Gleave saw the expression on Esmonde's face, one that said he knew perfectly well that his chances of coming back were almost nil – but he did not hesitate for more than a moment. Flak and fighters shot them all down as they went in.

These actions in early 1942 led to Myles receiving his second decoration, a Bar to his DFC, gazetted on 29 May:

> *This officer has participated in many sorties over Northern France and the English Channel. He is a cool and capable leader whose skill is reflected in the high standard of efficiency in his Squadron. He has destroyed at least 7 enemy aircraft.*

In June 1942 Myles was made leader of the Debden Wing, which at this stage comprised of the first American Eagle Squadron (71), 350 Dutch Squadron, 65 RAF Squadron and the second Eagle Squadron, No. 121. In due course, 65 and 350 moved away and in their place came the third Eagle Squadrons, No. 133. The plan was to hand over these three squadrons to the American 8th Air Force, now that America was in the war and starting to send men and aircraft to Britain. For some weeks Myles ran the Wing in consort with Colonel Chesley 'Pete' Peterson, who had been flying with 71 Squadron for some time. With the Americans, Myles became known as 'The Dook'.

The next bit of excitement was the Dieppe Operation on 19 August 1942. The idea was to capture and hold a French port for a day, in preparation for the time when the Allies would attempt a full scale landing somewhere along the French coast. Many lessons were learnt but although the RAF felt they had achieved a victory, supporting British commandos and Canadian troops during that day, the Luftwaffe definitely came out on top.

Myles led the Debden Wing over to Dieppe soon after the operation had begun, while it was not fully light. As the sun started to come up he could look down and see the armada of ships off the French coast. His orders were to cover the landing which he did for some forty minutes before being relieved, heading back to Gravesend where they were based for this operation. Later, as part of the Biggin Hill Wing, 71 Squadron, led by Myles, were over

Dieppe again, and some action ensued, and saw Peterson shoot down a Ju88, but the German gunner hit the American's Spitfire and he had to bale out into the sea. Fortunately he was soon rescued.

On another sortie, Myles led 232 and 124 Squadrons out and got bounced by a FW190, as he recalled:

'On my third sortie one German fighter dived out of the sun from a great height, attacked us head-on, and I did not see him until he was maybe 600 yards away and firing. Our closing speed was around 800 mph and I failed to react in the second and a half at my disposal. He shot down two aircraft in the squadron I was leading and both pilots were killed. We could do nothing but carry on and the squadron most commendably did not waver. The German's attack was skilful and right from the eye of the blazing sun in a cloudless sky.'

On one of these sorties to Dieppe, Myles remembered facing an unexpected surprise:

'One thing that scared the pants off me happened about five minutes after we arrived. Nobody had let me know about the new L.C.R. (Landing Craft, Rocket) which was used at Dieppe for, I believe, the first time on a combined operation. This craft carried, reputedly, 960 mortar-type missiles fired in sequence electronically and the whole salvo was discharged in less than a minute. I discovered that at least one such device was in use when the first 50 or so rockets passed through the squadron which I was leading. When I say through, I do mean that some went over the top of my head and some passed under my personal tail, and the L.C.R. miraculously did not score one Spitfire squadron – but only by virtue of one of those co-incidental miracles that makes one sweat slightly in retrospect.

'All the rockets continued in their apogee and duly plunged to earth somewhere off to port and a quick check showed that we remained not only intact but untouched. I managed some feeble jest about Mr Brock, having been enlisted in response to a (decorative) question from my No.2, enquiring about this phenomenon! Who needs enemies when we've friends like that, was another question which expressed our collective thoughts.'

* * *

Leading the Americans during August, Myles claimed a couple of successes, a FW190 destroyed on the 27th south of Gravelines, and a probable 190 two days later off Cap Gris Nez. His combat report for the 27th reads:

'I was flying east with 71 Eagle Squadron leading the Debden Wing at 18,000 feet, six miles south of Gravelines at 12.40 when I saw 14/16 FW190s 4,000 feet below, heading west. I turned to starboard and dived, and fired at one FW190 from 10° off astern, ½ ring deflection and at high closing speed. I broke away to starboard passing about ten feet underneath the enemy aircraft, having seen strikes on its fuselage near the cockpit. Enemy aircraft took no evasive action but turned gently to starboard after the attack and dived steeply. Squadron Leader Daymond flying Red 1, saw the aircraft dive for about 3,000 feet and then explode in mid-air and continue in a vertical dive completely enveloped in flames.'

This was probably Unteroffizier Friedrich Lindelaub of 1/JG26, who apparently managed to bale out of his falling 190 to survive, although severely wounded. He had only joined JG26 on 7 August.

Myles described to me another action resulting in the destruction of a 190:

'One day the weather wasn't awfully good, and not expecting to fly, most of the boys had pushed off to London. Then, out of the blue we were asked to run the Wing round Northern France to help divert enemy fighters from a bombing raid. So I had, what one might call, the "second team" made up of pilots still on the base.

'We were floating around Northern France in our, by now normal finger-four sections, when down below I suddenly saw a squadron in similar four section formations. I'd been warned that some Typhoons were around and when I first saw these aircraft, thought they were them. But for some reason I questioned it and got up-sun of them, I told the other two squadrons to stay up while I took 71 down to take a look. I slid down, keeping myself between the aircraft and the sun, and when I got nearer could see they were Germans. I called the boys and said, give me about 200 yards start – I want the leader. So they stayed up and I slid down into the formation and actually got right above the three aircraft above the leader, arriving then about ten yards behind him. I knew perfectly well that at that range I couldn't fire at him on the sight, I had to aim just up a bit – gave him a 2-second burst then broke away, calling the others to come on in.

'It created a little confusion among the German squadron for I'd hit the leader absolutely dead right. I blew both his wings off, which began to flutter down and then the fuselage nosed forward. The rest of the enemy fighters just paused a moment then my chaps were amongst them and we shot down about four others. We might have got some others but they went downhill so fast, I had to order them to break off and reform. When the other Wing pilots got back from London and found what we'd been up to they were absolutely furious.'

Myles now left the Wing. However, in September, 133 Squadron flew a long range mission out towards the Bay of Biscay and got caught in an unpredicted jet-stream, losing practically the whole outfit. Soon afterwards the Eagle Squadrons became the American 4th Fighter Group, USAAF, although it still flew Spitfires for some time. Duke-Woolley continued to be attached to the new formation and flew a few operations before the 4th were off on their own. Myles managed to claim one more victory with the Americans, which came on 2 October 1942. He was leading a show and found a small gaggle of 190s in the Calais area and in the subsequent fight three 190s were claimed shot down, one by Oscar Coen, another by Stan M Anderson, and a third, shared between Myles and Jim Clark. Myles remembered:

'Range estimation was absolutely essential. I worked at this so hard that in the last combat I had, on 2 October 1942, I declared the range as being 308 yards rather facetiously and determined I had error of range of 5 yards! I gave its estimated speed as being 325 mph, because you

Wing Commander R D M Duke-Woolley DSO DFC with the US 4th Fighter Group in 1943. His two companions are Lts Andy Anderson and Brewster Morgan.

can't work out a deflection unless you've got the angle and the speed. This FW190 had fallen in half just behind the cockpit and it did literally fall in half. My rounds had got to it after I'd stopped firing but I knew it was right, despite being upside down myself, the 190 being right way up. About three or four seconds later I saw his parachute.

'I had with me an American pilot [Jim Clark] and his combat film was off and he was firing the wrong way but we gave him a half share. I always felt it encouraged the up and coming pilot. His morale goes up and he knows next time he's in a fight, getting a Hun is possible. He later did very well.'

Jim Clark did indeed do well. Flying with the 334th Fighter Squadron during 1943, becoming its CO, and in 1944 flew as the group's operations officer. In combat he claimed ten enemy aircraft shot down, plus the half he shared with Myles. Oscar Coen also did well: he had several victories

Duke-Woolley after receiving the American DFC, 25 February 1943.

with 71 Squadron, more with the 4th, later commanding the 356th Fighter Group; in October 1941 he had been brought down over France but evaded capture and managed to get back to England in December. Stan Anderson went missing in April 1943.

On 25 February 1943, Air Marshal Trafford Leigh-Mallory, C-in-C of RAF Fighter Command presented sixty specially struck silver medallions to former Eagle Squadron members. The Commander of the 8th Air Force Fighter Command, General F O'D Hunter, presented American DFCs to some of the pilots, including Chesley Peterson, Gus Daymond – and Myles. He was, in fact, the first British recipient of the American DFC. He had also received the Distinguished Service Order, *London Gazette* 8 January 1943:

> *By his outstanding leadership and untiring efforts, Wing Commander Duke-Woolley has contributed much to the success attained by his Wing. Since June 1942, he has led his formation in many raids over enemy occupied*

territory, in the course of which 28 enemy aircraft were destroyed. Wing Commander Duke-Woolley has completed successfully a large number of operational sorties and has displayed outstanding qualities of airmanship and tactical skill. He has destroyed 10 enemy aircraft.

After a short period working as a liaison officer with 8th Air Force HQ, he moved in July to form a Mobile Control Centre for 84 Group, which soon became part of the 2nd Tactical Air Force, preparing for D-Day. When that day came he was soon in Normandy as the group's second in command. In January 1945 he attended the RAF Staff College and shortly after the war ended found himself in Turkey, instructing at the Air War College.

Command of RAF Acklington followed, instructor at the Staff College, then becoming the CO of RAF Debden before spending three years in the USA. He returned to work at Fighter Command HQ as a group captain in 1954. His wife Jocelyn (née de Satge Garnett) had become ill and her treatment needed warmer climes so he retired from the Service in 1961 and moved to Spain where he became a skiing instructor. After his wife died he returned to England and into the life insurance business, also marrying for a second time, Judy Healing. From 1973 to 1979 he served as Yeoman Usher of Black Rod to the House of Lords. He did not have the best of health in his final years, living in West Sussex, and died on 16 October 1991, aged 75.

Chapter 8

Squadron Leader J A A Gibson DSO DFC

Johnny Gibson caused mayhem against the Luftwaffe in France, and then went on to cause more during the Battle of Britain. John Albert Axel Gibson was born in the seaside town of Brighton, Sussex, on 24 August 1916, but four years later his family emigrated to New Zealand, and when his schooling began he went to Wellesley Boys' College, Curren Street School and Grafton, then attended Auckland Grammar School before moving to New Plymouth Boys' High School, Taranaki, on North Island. During his school days he enjoyed sport and became a champion rifle shot, something that came in handy a few years later.

Like many of his generation, he became fascinated by flying, and quickly discovered it was easier to join the Royal Air Force in his native country than in New Zealand. So, in 1938 he travelled to England on the RMS *Rangitata* and successfully applied for a short service commission in July. His commission was confirmed in August 1939 following his training with No. 4 E&RFTS, at RAF Brough. He then went to No. 3 FTS at South Cerney, but his first posting was into air co-operation work at Farnborough. However, when the Germans moved into France, he was sent to an operational fighter squadron.

As a matter of interest, Johnny Gibson appears to have been adopted by the Royal New Zealand Air Force, as

Flight Lieutenant J A A Gibson DFC. Like many RAF pilots they loved their pets, which often became squadron mascots.

in its official history it is noted that Gibson was born in Christchurch and had lived in Auckland.

Just as the shooting war began, Gibson was posted to 501 Squadron of the Auxiliary Air Force, his squadron being ordered to the Continent on the day the Germans launched its *Blitzkrieg* against France and the Low Countries. Leaving RAF Tangmere, 501's first base in France was at Bétheniville and then Anglure, Gibson only having flown a few hours on the aircraft with which it was equipped – Hawker Hurricanes.

The squadron had arrived to support the existing units of the Advanced Air Striking Force (AASF) and they were immediately heavily involved with enemy aircraft supporting their troops in their forward advance across France. Gibson had his first successful encounter on 27 May, operating from different airfields, running into thirty German bombers near Rouen, whilst flying from the airfield at Boos. 501 claimed several Heinkels shot down, including one by Gibson, plus another shared, but his own fighter was hit, so he was forced to crash-land in a field near Rouen. He escaped injury but his machine had to be abandoned. The bombers were from 1./KG53, three failing to return with one more damaged.

Johnny Gibson DFC seated in a Spitfire after the Battle of Britain, marked with his victories, although they were all scored in a Hurricane. Note the Donald Duck motif on the fuselage and the New Zealand shoulder patch.

Gibson was engaged with several He111 bombers over the next few days, claiming one on the 29th which was not confirmed, but another was on the 30th, in an action in which he also claimed a bomber damaged. He damaged another on 4 June, yet another unconfirmed on the 5th, plus a damaged. On 10 June, however, he attacked a Me109 near Le Mans and claimed it as destroyed but he was hit in the combat near Le Havre and had to bale out near Le Mans. He survived unhurt. The 109 belly-landed at Yvrench and was damaged beyond repair. The pilot, from I./JG76, escaped injury.

Four days later he possibly got another 109, but then 501 had to withdraw from France, flying to Jersey before heading back to England, where it reassembled at RAF Croydon. There is also the possibility that Gibson bagged another 109 over Abbeville on 8 June. The squadron continued to operate over France from the UK but France finally fell. Like everyone else the survivors from 501 awaited the next onslaught that would become known as the Battle of Britain.

Pilots of 501 Squadron at readiness. Standing: Pilot Officer Stefan Witorzenc, Flight Lieutenant George Stoney (KIA 18 August), Sergeant Franciszek Kozlowski; Seated: Pilot Officer Bob Dafforn, Sergeant Paul Farnes, Flying Officer Ken Lee, Flight Lieutenant Johnny Gibson and Pilot Officer Hugh Adams (KIA 6 September).

His squadron had acquitted itself well over France, achieving around forty-five victories. Several of its pilots had scored heavily, including Ginger Lacey, Bob Dafforn, Paul Farnes, Ken Lee, Don McKay and Percy Morfill. They would continue to do so.

* * *

When the Battle began, 501 were at Middle Wallop. In one of their first encounters on 9 July, Gibson damaged a He111 over Portland, and on the 13th destroyed a Dornier 17 over the same location, although this may have been a Me110. Pilots were sometimes confused as the Dornier and the 110 both had twin rudders.

However, there was no mistaking the distinctive shape of the Ju87 'Stuka' dive-bomber, which 501 encountered on 29 July. Stukas of II./StG 1 were engaged over Dover early in the day and 501 and 41 Squadrons got in amongst them, shooting down four and damaging another. Gibson was credited with one, and another as damaged. His report noted:

'Sighted enemy aircraft approaching Dover Harbour – engaged a Junkers 87 as it broke away from attack on the ships. Saw enemy machine dive steeply with black smoke pouring from it. Broke off attack as I saw a Spitfire with another Junkers 87 on its tail. Fired at this dive-bomber which burst into flames and plunged into the sea.'

On the 31st Gibson damaged a Dornier near Folkestone. He was in combat with Stukas again on 12 August, claiming one and a damaged, but he may have been a trifle over-optimistic as no Ju87s were lost on this date. He may have done better this same day by claiming a He113 shot down. Although this was, of course, a Me109, He113s never flying over England, nearly a dozen 109s did fail to make it home. The down-side to this day was that landing at RAF Hawkinge where the runway had been damaged, Gibson tipped up in a crater. But he was not hurt and his fighter could be repaired. Ginger Lacey did the same thing.

There was no let-up. On the 15th, ever increasing numbers of enemy bombers and fighters headed across the English coast, with a tiring Fighter

Command opposing them. Stuka dive-bombers were again in evidence, Gibson leading a section against a formation of twenty at approximately 11.30 am. The three RAF pilots each claimed a Junkers shot down, Gibson seeing his victim burst into flames and crash into the sea. He was then recalled to Hawkinge as the base was under attack by more Stukas. Gibson went into the attack and damaged one, but fire from one of the German rear gunners set his Hurricane on fire and he quickly undid his safety harness and radio lead and baled out. Once again he suffered no injury.

Johnny Gibson was having a charmed life but he was back in action just after lunch on 24 August, this time tangling with a Ju88. This appears to have been the aircraft of 5(F)/122 on a reconnaissance sortie, which failed to return from its mission along the Channel. On the 28th he damaged a 109 over Folkestone, but the next day he was credited with a 109 confirmed destroyed. The squadron had encountered 109s from JG3. This unit suffered at the hands of 501 and 85 Squadrons, losing seven of its fighters during the day, with others damaged. However, in the fight Gibson's Hurricane was hit and once again he found himself dangling on the end of his parachute lines. His machine crashed at Ladwood Farm, while he came down at Mill Hill Farm, Ottinge, although this time he was slightly injured. He reported:

'There were about twenty bombers escorted by some thirty fighters above and behind them. A dogfight started and I managed to position myself on the tail of a Messerschmitt and gave him a short burst. He wobbled and then dived to the ground and crashed near Kingswood.'

Gibson had now been made a flight commander and his actions were rewarded by the announcement that he had been the recipient of the Distinguished Flying Cross. It was officially announced in the *London Gazette* on 30 August:

In August, whilst on an offensive patrol over Dover, this officer engaged and destroyed a Junkers 87 and was afterwards shot down himself. Although his aircraft was in flames he steered it away from the town of Folkestone and did not abandon the aircraft until it had descended to 1,000 feet. Pilot Officer Gibson has destroyed eight enemy aircraft, and has displayed great courage and presence of mind.

Despite his slight injury, Gibson was back in action on 2 September, damaging a 109 near Maidstone. Four days later he destroyed one over Ashford while leading 501, then on the 7th he damaged yet another. He received another slight wound and was taken to hospital, and returned when the squadron went back to Filton, where, in April 1941 it began to re-equip with Spitfires. But Gibson was now due for a rest, so on 28 May he was posted to be an instructor at No. 53 Operational Training Unit at RAF Heston.

His flight commander rank was confirmed in September 1941 and towards the end of the year he received notification that he would soon be joining No. 457 Squadron at Jerby, on the Isle of Man. This was an Australian squadron engaged mostly on convoy patrols over the Irish Sea. In the spring of 1942 the squadron was moved to Redhill and began operations over France, but in May it was sent north, to Kirton-in-Lindsay where it was to prepare for overseas duty – in this case, Australia.

With the Japanese entering the war in December 1941, and making steady advances in the South Pacific regions, northern Australia was in danger. The Australian government asked Winston Churchill for help, which resulted in a wing of Spitfires being made available. Two were Australian-manned squadrons, 457 and 452 Squadrons, plus 54 Squadron RAF. However, Gibson was not to become part of this move, for the period of his short service commission had come to an end, and he decided to return to New Zealand, being made RAFO – Reserve of Air Force Officers.

In June he became attached to the Royal New Zealand Air Force, and was posted to the newly formed 15 Squadron RNZAF at Whenuapi, although it had no aircraft. It was supposed to have had Curtis P40 Kittyhawk fighters, but these had been diverted to North Africa due to that theatre's urgent need. The Americans had asked for support in the South Pacific theatre so 15 Squadron prepared itself and eventually sailed from Wellington on the USS *President Jackson* on 23 October, reaching the island of Tonga four days later. Here it took over the P40s and equipment of the American 68th Pursuit Squadron on Fuamotu airfield. Despite the poor state of the aircraft, they persevered with their training and finally took over the defence of the island.

Gibson now found himself back in New Zealand in mid-December 1942 in order to take up an appointment at Air HQ, Control Group. In April 1943 he was promoted to acting squadron leader and after about a month was sent to the Army Staff College at Palmerston North, before returning to staff duties. Gibson returned to 15 Squadron on 15 December as commanding officer, taking over from Mike Herrick DFC, who had been a night-fighter pilot with the RAF in 1940.

The squadron was now based on New Georgia, in the Solomon Islands, and it took part in heavy fighting that supported the landing on Bougainville. Once this had been taken, the squadron moved to the island itself, flying from the airfield of Torokina. There were not too many opportunities to engage enemy aircraft, but on 23 January 1944, leading his squadron as escort to American Avenger bombers to the huge Japanese base at Rabaul, the force was attacked by Japanese fighters. Gibson attacked a Zero that had been going after the bombers, and shot it down into the sea. On the 11th, the squadron returned to New Zealand for a rest.

This lasted until May, at which time Gibson took his squadron back to the battle front, to the island of Guadalcanal, moving from there in June back to Bougainville. His acting rank was confirmed on 1 July and at the end of the month, its tour completed, 15 Squadron once again returned to New Zealand. In mid-August he was posted and by the end of October was on his way back to Britain. He was awarded the Distinguished Service Order, gazetted on 11 March 1945, for his command of 15 Squadron.

The recommendation had been put forward by Government House in Wellington, NZ, on 20 October 1944. The wording of it is as follows:

Since being awarded the Distinguished Flying Cross for his achievements as a fighter pilot in the Battle of Britain, this officer has further distinguished himself both in England and more recently in the Pacific, where he has made three tours in the Solomons area. He has destroyed a total of 14½ enemy aircraft, adding to his earlier record one Japanese fighter which was fiercely attacking an Allied formation over Rabaul Harbour. Acting Squadron Leader Gibson, who is a brilliant pilot and a born leader, has to his credit the exceptional total of 669 hours of operational flying covering 382 missions. On his two latest tours in the Pacific this year, he has commanded a Squadron, and his enthusiasm and fearless leadership have been outstanding. His personal courage, both in aerial combat and in ground strafing and fighter–bomber missions, and his long experience, have been of inestimable value to his Squadron, which has earned the high praise of Allied Commanders.

The war had not finished with him yet, and he found himself back in Europe flying with 80 Squadron at Volkel, Holland, a unit flying powerful Hawker Tempest fighters, during the final weeks of the Second World War. This unit was part of the mighty RAF Second Tactical Air Force (2nd TAF), its Tempest squadrons ranging far and wide attacking anything Germanic that dared show any sign of a presence. Trains, MT, ground troops, enemy strong points, all were fair game for the Tempest's four 20 mm cannon. In March 1945 came the crossing of the River Rhine. It began on the 23rd and Gibson was part of it. On the 25th his Tempest was hit by flak south east of Helmond; his windscreen was covered in oil and the engine stopped. However, he managed to re-start it sufficiently to get back over the Rhine and make a forced landing. The Tempest broke its back, and Gibson damaged his right shoulder, but he had survived yet again.

* * *

During the war Johnny Gibson had married Ethel Formby, the sister of the popular and well known George Formby of ukulele fame, soon after the war started. They had a son, Michael. Ethel was a star in her own right, starting out as a stage dancer but like her elder brother took up playing the ukulele, as she found it easier. During the war she lived with Johnny in New Zealand while he was there, later going to Australia where she appeared in a number of shows at the Tivoli Theatre in Melbourne. However, their marriage was dissolved and later Johnny married Isobel Sharpe.

Gibson – by now given the nickname of 'Hoot', after the American rodeo champion and cowboy film actor – transferred to the RNZAF on 1 December 1945 but a year later relinquished his commission and rejoined the RAF. He became the personal pilot for Field Marshal Bernard Montgomery, and later personal aide and pilot to Marshal of the RAF Lord Tedder. He retired from the RAF in 1954 and went to live in South Africa, where he became a commercial pilot with the Chamber of Mines in Johannesburg. They had several DC3 and DC4 aircraft, Gibson taking on the role of Chief Flying

Instructor, as well as airline captain until 1965. He then formed and became general manager of the first national air carrier for the country, Bechuanaland National Airways, which also flew DC3s and DC4s.

Between 1969 and 1970 Gibson flew with the Rhodesian Air Services during the Biafran war, ferrying refugee children out of the danger areas, while also flying in much needed supplies. His landing strip was a disused but widened former road. All flights had to be made during darkness and often in bad weather, with very few navigational aids. His son Michael also flew as co-pilot on occasions. After this he formed Jagair air charter company, operating a Cessna 310 from Kariba in Rhodesia.

He finally retired, or semi-retired, in 1974 but continued to fly with the Rhodesian Air Force until the end of hostilities in late 1979, at which time he lived in Salisbury, Rhodesia. He then became operations manager in the Department of Civil Aviation in Rhodesia/Zimbabwe, until he finally retired from flying in 1982. Five years later he returned to England, retiring to Nottingham. He died in July 2000, aged 83.

Chapter 9

Squadron Leader C Haw DFC DFM
Order of Lenin

When I met 'Wag' Haw at his home in Farnham, Surrey, I found him busily engaged in making children's dolls houses. This seemed a far cry from RAF fighter pilot, but I could see he was totally engrossed in making these quite splendid toy buildings. However, he was able to drag himself away long enough to tell me about his war.

Charlton Haw had been born in York on 8 May 1920 and, like so many other young boys, became enthralled – at the age of ten – by not only seeing Sir Alan Cobham's famous Flying Circus, but actually having a ride with him in his aeroplane. It had cost him, or perhaps his father, ten shillings, but it was money well spent.

His entry into the world of flight, while engendered, was not immediate. Following his education, which began at Tang Hall School, York, he took an apprenticeship as a lithographer in Leeds, but with war looming, he decided to joined the RAF Volunteer Reserve and undertake pilot training.

Accepted, he went through his pilot training, received his 'wings' and in June 1940 was posted to 504 (County of Nottingham) Squadron, an auxiliary squadron based at RAF Wick in Scotland, whose task it was to protect the British base and fleet at Scapa Flow. They had had a trying time in France and welcomed the break. Although auxiliary pilots generally stuck together and were sometimes suspicious of newcomers, Wag Haw was made welcome because he was able to play the piano!

With the Battle of Britain raging down south, 504 were eventually required to reinforce squadrons wearied by constant fighting or suffering casualties, so on 5 September the squadron was ordered to fly their Hurricanes down to RAF Hendon. His CO was Squadron Leader John Sample DFC. Two days later they were flying operations.

That first day 504 had its first casualty, Pilot Officer K V Wendle, who was shot down and killed over Faversham; another pilot had to make a forced landing. On the 11th, the squadron suffered another loss, but on the 15th, it was hit hard. Attacking Dornier 17 bombers, around noon over London, one pilot was killed, and another had to take to his parachute. The latter was Sergeant R T Holmes, who became famous in this action by shooting down a Dornier that crashed into the forecourt of Victoria railway station. With his Hurricane damaged, Holmes baled out over Chelsea, landing in a dustbin. The Dornier was from 5/KG3, one of at least three brought down by 504.

The squadron's next casualty came on the 27th, this being Haw himself. On this day the Germans were attempting to destroy the Bristol aircraft factory at Filton. It had been attacked on the 25th and it was embarrassingly unopposed by RAF fighters. The next day, 504 Squadron were ordered to fly from Hendon to Filton, a 10 Group sector station, whose own squadrons were at Exeter, defending Plymouth and the Devon radar stations. On the 27th, the Luftwaffe again went for Filton, with 30 Heinkel He111s of KG55, preceded by nineteen bomb-carrying Me110s of *Erprobungsgruppe 210* (Erpr.Gr.210), with an escort of 27 Me110s of III./ZG26.

However, 10 Group fighters were not to be caught out again, and the group commander, Air Vice-Marshal Sir Christopher Quinton-Brand KBE DSO MC DFC, had five squadrons, including 504, ready for them. These fighters engaged the Heinkels over Yeovil, forcing them to abandon their assault and jettisoning their bombs around Sherbourne. However, EG210's Messerschmitts pressed on alone and were hammered by RAF fighters, losing four of their number, including its Gruppenkommandeur, Hauptmann Martin Lutz, and the second staffel's captain, Oberleutnant Wilhelm Roessinger. Haw was credited with one Me110 destroyed, but was then himself shot up, by a Me109, possibly Oberleutnant Gustav Rödel of 4./JG27, and was forced to make a forced landing at Gammons Farm, Kilmington, Axminster. His Hurricane, P3415, although damaged, was repairable and Haw himself was not injured. Rödel had flown during the Spanish Civil War and shot down his first victory over Poland on 1 September 1939. He was by this time a *Staffelkäpitan*, and would survive the war with ninety-eight victories, most being claimed in the west. He received

A group of 504 Squadron pilots towards the end of 1940, with some of their trophies. From left to right: Flying Officer P T Parsons (KIA in 1942), Flying Officer M E A Royce, Sergeant Charlton Haw, Sergeant D Haywood (PoW in 1943).

the Knight's Cross with Oak Leaves, and rose to the rank of general in the post-war Luftwaffe.

No.504 Squadron continued their actions during the late stages of the Battle, remaining at Filton till the end of the year. Haw was able to record another success on 17 January 1941. He and another pilot were sent off to intercept a raider, finding a Ju88 of I./LG1. Although they identified it as a Heinkel 111, and claimed to have only damaged it, the bomber in fact failed to return to its base.

The squadron moved to Exeter for the first half of 1941, but in July 'A Flight' became the nucleus that helped reform 81 Squadron at RAF Debden. With Russia having entered the war, Britain was asked to provide help, and the Air Ministry were asked to provide some fighters to go to Russia, to help train Russian pilots who would be receiving RAF fighters – Hurricanes and American Bell Aircobras – and to assist in some air defence actions. The RAF therefore formed 151 Fighter Wing, which included 81 and 134

Squadrons. 81 Squadron was commanded by Squadron Leader A H Rook (qv) and 134 by Squadron Leader Anthony G Miller.

Anthony Rook had been made CO of 504 Squadron in March 1941 and it was he who took A Flight to become 81 Squadron. Rook's cousin, Michael Rook (qv), had also been with 504, but was posted to 134 in July 1941, forming in readiness for Russia. Anthony Miller had been with 17 Squadron in 1940 and led it until July 1941, at which time he was given command of 134. Now located at RAF Leconfield, the pilots prepared for overseas duty, embarking on the aircraft carrier *Argus* at Glasgow on 18 August, sailing the next day. Picking up escorts the carrier left Scapa Flow on the 30th and headed for Murmansk via Iceland. After something of a tortuous journey the Hurricanes were flown off on 7 September and headed for Vaenga airfield.

They were met by a number of Russian pilots who made everyone welcome and in the following days everyone busied themselves making their accommodation liveable and the maintenance areas workable. The Wing became operational on the 11th. On the afternoon of the 12th, 81 Squadron claimed two Me109s shot down, and damaged two more. There had been five 109s, escorting a Hs126 of 1/(H)32. One of those destroyed was claimed by Haw west of Murmansk. These were from 1./JG77 who lost Leutnant E von der Lü.

On the 17th the Wing bagged four German aircraft, and again Haw was credited with another Me109 confirmed, and in the same area. Again it was JG77 which suffered, with Feldwebel J Stiglmair missing. Eight Hurricanes of 81 Squadron were on a defensive patrol in order to cover the return of Russian bombers from a raid. Two 109s bounced the Hurricanes. In the fight that ensued, one was shot down by Squadron Leader Rook, and shared with Sergeants P Sims and A A Anson. Haw engaged the other one, chasing it and, having closed the range, opened up, and the 109 began to leave a smoke trail from its engine. It then went into a vertical dive and the pilot baled out, being reported a prisoner.

Bad weather in Russia was the main obstacle for the Wing, but it was possible to fly a few escort missions. The main problem Haw and his companions found was that it was hard going to keep up with the Russian Petlyakov Pe-2 bombers (at first glance looking similar to German Me110s) that seemed able to fly at an incredible speed: 335 mph at 16,400 feet. On the 26th, 81 Squadron were jumped by 109s while escorting bombers and were fortunate to not only survive receiving any damage but managed to claim three Messerschmitts shot down. Next day another escort and more 109s engaged, this time 81 claiming two more, Haw being one of the victors. Haw reported:

'I was White Leader in a formation of four Hurricanes when I sighted four Me109s approaching us from the west. The leader of their second section tried to do a beam attack on me but I turned towards him and after about three complete turns I was on his tail. I gave him several shorts bursts and while doing this we lost height down to 3,000 feet. As I fired the last burst but one, the enemy aircraft came out of its turn, climbed steeply, and then stalled and went into a spin, white and black smoke pouring from it. I did not see what happened to it, as there was an enemy aircraft on my tail. I got rid of this and returned to base.'

The Order of Lenin. Haw and his CO, S/Ldr A H Rook (qv), both received this Russian decoration for their work with 151 Wing.

The kill was later confirmed as crashed. Haw had now accounted for three Me109Es in two weeks. In total the wing had claimed twelve Germans shot down to date, for the loss of one pilot.

All the air combat glory had gone to 81 Squadron, but finally 134 were able to claim some kills on 6 October. A German attack on the aerodrome by 14 Ju88s with 109s as escort was intercepted by 134, who claimed three victories and several damaged. The RAF pilots were now busily showing Russian pilots the rudiments of the Hurricanes, in readiness to hand them over to the Soviets before they left to return to England. When they did so, the Russians were able to form a wing of their own men. One thing Wag Haw told me about Russia was that they had mostly to fly low down, below 5,000 feet most of the time, because of the risk of leaving con-trails. If these trails started, the pilots had quickly to reduce height to get rid of them, because they stood out like the proverbial sore thumbs.

The Wing's last operation came on 17 October, with 134 escorting Russian bombers to bomb east of Petsamo, but saw no hostile aircraft. The RAF pilots began to return to England by sea in late November. The Wing had flown 365 sorties. It had been quite an experience. There had been some 550 RAF airmen plus 50 or so pilots, and as it was beginning to get really cold, it was a good time to go home. They docked on 7 December, the day Japan attacked the American Air and Naval Base at Pearl Harbor.

Some decorations were awarded. Firstly the Russians presented four pilots with their Order of Lenin. To Wing Commander H N G Ramsbottom-Isherwood AFC, Squadron Leader A H Rook, Squadron Leader A G Miller, and Flight Sergeant Haw. In addition, Squadron Leader Rook, and the wing leader, Wing Commander H N G Ramsbottom-Isherwood AFC, both received the DFC while Charlton Haw was given the Distinguished Flying Medal. It came with an excellent recommendation by Tony Rook:

[This airman] joined No.504 Squadron in June 1940, and since then has been an operational member of the squadron, participating in the Battle of Britain all of September and dealing with raids on Filton aerodrome in late September, 1940. He has done numerous convoy duties and escort for daylight raids on Le Havre, Cherbourg and Brest. In July 1941, he was transferred to No.81 Squadron for overseas duties in Russia where he carried out his duties admirably, shooting down three enemy aircraft for which he was awarded the Order of Lenin. Sergeant Haw has always flown under me, first as his Flight Commander and secondly as his Commanding Officer and I strongly recommend him for the Distinguished Flying Medal. In all, he has done 280 hours operational flying and numerous hours training new pilots.

* * *

In the meantime, the Russians recorded the following with their Order of Lenin:

To pilot of the Royal 'Military' Air Fleet of Great Britain, SERGEANT HAW, C.F.

I congratulate you with the high Government award of the Union of Socialist Republics, the 'Order of Lenin'. Your manliness, heroism and excellent mastery in battles of the air have always assured victory over the enemy. I wish you new victories in battles against the common enemy of all progressive nations, i.e. German fascism.

Charlton Haw was commissioned in March 1942, returning to 504 Squadron, but then in May he was made a flight commander with 122 Squadron, flying Spitfires. 122 was commanded by a Belgian pilot, Squadron Leader Leon Prevot; he was shot down over France on 30 July, but managed to evade capture. Because of his absence his place was taken by Squadron Leader J R C Kilian until November 1942, at which time Squadron Leader Don Kingaby DFM took over. Finally, in February 1943, Haw was given command of 611 Squadron. Wag Haw told me:

'I was a flight commander in 122 under Don Kingaby where we were engaged in a lot of sweeps, and escorts to US Marauders and Mitchells. When I went to Biggin Hill with 611 Squadron we began to receive the Spitfire IXB. They were better low down than the IXA had been. They had been fine above 20,000 feet but the IXBs were a match for the FW190 at all heights, but especially lower down. This was good because the air battles were beginning to come down by then.

'Rhubarbs were something that many pilots didn't like. They were very costly and largely a waste of time. I was flying with Paddy Finucane [Wing Commander B E F Finucane DSO DFC] when he was killed [15 July 1942]. We had attacked an army camp just inside France and he was hit the moment we crossed the coast. He was streaming a little bit but on the way out, he'd got over the Channel and couldn't fly on. He put his flaps down, hit the sea and went straight in. The night before, one of our pilots ditched in similar fashion, but the sea was flat calm, just like a mill pond. He'd been hit on his first trip, beating up shipping. However, he left his flaps up, bounced two or three times, settled on the water and climbed out. So there was Paddy Finucane, an experienced pilot, trying to ditch but on a sea that was a bit choppy, flaps down, and went straight in. Force-landing on the sea was a risky business at any time.

'Don Kingaby was a great chap. I confirmed his last Hun he shot down with us. We were over Cap Gris Nez and it was a lovely climbing shot. We were at 25,000 feet when Don chased this fighter which then began a gentle climbing turn to the right. Don pulled round after it, cut inside and fired and that was that!

'During the Dieppe operation on 19 August 1942, I had a go at a 109, but then I was surrounded by about six more. I was yelling for help and Griffiths [F/Lt L P Griffiths], the other flight commander, who was a New Zealander, came to my rescue and they all sheared off. I then headed home, all on my own, and came up right behind a Dornier 215 that was preparing to go after some small ship. I closed right in behind it – the crew didn't see me – and pressed the button. Nothing! My guns were empty.

'All Fighter Command was really doing in 1942-43 was pinning a lot of fighters down in France by our sweeps etc., although the Germans didn't like to mix it much. I remember I was chasing a FW190 and was slowly catching it up, when out of the blue this Spitfire arrived between me and the 190. It rolled upside down, shot the 190 down, then rolled right way up. As he regained level flight I could see it was our wing leader. When we got back I said I'd been amazed at his manoeuvre to which he replied, "Well I had to lose some speed, didn't I?" It was brilliant shooting.'

Flight Lieutenant C Haw DFC DFM (2nd from the left) with his CO, S/Ldr Don Kingaby DSO DFM, 122 Squadron, 1943.

Squadron Leader C Haw DFC DFM OoL, as OC 65 Squadron post war.

The Wingco was probably New Zealander Al Deere DSO DFC. The only chance Haw had to increase his score was when he damaged a Me109F off Daro on 20 January.

In April 1943 he left 611 to undertake a six-week lecture tour and was then posted to the Fighter Leaders' School until November. He was then given command of 129 Squadron, initially on Spitfires again, but then with Mustang IIIs. From March 1944 his squadron was part of one of the Polish wings at Heston. Following the invasion of France, Haw returned to the Fighter Leaders' School in July that had now become part of the Central Flying School at RAF Tangmere. It was here that he received the Distinguished Flying Cross. This was gazetted in October 1944 and had been in the works for some time. The original recommendation for an award was made sometime in May of that year, which noted that he had flown a total of 502 hours on operational flying during approximately 300 missions. Since his DFM award he had flown 280 hours during 168 sorties. The citation read:

This officer is now carrying out his third tour of operations. During his last tour he was a flight commander for 6 months with No. 122 Squadron and Squadron Commander for 3 months of No. 611 Squadron. He was awarded the D.F.M. in December 1941 and subsequently carried out 135 sorties during his second tour and, during his third tour, has to date carried out 33 offensive sorties.

On the recommendation for this award were the words of the Wing Commander Flying, a famous Polish fighter pilot, Wing Commander Stanisław Skalski VM KW DSO DFC, dated 2 June 1944, just four days before D-Day in Europe:

'He is [an] exceptional Squadron Commander and very keen leader. He impressed upon his pilots to engage the enemy!'

This in turn was endorsed with the remarks of the officer commanding the sector, another Polish ace, Group Captain Aleksander Gabszewicz VM KW DSO DFC, dated on D-Day, 6 June:

'S/Ldr Haw is a very good pilot. During his career as a pilot he has shown great courage and eagerness to engage the enemy. Since last being decorated, he has "collected" over 300 points.'

The final endorsement came from the AOC 84 Group, 2nd TAF, Air Vice-Marshal L O Brown CBE DSC AFC, who wrote: 'Very strongly recommended. This officer has just completed his third tour.'

* * *

Regarding the Mustang, Haw told me:

'The first Mustangs had enclosed cockpits, not the bubble hoods which came later. We did a lot of dive-bombing, sticking a couple of bombs under the wings. We'd attack trains, crossroads, etc., whatever one saw; we just rolled over and dived. We did all of our practice dive-bombing over France – live! We also attacked shipping, and did about ten escorts to American heavies while I was in command.

'When converting, we had an American help us. The machine had a 'pee-tube' which could be brought up between the legs where the pilot could undo flying suit and put his "equipment" into it. This was often necessary for long range work! Our American friend tried one out one day only to find he couldn't get it off! Because of the suction at the back, this thing had locked on him. There he was, tugging away and eventually he had to stall the thing to stop the airflow so he could pull it free. We all stood watching him roller-coasting across the runway! Then they had to alter the position where the urine drained out to avoid this tremendous suction.

'We had one of our pilots killed at Coolham which was entirely his own fault. He took off but forgot to tighten the knob which kept the throttle from moving back with the vibration. He had bombs on and just sort of sunk in on take off. Another pilot at Coolham, which was all Sommerfelt tracking, burst a tyre on take off. Either side of the runway we had latrines, just four poles with some hessian wrapped round them. This Mustang careered off and its wing knocked this thing down and as it happened there was a Polish airman on the "throne", trousers round his ankles, and the wing just missed his head. It left him with a very surprised look on his face, and the Mustang ended up in a ditch. I don't know if the poor fellow was constipated but that must have cured him!

'During the Invasion, we were on ground attack again, all in support of the army, just attacking anything which moved. On D-Day itself we flew high cover but although briefed late the previous evening, we had to sit around very frustrated, until about tea-time on the 6th. We became part of a huge air umbrella over both the beaches and the ships. An impressive sight.

'I don't think anyone of us managed to fire at a German aircraft on the long range escorts. By now, of course, the Germans were mostly doing those head-on attacks on US bomber formations. One moment they were just dots, the next they were gone and rolling away and down.

'But we went a long way over – we even flew to Berlin once, and Frankfurt. It took us five hours to fly to Berlin. On that escort we went out with them then came straight back, because naturally we did a lot of weaving about during the journey. The relief escort would then fly direct to Berlin and bring the bombers home. Over Berlin we only saw some smoke and low cloud but it was a great feeling to know we were there and that Berlin was below us. However, it was a long time sitting in a single-seater.

'During the war I flew Hurricanes, Spitfires and Mustangs, which were all super aeroplanes. On the whole I think I would favour the Spitfire with its better overall performance. The Mustang, however, did have better acceleration, especially if you rolled it upside down and dived it with two bombs on. Certainly we found the ground coming up pretty quickly. I had a bomb hang-up once and after trying everything to get rid of it, was finally told to land at Tangmere. Then, as I crossed the coast, it fell off, just missing Littlehampton.'

* * *

In the final months of the war Wag Haw once again went to the Fighter Leaders' School, part of the Central Flying School at Tangmere. He later took an admin post at Horsham St Faith. Post-war he received a permanent commission in 1948 after commanding 65 Squadron with Spitfire XIVs and later, in 1947, helped to convert the squadron onto the de Havilland Hornet. However, his eyesight was letting him down which caused him to lose his flying category and consequently he left the Service in 1951.

For the next six years he and his wife ran a public house in Sussex, before owning a boarding kennels. Then they developed a pet food wholesale and retail business, which he ran for 25 years until he retired in 1985. That same year he visited Moscow for the celebrations for the 40th anniversary of the ending of the war. He resided in Farnham, Surrey in his last years until his death in December 1993. He left a second wife Audrey, and a son, and he was aged 73.

Chapter 10

Wing Commander K T Lofts DFC & Bar

Pilot Officer K T Lofts RAuxAF, 615 Squadron, pre–war.

Born in the city of Canterbury, Kent, on 8 February 1918, Keith Temple Lofts, was the son of Algernon K and Mrs Ethelind M Lofts; his father died in November 1929. There was a brother, Michael Henry Lofts, who was some two years younger. Keith was educated at Haileybury College, near Hertford, between 1932 and 1937. In 1938 he joined No. 615 (County of Surrey) Royal Auxiliary Air Force Squadron being called for full time service on 24 August 1939. In mid-September he was attached to 11 Fighter Group's Pool for Hurricane training.

Back with 615 at Croydon, the squadron prepared to go to France, flying out on 15 November to Merville, not as one might suppose with Hurricanes, but with Gloster Gladiator II biplanes. Before the year was out it was based at Vitry with a detachment at St. Inglevert till April 1940, then to Abbeville with a detachment at Le Touquet, where they began converting to Hurricanes.

The squadron's main task was patrolling over the Channel ports as ships from England arrived with supplies and so on, and this continued until the German *Blitzkrieg* began on 10 May. For the next ten days the squadron was engaged in a few combat skirmishes, ground attack sorties against advancing German troops, and a few escort trips. Lofts appears to have got in a few fights with hostile aircraft and damaged a couple, but by 21 May it was all over and the squadron were pulled out and reformed at RAF Kenley, in Surrey. It took a month to get themselves together, while also flying a few sorties over France. During one of these missions, Lofts intercepted and damaged a Ju52 transport aircraft on 22 June.

As the Battle of Britain began, 615 took its place in the battle order, with a detachment based at Manston. Keith Lofts had his first confirmed success on 14 August, shooting down a Ju87 dive-bomber and damaging a second over the Channel. These were aircraft from 10/LG1, four being shot down by 615 and 610 Squadrons, although this may have been over-optimistic. The next day he shared in the destruction of a Me109 from 2./JG54, together with Flying Officer Tony Eyre, south-east of Folkestone, while on the 16th he got a Heinkel 111 bomber during a fight with II/KG55.

The squadron's base at Kenley was raided on the 18th, a day that is remembered each year by the squadron's Association. That day the squadron lost six Hurricanes destroyed on the ground, four shot down in combat, and one pilot killed. 615 did get in amongst enemy bombers and claimed a couple of Dorniers. Lofts managed to put some holes in another one.

The almost decimated squadron began operating from Croydon, and on 20 August Lofts shot down a 109, and then claimed another as a probable on the 29th. The former was a machine from 1./JG51 which he attacked and sent into the sea. Its pilot, Feldwebel Maul, was later rescued by a German He59 aircraft of the air sea rescue service of Seenotflugkdo.3, but the rescue aircraft seriously damaged a propeller when taking off.

The squadron were now in desperate need of a rest, and were pulled out of the line at the end of August and sent north to Prestwick. However, within a few days Keith Lofts was posted back south, to join 249 Squadron at North Weald. He arrived on 10 September and was in action on the 15th, sharing the destruction of a Heinkel to the south of London, but he was shot up by return fire and had to force land. His report stated:

'Whilst on patrol with Yellow Section we were detailed to intercept a raid coming in from the south-east, which consisted of about 20 Dorniers. When the interception was made, I was situated about 2,000 feet below the Dorniers which had an escort of Me109s who started diving on me.

I broke away from this attack and when well clear regained height and found a large formation of He111s on my right, slightly below. I picked out one and did an attack from about 2,000 feet above. I gave one long burst and noticed this e/a break formation and start diving. It was then attacked by several other Hurricanes. It eventually force-landed at West Malling. Damage to my aircraft was due to return fire.'

The Heinkel was from 5/KG53 and had been part of a formation of twelve bombers going for the docks of the Thames estuary. It had started to lag behind due to a problem with one engine which then cut out, and then the fighters attacked. The pilot, Feldwebel Kurt Behrendt, with two of his crew dead and two others wounded, made a forced landing in the western corner of West Malling aerodrome.

Keith Lofts while serving with 249 Squadron in 1940.

The official report says that Keith's aircraft was damaged by an attack by a 109, forcing him to crash land at West Malling. Either he did not see the 109, or he preferred to believe he was hit by return fire.

He wrote about another combat report on 27 September, having a share in a Me110 shot down over south London:

'Whilst on patrol with A Flight we encountered a formation of Me110s in a defensive formation. The leader attacked and was followed up by the rest of the flight. I picked on one and gave him a short burst from underneath. He immediately broke away and was then followed by the other Hurricanes who followed and gave him another burst. He finally crashed near Lingfield, Surrey.'

The other pilots were Pilot Officer J R B Meaker and Sergeant H J Davidson, Meaker noting that they received no return fire from the Messerschmitt. This 110 came from 15./LGI on a free-lance patrol, and had already been hit by other fighters. With both engines damaged by 249's attack, its pilot, Oberleutnant Otto Weckeiser force landed near Socketts Manor, Oxted, which is about five miles north of Lingfield. His gunner, Gefreiter Horst Brüggow had been wounded. This German unit did not fare well this day, with seven of its 110s lost.

October started fairly quietly for 249. Some new pilots arrived, one being a Polish chap, Michel Maciejowski (qv). Within a few days some awards were announced, one going to Keith Lofts, although this was mainly for his success in 615. The citation in the *London Gazette* for 22 October read:

> *This officer has participated in numerous engagements against the enemy in Belgium, France and England. He has displayed great determination and coolness and has destroyed eight enemy aircraft.*

He was able to add slightly to this total on the afternoon of 16 October. He was leader of a two-man patrol which was vectored on to a lone raider. His wingman was a Frenchman, Adjutant H J Bouquillard. The raider was approaching Maidstone from the south at 12,000 feet, and within a few minutes Lofts spotted it coming straight for them. The German pilots saw the Hurricanes too and turned steeply in order to make for some clouds above. Keith later reported:

> 'I detailed Red 2 to go above and myself entered the clouds on the same course as the bandit. I flew for a few seconds and then sighted him straight ahead. I closed to rather a too close a range and opened fire with a burst of about ten seconds. The Do215 dived slightly to the right and I noticed smoke coming from his port engine; he then started to lose height. I then felt a thud against my aircraft and shortly afterwards my engine stopped – no oil pressure. The cockpit filled with flames and smoke but they were not sufficiently overcoming to warrant an emergency descent.'

Lofts made a successful force-landing at Rolvenden, near Tenterden. Later he discovered that his wingman had also made an attack, and during it saw the rear gunner of the Dornier firing back, but then appear to stop. He too could see the smoke from the port engine as the Dornier lost height and disappeared into cloud. They were credited with a shared probable. Lofts' Hurricane was a write off. The Dornier, a 17z, not a 215, was most likely an aircraft from 6/KG2 which force-landed at St Leger, with one crew member wounded. It suffered, as the Germans liked to assess these things, with 40 per cent damage.

On the afternoon of the 29th, the squadron had been scrambled to patrol base at 15,000 feet but as they started to get airborne, about a dozen bomb-carrying Me109s from II(S)/LG2, from Calais/Marck, caught them in their most vulnerable state, and commenced bombing the airfield. One bomb fell in the middle of the aerodrome just as Yellow Section left the ground and Lofts' aircraft was damaged by blast and debris. He was not hurt and managed to land back safely, but it had been a close thing. Another pilot, from 257 Squadron that shared the base, was not so fortunate. His Hurricane was hit and bellied in; the pilot was burned to death in the cockpit.

* * *

This was the end of Lofts' participation in the Battle of Britain, but he remained with 249 for a while longer. On 16 January, he, along with Wing Commander Victor Beamish AFC, Squadron Leader R A Barton DFC, Flight Lieutenant T F Neil DFC and Pilot Officer B Beard DFM, travelled to RAF Duxford to receive their recent awards from His Majesty King George VI. On 18 February his time on 249 came to an end with a posting to No. 56 Operational Training Unit at RAF Debden.

He was retained as an instructor here till the end of July 1941, and later was posted to RAF Turnhouse in November in order to form and command 340 Squadron. This was to be the first Free French fighter squadron in the RAF, equipped with Spitfire IIs. It began its operational duties flying convoy patrols along the east coast, using Drem as a forward base. This lasted until January 1942, Lofts being posted to command 134 Squadron at RAF Eglington, outside Londonderry, and later at RAF Baginton, south of

Coventry, until April. 134 had recently been part of 151 Wing, along with 81 Squadron, that had operated on the northern Russian front, at Murmansk.

Things took on a rosier hue in May 1943, as he was put in command of 66 Squadron at RAF Skaebrae. Soon after taking over 66, which had Spitfire VI as its equipment, it moved to Church Stanton, Somerset (perhaps better known as Culmhead, as it later became). For the rest of the summer the squadron alternated between the West Country and 11 Group's RAF Kenley and Redhill, flying operations over France and over the sea of the Western Approaches.

Leading a sortie on 8 October 1943, west of the German naval base of Brest, they ran into a Me110 which Keith attacked and damaged before it escaped into cloud. A few days later, the squadron found a Ju88, and several pilots attacked and shot it down. Keith and five of his pilots were credited with one sixth of a victory each. Less than a month later came the devastating news that his brother Michael had been killed in action on 11 November. He had been a major with the Hertforshire Regiment, serving on the Italian front.

Towards the end of his year in command of 66 Squadron, he claimed his final combat success by damaging a Me109 on 19 May, flying a Spitfire IX. Two days later, on the 21st, his luck finally ran out. A morning Ranger operation over France was met by German anti-aircraft fire over Bayeux, and he and one of his pilots were both hit and shot down. The other pilot got back to the coast before he dived straight into the sea off Normandy, while Lofts was forced to crash-land his Spit IX (MJ182) north of Bayeux. However, he still had a bit of luck left, for he was able to get clear of his downed fighter and disappear into the countryside without being challenged by German soldiers. He spent the next couple of weeks evading German troops with the help of French Resistance workers, and then the Allies landed in Normandy. As luck would have it, this was not too far from his own location, and then it was just a matter of waiting until British or American troops over-ran the area in which he was hiding. This is exactly what occurred, although it was Canadian troops he met up with, on 19 July; soon he was on his way back to England.

Following a spot of leave he became Wing Commander Flying at RAF Hornchurch. He ended the war as a Wing Commander and in early 1945 was awarded a Bar to his DFC, the recommendation reading:

This officer has a long record of operational flying. He was awarded the Distinguished Flying Cross in 1940. Now on his second tour of operational duty, he has led his squadron on many sorties and several times led the Wing. In May 1944, his aircraft was shot down. Squadron Leader Lofts evaded capture and, showing courage and initiative, hid until able to return to our lines. He has destroyed at least eight enemy aircraft and damaged others. In addition, he has inflicted considerable damage on enemy vehicles and locomotives.

The other bit of news in this year came in October when he and his fiancée, Dawn Malet, daughter of Mr & Mrs Cecil Malet of Beaconsfield, announced their engagement.

Keith Lofts finally left the Service in 1946, but rejoined the Royal Auxiliary Air Force in 1948, taking command of 604 Squadron, which was equipped with De Havilland Vampire jets. Under his leadership, the squadron regained the coveted Esher Trophy in 1949. This trophy was competed for each year by AAF squadrons, marks being awarded for bombing, formation flying, piloting ability, landing on a mark, gunnery, etc. This dated back to the mid-1920s.

On Sunday 20 May 1951, Keith was taking part in the Cooper Trophy Air Race for auxiliary pilots, at RAF West Malling, Kent. Lofts was flying a Vampire III (VG700). The first heat of the race had already taken place and the second heat was going to start shortly after 3 pm. Group Captain H S Darley DSO, the station commander and former Battle of Britain pilot who had commanded 609 Squadron in 1940, had had lunch with Lofts who, he said, appeared '…to be very fit'. At around 3.20 pm, Darley was on the aerodrome, and saw Lofts seated in his aircraft, and as he passed, remarked to him that his aircraft seemed to be in excellent trim. Lofts smiled back in reply and a few moments later the Vampire taxied by. Some time after Lofts had taken off, Darley saw the Vampire pass over the airfield having completed one circuit of the 50 or so mile course, and disappear from his view. There were three aircraft in this heat and when only two aircraft later reappeared Darley knew it was Lofts' machine that was missing. According to eye witnesses, Lofts attempted to cut inside the turn made by the two planes in front of him and the stresses placed on the airframe caused the top nose cowling to detach itself and strike the cockpit canopy. The Vampire climbed vertically while making a slight turn, stalled at around 2,000 feet, and went into a spin. The pilot seemed to manage a recovery but pulled out too harshly, causing a second stall and spin. Moments later the Vampire struck the ground.

The gravestone of Keith Lofts, shared with his father and brother.

One of the first people to reach the scene of the crash was Police Sergeant William Albion, on duty at Cranbrook, and he had seen the crash. He found the aircraft burning furiously and spotted the top of a skull lying near the wreckage. With some help from others who had arrived they extricated the body from the cockpit. The injuries sustained made it obvious that the pilot had died instantly. He was 33 years old.

Group Captain Darley received the news that Lofts had crashed at Swifts Park, Cranbrook, at about 4.20 pm, and he quickly went to the scene. Seeing the wreckage of the Vampire he identified it as being Keith's and recognised too a particular blue shirt he had been wearing prior to the race, on the body which lay nearby.

Chapter 11

Wing Commander A D J Lovell DSO & Bar, DFC & Bar, DFC (US)

Anthony Desmond Joseph Lovell was the son of C A Stuart Lovell and Mrs Clare Mary Lovell, of Portrush, Northern Ireland, born on 9 August 1919. He was educated as a boarder, at Ampleforth College, North Yorkshire, run by Benedictine monks and lay staff from Ampleforth Abbey.

Completing his education, he decided to join the Royal Air Force and was successful in obtaining a short service commission in November 1937. After basic ground and flight training he was sent to No. 6 Flying Training School at Sywell, after which he was posted to No. 41 Squadron, based at Catterick, flying Hawker Fury fighter biplanes. When war came their station was moved to RAF Wick in Scotland, in October 1939, but quickly returned to Catterick where it remained until the time of Dunkirk. By this time it had changed over from the Fury to the Supermarine Spitfire I.

Tony Lovell saw his first actions over the Dunkirk evacuation in May 1940, the squadron having moved south to Hornchurch. On 31 May, flying with his flight commander, J T Webster, they engaged and shot down a He111 bomber, each credited with a half share. It was an early morning patrol over the beaches. The next day he shared another Heinkel, this time with Pilot Officer O B Morough-Ryan, mid-morning.

In the opening rounds of the Battle of Britain, 41 Squadron, now back at Catterick, sent up a section on Monday 8 July to investigate a possible raider, while 249 Squadron did the same. 41 Squadron, when they found and engaged it over the Yorkshire countryside, identified it as a Junkers Ju86, although it fact it was a Ju88 from 9/KG4 (coded 5J+AT) looking for British shipping off the east coast of England. Both squadron aircraft made attacking passes, but most of the credit appears to have gone to 249 Squadron. Flying Officer D G Parnell of 249 spotted the Junkers off Flamborough

Head at 17,000 feet. He closed in and was about to begin his attack when he saw a Spitfire make an attack, appearing to open fire for about three seconds. No evasive action came from the 88 and as the Spitfire broke away the bomber was trailing smoke from the port engine. Parnell and his two pilots made attacking passes at the damaged aeroplane before losing it in cloud. Riddled with bullets and one engine stopped, then the port engine catching fire, the pilot jettisoned his bombs, turned towards the English coast, and ordered his crew to bale out. The bomber crashed and exploded before the pilot could leave. He was the Staffelkapitän, Hauptmann Kurt Rohloff. His three crewmen survived although

Flight Lieutenant A AD J Lovell DFC, 41 Squadron, 1940.

wounded. The 88 came down at Hornsea, near Catfoss, at 11.42 am. Lovell was given credit for a fourth share with the three men of 249 Squadron.

If Lovell had survived this far on luck, it ran out a little on 28 July. The squadron was in action with Me109s near Dover and Lovell, flying Spitfire P9429, was wounded in the thigh by an attacking 109 apparently flown by the leader of JG51, Major Werner Mölders, a pilot with a score of around thirty by this date. Moments later, as the air fight developed further, the German ace ran into 74 Squadron's Spitfires, and its leader A G 'Sailor' Malan DFC shot down one 109 and then raked another, this being flown by the German ace. Mölders was wounded but was able to get back to his home base, Wissant, where he crash-landed. Lovell too, despite his wound, made it back to Hornchurch where he too crash-landed. However, it is also believed that it was John Webster who shot-up Mölders in this action, one of two 109s he damaged. Pilot Officer G H Bennions of 41 also shot down a 109 into the sea from JG51, the first of twelve kills 'Benny' claimed in the Battle of Britain.

It would be more than a month before Lovell got back from hospital and scored again. Being at Catterick, in 13 Group, most of the action was down

Group of 41 Squadron pilots. From left to right: Flying Officer N Mackenzie DFC, Tony Lovell, S/Ldr D O Finlay DFC, Flight Lieutenant E N Ryder DFC (qv), Pilot Officer R C Ford.

south, in 11 Group's territory, but on 15 August the Germans decided to make attacks in the north, hoping that the RAF defences would not be so concentrated over Yorkshire. They were wrong, and of course flying over from Norway and Denmark they came without suitable fighter escort: twin-engined Me110s, instead of the more effective Me109 single-seaters. It was becoming evident that the 110s, while still dangerous, were not generally as lethal as the 109s.

By late morning, Fighter Command controllers were seeing German aircraft heading in to the south coast, but shortly after mid-day British radar spotted the first signs of hostile aircraft coming across the North Sea and fighters were scrambled. 41, 72, 79 and 605 all became airborne to intercept He111 bombers of KG26, escorted by the 110s of I/ZG76. A little further south, 12 Group's radar began picking up a further raid, and sent Boulton-Paul Defiants of 264 to fly cover to a convoy, while 73 and 616 Squadrons were scrambled. Tony Lovell engaged the escorting 110s of ZG76, being credited

Wreckage of a Me110 of 1/ZG76, shot down by Lovell on 15 August 1940.

with one down near Barnard Castle, and another probably destroyed. The 110 crashed landed at 13.36 and as it slithered along the ground beside an army camp, it came to the road and the rear fuselage wrapped itself around a telegraph pole. Oberleutnant Hans-Ulrich Kettling and Obergefrieter Fritz Volk were taken into captivity.

The other raids were all intercepted and the Luftwaffe suffered a major defeat this day. Dowding's decision not to denude Fighter Command in the north in order to have more squadrons down south, was vindicated.

* * *

No. 41 Squadron moved south to Hornchurch in early September, but almost immediately lost their CO, Squadron Leader H R L Hood, on the 5th. He and John Webster, who had just received the DFC, collided during an attack on a Dornier 17. Hood was killed and Webster baled out but fell dead. This was a massive loss to the unit.

It was not the only misfortune that befell 41 that day. Lovell was also shot down in Spitfire R6885, baling out near Benfleet, Essex. Flying Officer R W

'Wally' Wallens was wounded in one leg and force-landed, and Sergeant R A Carr-Lewty was also shot up and had to force-land at Standford-le-Hope.

The new CO arrived, Squadron Leader R C F Lister, but he was shot down and wounded on the 14th. A new Boss, D O Findlay, who had been an Olympic hurdler at the Berlin Games in 1936 winning a silver medal, took over.

On the 6th, the day after he himself had been shot down, Tony Lovell shot down a Me109 north of Manston, possibly a machine of JG53, and another on the 15th south-east of Canterbury, plus a probable south-west of Hornchurch. The confirmed claim on the 15th was a machine from I./JG53, Feldwebel Herbert Tschoppe baling out badly burned at 12.09. The German was in a section of five on a freelance patrol, three in a line with the other two above and behind. Tschoppe, who told his captors he had only arrived at his unit the previous evening, had his fuel tank hit and the contents set on fire.

Lovell's final claim in September was a Dornier 17 that he damaged, on the 30th off Hastings. KG2 and KG3 had several of their aircraft return home damaged. Lovell was also promoted and made a flight commander.

During the dangerous days of October, as the Germans switched from massive raids of bombers to nuisance raids with bomb-carrying Me109s, escorted by other unencumbered 109s, Lovell scored again. On the 1st he shot down Feldwebel Edward Gernith of 1./JG51, whose fighter crashed at 'Chequers', Shadoxhurst, near Ashford at 16.50. Garnith survived by parachute and was taken prisoner. He was flying one of six 109s on an escort to a Dornier reconnaissance aircraft and was at 26,000 feet when attacked by a dozen Spitfires. Gernith was hit in the engine, which caught fire leaving the pilot no choice but to bale out. This had been the German's second sortie of the day, having escorted bomb-carrying 109s during a morning operation to the south-west of London. He was on his 20th sortie in the Battle and had also seen action during the French campaign.

On the 20th Lovell got another 109, this being flown by Oberfeldwebel Albert Friedemann of 6/JG52. Lovell got him over Welling, near Bexleyheath, his 109 exploding at 13.45. Friedemann fell from his disintegrating fighter but his parachute was not deployed. Lovell damaged another 109 on the 30th and was lucky to survive the fight. His number three on this date was

New Zealander John Mackenzie and as they became engaged with around thirty Messerschmitts, Mackenzie attacked one as it slid behind Lovell's tail. The 109 nosed down, Mackenzie half-rolling after it, firing until bits flew off, and it streamed smoke, crashing below. These 109s were from JG26 that lost one pilot; but later in the afternoon, JG26 had their revenge, shooting down two of 41's Spitfires near Maidstone. One pilot was killed, the other wounded.

Although we say today the Battle officially ended on 30 October, the fighter pilots did not know this at the time, and as far as they were concerned it was business as usual in November. Lovell bagged yet another 109 on the 17th north of Herne Bay, and shared yet another on the 27th near Tonbridge. These victories brought his score to five destroyed, five shared destroyed, two probables and two damaged. He had recently been awarded the DFC, this citation appearing in the *London Gazette* on 26 November:

> *This officer had flown on active operations against the enemy since war began. He has shown a fine fighting spirit and has led his flight and on occasions his squadron with great courage, coolness and determination. He has destroyed seven enemy aircraft.*

He received the award from the King at Buckingham Palace on 11 March 1941, accompanied by his mother, and sister Claire.

Lovell remained with the squadron until the early spring of 1941, during which time he managed to intercept and damage a He111 on 22 January, shared with another pilot, and on 30 March shot down a Ju88 near Ouston, this being a machine from I(F)/23. On 1 April he and another pilot damaged another He111 north-west of Leeming airfield.

It was now time for a rest, although many pilots did not think being a flying instructor either a rest, nor less dangerous than operational flying. However, everyone had to go through these periods, and Tony Lovell went off to No. 58 Operational Training Unit at Grangemouth, on 23 May, to impart his knowledge and experience to the coming generation of fighter pilots. Nevertheless, he managed to slip this particular noose in mid-June with a posting to Catterick and a job as Operations Room Controller. A much better, and much safer job.

In October he was given command of 145 Squadron, taking over from Stan Turner DFC (qv). There was little in the way of operations but he did manage to shoot down a Ju88 north-east of Hartlepool on 16 November, in a Spitfire IIb; on 19 January 1942 he got another, off Newcastle, flying a Spitfire Vb. These successes brought him a Bar to his DFC, gazetted on 10 February:

This officer is a fearless and skilful fighter pilot. His keenness to engage the enemy, combined with fine leadership, both in the air and on the ground, have set an inspiring example. In November 1941, Squadron Leader Lovell shot down a Junkers 88 some 35 miles off the Yorkshire coast. In January 1942, in the same area and in difficult weather conditions, he intercepted another Junkers 88 and shot it down into the sea. This officer has personally destroyed at least 11 hostile aircraft and has damaged others.

Lovell's squadron was now slated for overseas service and his next job was to prepare for the move. They left in February, going to Helwan, Egypt, but once the move was made Lovell was sent to HQ RAF Middle East in May, initially as a controller with 252 Wing, moving on to the 13 Sector's Ops Room in October. Eventually he was allowed back into front line service, being flown to Malta to command No. 1435 Flight on 21 July. This flight had previously had night-fighter and day-fighter duties with Hurricanes, but with the Battle for Malta still raging, it had been enlarged to a full squadron and re-equipped with Spitfires. No sooner had he begun this task than he was made wing commander of the Safi strip base.

Two days later Lovell shared two Ju88s damaged with other pilots and on the 26th damaged an Italian Macchi MC202

Wing Commander Tony Lovell DFC & Bar.

and a German Me109. On the 28th he shared in the destruction of a Ju88 of II/KG77 near Kalafrana Bay. Flight Lieutenant R I A Smith, a Canadian, had initially attacked this bomber which then suffered further attacks by Lovell, Pilot Officer J G Mejer, a Belgian pilot, and Wing Commander G H Stainforth. The latter was the CO of 89 night-fighter Squadron, but who on this occasion had borrowed one of 1435's Spitfires and gone 'along for the ride'. The 88, hit badly, headed towards the sea, two of its crew baling out. The pilot, Unteroffizier Albert Führer (he must have suffered with a name like his) did not survive but three others were rescued by seaplane tender from Malta. George Stainforth AFC had been a Schneider Trophy pilot in the late 1920s, and in 1931 had been the first pilot to exceed 400 mph. He was to die in action near the Gulf of Suez in September 1942.

In August, 1435 Flight became 1435 Squadron. This was the time of Operation Pedestal, the gallant ship convoy that pushed to Malta from Gibraltar, suffering severe losses, but getting its precious tanker through, the *Ohio*.

Lovell was in action over the convoy on the 13th, shooting down an Italian Ju87 dive-bomber of 209° Squadriglia, piloted by Serg-Magg. Guido Savini, surviving a ditching with his gunner, 1° Av. Arm. Nicola Patella. Lovell was over the convoy in the late afternoon, giving all his attention to a Savoia S-84 bomber, shooting this down into the sea. The next day Lovell led his pilots in another cover patrol over the few remaining ships, in company with 229 Squadron. Italian aircraft made an approach towards the struggling *Ohio*. Lovell made the following report afterwards:

'As we arrived I saw one Ju87 diving and went for it, overtook it rapidly, opened fire at 300 yards and broke away at 30 yards. Saw strikes all over the engine and fuselage. White smoke poured from both sides. He lost height, smoke stopped and he did a steep turn to port and flew west losing height. I turned back towards the convoy and saw the Ju87 crash into the sea. I claim half share with Sgt. Philp.' [Sergeant G Philp was his wingman.]

The Italian Ju87, from 239° Squadriglia, was crewed by its CO, Captain Antonio Cumbat and 1° Av. Arm. Michele Cavallo. Although Cavallo had been badly wounded, they survived in their dinghy and, together with a downed Macchi pilot, were later rescued by a Dornier flying boat. They had a long tale to tell of Spitfires, Beaufighters and finally the Dornier.

Lovell continued to be very active over the next few weeks, although his next claim did not come until October. On the 1st he damaged an Italian R2001 fighter, then damaged a 109 on the 11th. His wingman, Pilot Officer W C Walton, had to shoot another 109 off his tail. This was followed by a Ju88, destroyed north of St Paul's Bay on the 12th. The Axis aircraft were having what turned out to be a final 'blitz' on the island, and this action took place during the fifth raid of the day. At about 15.30 pm some 50-60 enemy aircraft made an approach to the island, of which one group were five Ju88s. Lovell and his pilots intercepted them half-way between Sicily and Malta. Lovell recorded:

'While closing in rapidly on the starboard bomber I fired a two-second burst from a range of 300 yards and large pieces flew off, and flames came from the starboard engine. I then broke away sharply. P/O Walton and F/Sgt Scott witnessed the aircraft on fire.'

Over these five raids the Germans suffered heavily, LG/1, KG77, and KG54 losing aircraft, while JG53 and JG77 lost three Me109 pilots. Before the month was out, Lovell had made a claim for a Ju88 damaged on the 17th and a 109 damaged on the 26th. His final aerial victory from Malta came on 7 December, another Ju88 destroyed over the sea, and during an attack on the Italian airfield on Lapedusa on 17 December Lovell strafed and destroyed a S-79 bomber. Before these last couple of claims, Lovell had been awarded the Distinguished Service Order, gazetted on 3 November 1942:

This officer is an outstanding squadron commander who has played a considerable part in the defence of Malta. One day in October 1942, he led his squadron in an attack against six Junkers 88s escorted by a number of fighters. In the combat, Squadron Leader Lovell shot down a Junkers 88, bringing his total victories to nine. On many occasions, his skilful leadership has enabled his squadron to intercept enemy air formations bent on attacking

Malta. This officer's gallantry and determination have set an example worthy of the highest praise.

Lovell was also awarded the American DFC on 14 November 1944. In early December he moved to No. 322 Wing as Wing Commander Flying, leading this during the assault on Corsica in March 1944, and once established here, operations began over north-west Italy as well as the south of France. On 3 May, in a fight over Sienna, he shot down a FW190 and damaged a second, aircraft of I/SG4. On the 15th he shot down a 109 over Lake Bolsena and exactly one month later, over Piacenza, claimed a MC205, but it was probably a Fiat G55 of I° Gruppo RSI, one of two this unit lost on the 15th. These were his last fighter claims, which now totalled sixteen destroyed, six others shared destroyed, and a number of probables and damaged.

As the landings on the French coast began, he was sent in August to join No. 1 Mobile Operations Room unit of the Mediterranean Allied Air Force. He now commenced a fifth tour of operations in November as wing leader of 244 Wing in Italy, and received the American DFC at this time.

In December 1944 he was given a break with a posting to 71 OTU at Ismailia as Chief Instructor. It was while here he learnt that he had been awarded a Bar to his DSO, gazetted on 23 February 1945:

Since the award of the Distinguished Service Order this officer has taken part in many more operational sorties and has destroyed at least a further three enemy aircraft, bringing his total victories to 19 enemy aircraft destroyed. He has led his wing on many low level attacks against road targets in the face of intense enemy fire. His enthusiasm and fine leadership have been reflected in the success achieved by the wing since April 1944, which has destroyed 30 enemy aircraft and over 1,000 enemy vehicles, besides damaging 50 enemy locomotives. Both in the air and on the ground, Wing Cdr. Lovell has set an inspiring example of courage, skill and devotion to duty.

With the coming of peace in Europe he was posted back to England in June 1945 joining the School of Air Support at RAF Old Sarum as a supernumerary until taking command of No. 5 Co-op Wing in August.

At around 11.30 am, on 17 of August (just two days after Japan surrendered) he took off for some local flying, taking a Spitfire XII (EN234) of the station's Communications Flight. Witnesses said later that as he did so he went into a slow roll. As he started to level out it looked as if he was about to perform a second one, but his Spitfire had hit some telephone wires. Then, having stalled, it scraped some fencing, bellied into the ground and disintegrated. Lovell was killed instantly. It seems inconceivable that such an experienced fighter pilot would have carried out such a manoeuvre. The Spitfire XII was a type he was new to, so whether inexperience on type or perhaps some mechanical malfunction occurred, the true reason for the accident remains speculative.

* * *

Lovell was not the usual run of fun-loving fighter pilots, and being a devout Catholic he rarely caroused with his brother pilots, so in some respects this resulted in his spectacular achievements being overlooked. He did, however, fly operations throughout the war, received five decorations, and there can be few pilots who flew more fighter tours and operations than Tony Lovell. He had nearly 1,200 flying hours in Spitfires alone.

His remains were buried in Portrush Cemetery, Country Antrim, Northern Ireland. He was 26 years old. His older brother Flight Lieutenant Stuart James Lovell was 27 when he was killed in action with 183 Squadron on 29 January 1944 and is buried in Kerfautras Cemetery, Brest. His Typhoon was shot down by ground fire during a Rodeo operation to Guipavas airfield.

Chapter 12

Flight Lieutenant M K Maciejowski VM KW & 3 Bars DFC DFM

There are occasions when pure chance results in meeting someone pretty special, someone it would be difficult to meet under normal circumstances. In the summer of 1966 I was a training officer with the Air Training Corps, and my squadron's summer camp was at RAF Gaydon, in Warwickshire. It was August, and it was soon apparent that the Station was preparing for a Battle of Britain open day the following month. Gaydon was part of RAF Training Command and had Varsity aircraft that equipped the Air Navigation School there. If I may digress slightly, I was given a ride in a Varsity one evening, which was the first time I had ever been in an aeroplane at night. As we taxied out the sun was setting and by the time we lifted off it had gone down. Once airborne, the sun reappeared as we gained height, setting again several minutes later, so my first flight at night gave me two sunsets.

Fairly early on at Gaydon I noticed an RAF officer in the Mess, who had more than the average collection of medal ribbons beneath his RAF wings, but did not like to approach him without first finding out his name. When I asked the RAF officer who was looking after the ATC units on base, I was told he was Flight Lieutenant Manson. I had already noted that this man had a rosette on his 1939-45 Star, which denoted he had been in the Battle of Britain, but the name rang not the slightest bell with me.

A day or so later, some of my cadets asked me who this man was. I had to admit I had no idea, which was a bit of a let-down for the boys but I said I would find out more about him. What had fascinated the lads was that in the airmen's mess, where they ate, this highly decorated pilot was helping – in shirt sleeves – to dish out grub from behind the food counter.

Once again I spoke to our 'tame' liaison RAF officer, who told me that Mike had been in the Battle of Britain, was Polish by birth, and he was also helping the Station with the coming BofB Day preparations. Still not sure of how I should approach him, for he looked fairly stern and unsmiling, I waited until Friday. It was the last day, and that night, traditionally, the officers would have a bit of a party in the Mess. Time was running out but suddenly he appeared at dinner. It was now or never. I was still in uniform so felt a little safer when I went up to him and asked him which squadron he had been with in 1940. He replied that it had been 249 Squadron, but this did not help. When I said I did not recognise the name of Manson as being in 249, he smiled. Of course not, he said, in those days I used my Polish name – Maciejowski. Now that was a name I did recognise.

Micheł Karol Maciejowski came from Gródek, Jagielloński, Poland, born 29 October 1913, so he was approaching his 53rd birthday. Upon graduation from secondary school he apparently joined a Catholic seminary, but left two years later, before he became ordained. During his compulsory military service as a drafted soldier, he volunteered to join the air force. Between 1935 and 1936 he took pilot training at the 6th Air Regiment in Lwów, subsequently serving with the regiment as a pilot. During March to July 1939 he became a corporal instructor at the flying training school of the 6th Air Regiment but failed to get into combat following the German invasion. He was evacuated to Rumania and following a short internment left by sea, arriving in the French port of Marseille in February 1940. He may well have attempted to get into the fighting but when France fell in June 1940, he, like so many other Polish airmen and soldiers, managed to get to England in order to continue the fight. However, his method of escape was a little different to most, for he and three other Poles stole a French aeroplane and flew it across the Channel.

* * *

I was still in somewhat of a daze at having discovered who Flight Lieutenant Manson was, knowing too that I had so very nearly missed speaking to him, so when he asked me a few questions, and realised that I had more than a passing interest in the RAF during World War Two, he wondered if I would like to come to his quarters for a chat. I needed no further persuading, and off we went. Once in his room he produced his old wartime flying log book, and then, to my complete surprise, rummaged in a drawer and pulled out an old Registered Post envelope, complete with blue lines down and across, and tossed it in my direction. It sort of rattled and, tipping out the contents, I found the actual medals that equated with the ribbons on his uniform. In my hands I held the Polish *Virtuti Militari*, the *Krzyżem Walecznych* (KW) *with three Bars*, together with the British Distinguished Flying Cross and Distinguished Flying Medal, plus the normal array of campaign medals. Little wonder my cadets had been impressed by this disher-out of food. Despite what I took initially as a dour expression, Mike Maciejowski – Manson – was very helpful and forthcoming, and I was allowed to thumb through his log book asking various questions, most of which he was able to answer. If only I had had my tape recorder with me.

One of the first things he mentioned was that after the war he had had some problems with being recognised as a Battle of Britain participant. But after forwarding copies of his log book pages for September and October 1940 to the Battle of Britain Association, he was finally given his place on the official list.

Once he had arrived in England in 1940, he told me, he had gone through a training regime at No. 5 Operational Training Unit, Aston Down, and then was posted to 111 Squadron, to fly Hurricanes, on 10 September, based at Northolt. Towards the end of the month, he was moved to join 249 Squadron at North Weald. Maciejowski, known as 'Miki', or sometimes 'Mickey Mouse', flew a number of sorties but on 25 October became separated and lost during an interception of a dozen Me109s and landed at Colchester. Flying Officer K T Lofts (qv) later flew the squadron's Magister over and led Miki back to their base.

In the late afternoon four days later, the 29th, the squadron was ordered up to patrol over base at 15,000 feet, together with Hurricanes of 257 Squadron, but as they became airborne some twelve Me109s from II/LG2 suddenly appeared and began to dive-bomb the airfield. One bomb which landed in the middle of the field damaged Keith Lofts' fighter although he was unhurt. Another Hurricane was also hit by debris, knocking off part of its propeller, but the pilot managed to get back down despite his aircraft shuddering madly. One pilot of 257 Squadron was killed as his Hurricane crashed and burned. Another 257 machine became airborne but the pilot had to bale out, doing so safely. On the ground a number of people were either killed or injured.

The Messerschmitts began to head for home but Red Section, led by Flight Lieutenant R A Barton gave chase as they skimmed across the ground at low level. Barton fired at several 109s, claiming hits on some and definitely got one, its pilot baling out mortally wounded. Mike Maciejowski was also behind a 109 as his report shows:

Sergeant M K Maciejowski, 249 Squadron, 1940.

'I followed Flt Lt Barton, as leader, attacking one of a formation of five at about 4,000 feet. Two of this formation separated and I pursued them. They dived into cloud and I cut through the clouds and found myself 50 yards behind both of them. I gave one of them five-to-ten seconds burst stern attack and it immediately burst into flames and fell to earth, where I saw it burning about 200 yards from the seashore, on land. I could not tell whether it was by the Blackwater River. There were some small boats nearby. I gave the second about five seconds burst but I then lost it in the clouds.'

The German pilot was Oberfeldwebel Josef Harmeling, of 4/LG2, who force-landed his 109 at Langenhoe Wick, near Colchester, was wounded and taken prisoner. This 109 was later put on public display, complete with bullet holes. No doubt the fighter Miki had seen burning was that shot down by Barton. Two other pilots also scored hits on 109s, one going into the sea off Southend. Miki was credited with one Me109 destroyed, which is noted in his log book. On the 29th LG2 lost a total of three aircraft and had another crash-land at Wissant, France. Strangely Miki also records a 109 destroyed on the 22nd, but there does not appear to be any action by 249 on this date.

The following day, Maciejowski was again in combat with 109s but in chasing them out to sea he ran short of fuel and had to make a forced landing at Stoney Field Farm, near Herstmonceux, Sussex. The locals came over to his machine as he got out and he asked in his broken English where he was. Despite the RAF markings on his machine they took him to be a German, but eventually things were straightened out and with some fuel put into the fighter he was able to take off and head back to base.

As November began, 249 and other southern-based fighter squadrons were continuing the fight against bomb-carrying Me109s, the German bomber force more or less out of the actions now. It was a dangerous time, for the mainly blue skies of summer had changed to more cloudy conditions that made it more difficult to locate the German fighters, and equally dangerous for the British pilots as they could be surprised by 109 pilots using cloud to approach unseen.

Miki's next claims came on the 7th, 249 being scrambled to intercept German dive-bombing Ju87s of I/StG3, escorted by 109s from JG26, JG51 and JG53. Quite a dog-fight developed but the Stukas got away with just one of their number damaged, by Pilot Officer T F Neil DFC. Seven Me109s were claimed shot down (three destroyed and four others damaged) but in the confusion of the air battle and the cloud, only one Me109 of JG26 actually failed to return. Maciejowski's report stated:

'In position Yellow 4 after patrolling the Thames Estuary, e/a were sighted attacking convoy. The squadron dived to attack and split up. I sighted five 109s attempting to bomb the convoy. They eventually split up into pairs, leaving one straggler in the rear. I attacked the single from behind and above, pouring into him from very close range, approximately a six-second burst. The e/a made no attempt to escape and burst into flames. The pilot did not jump. E/a crashed in flames in the sea about eight miles north-west of Margate.'

In his log-book Maciejowski noted two other 109s as probables.

His next engagement came on the 28th, Miki being part of a 12-man patrol over Kent in the afternoon. Several Me109s were seen above; JG26 again. The Hurricanes began to climb towards them but the 109 leader,

Oberstleutnant Adolf Galland, dived and shot down Flying Officer P H V Wells, whose fighter caught fire and went down. Although badly burned, he managed to survive by taking to his parachute. Meantime, Maciejowski attacked one of the Messerschmitts, claiming it probably destroyed near Maidstone. In the event, two 109s failed to get home, but 19 Squadron's pilots also got into this action and also claimed 109s destroyed.

Miki's next combat report was dated 5 December:

'Having patrolled Maidstone with the squadron, south-west towards Dungeness, I saw about 5 Me109s about 2,000 ft above us, we being at about 19,000 ft. We formed a circle going lower and lower, while the enemy followed us down.

'Two Me109s dived and attacked. I turned left out of formation and I saw one Hurricane shot down. The Me109 that had shot it down diving steeply, pulled upwards and climbed. In this climb he passed before me and I gave him two short bursts, as he was climbing almost vertically before me. He went into a spin and crashed into the sea about 500 yards from the shore.'

* * *

With the ending of 1940, and the arrival of winter, operations slowed down, although most believed that the spring would see a return of German aircraft over southern England. However, Fighter Command were determined to attempt hitting back themselves and as 1941 indeed was to prove, Fighter Command began a serious regime of operating over northern France. For Maciejowski, 10 January saw his resumption of hostilities against the Luftwaffe.

On this day Fighter Command launched the first cross-Channel Circus Operation, fighters escorting a handful of Bristol Blenheim light bombers over to France. 249 and 242 Squadrons acted as forward support, while other units provided top cover and close escort. A few Me109s did sniff around but no engagements occurred until the force was heading back. First gunfire from four small patrol boats off Calais damaged two Hurricanes, but the North Weald Station Commander, Wing Commander Victor Beamish DFC

AFC, went down and shot them up. One Hurricane was then shot down by a 109 and as 249 Squadron landed, they realised that Sergeant Maciejowski was missing. However, he turned up later and was able to report the following adventure:

'I was on a sweep patrol in the neighbourhood of St Inglevert aerodrome and got temporarily separated from my section, when I saw five Hs126 [aircraft] in line at the south-east corner of what I have since verified through photographs was the Guînes-la-Place aerodrome. I came down to between 200-300 feet and machine-gunned the line of aircraft but did not have time to observe the results. I saw two Me109s at about 300 feet flying NNW and climbing. I climbed to 1,000 feet and then attacked the rear Me109, giving him one long and two short bursts from above, 150 yards from behind and above slightly from the right-hand side. He turned steeply and dived vertically towards the ground as if the pilot had been hit.

'My throttle had jammed full open and as the other Me109 was climbing steeply, I was unable to follow, so I came down to ground level and made for the coast which I crossed between Cap Gris Nez and Boulogne. As I was approaching the coast, I was fired on by machine-gun posts and Bofors, and from ships as I was almost at sea level. My throttle was still jammed and I came over Hornchurch and switched off the ignition and landed. I later returned to North Weald and landed at 15.15.'

In his flying log book Mike claimed one 109 destroyed and five Henschels damaged on the ground. His next log-book entry regarding combats was noted exactly one month later, on 10 February:

'I was flying at 1,000 feet higher than the leader, who was at 14,000 feet. I saw three Me109s attacking the formation below me. I dived down and did a steep climbing turn and delivered a three-quarter stern attack with deflection. The e/a turned on its back immediately and the pilot baled out although the aircraft had given no sign of injury.'

The operation was another Circus – Circus No.4 – six Blenheims attacking the docks at Dunkirk. The attackers were 109s from IV/JG51 and I/LG2, which bounced 249, shooting down one Hurricane whose pilot baled out and was taken prisoner. In the subsequent air fight, Maciejowski, Sergeant G C C Palliser[3] and Sergeant S Brzeski each claimed a 109 shot down. Miki had accounted for Unteroffizier Karl Ryback of LG2, who crashed into the sea. He did not bale out, so Miki may have seen the 109's canopy jettisoned and assumed the pilot would quickly follow. Two other Hurricanes were damaged by pilots of JG51. Until now, 249 had been soldiering on with Hurricane Mark Is but the arrival at this time of Hurricane Mark II was to be a marked improvement.

Miki was posted to 317 Polish Squadron on 18 February (arriving on the 25th) which was in the process of being formed at RAF Acklington. Once operational the squadron became engaged on convoy patrols with the odd abortive scramble. He had missed the upgrade to the Hurricane II with his posting from 249 but these arrived on 317 in July, and by the autumn they began changing over to the Spitfire Vb. The squadron's first two COs had been British, but in June Squadron Leader Stanisław Brzezina took command and in August, Squadron Leader Henryk Szczęsny. In the Battle of Britain both these men had been with 74 Squadron, known as 'Sneezy' and 'Breezy'.

In April Miki was awarded the Polish Cross of Valour, followed by a second Bar to his KW in August, and the British Distinguished Flying Medal in the spring. The recommendation for the DFM was put forward by Wing Commander Beamish on 12 February 1941. It stated:

---

3. Later Flight Lieutenant G C C Palliser DFC, who flew with 249 in England and Malta. He died in 2011 but not before writing his story in *They Gave me a Hurricane*, Fighting High Ltd, 2012. He recalled Maciejowski: 'Mickey was a funny lad, full of good humour and full of stories about his journey and subsequent arrival at No. 249. He could never wait to go to the local village or even into London when he was off duty, proving to be a real terror with the ladies. One night he returned to the hut in our last week, very late. He jumped into bed and refused to switch the light off. A big argument commenced, to be finished when John Beard [later Squadron Leader J M B Beard DFM], who was the senior in the hut, produced a revolver and shot the light off.'

'This Pilot N.C.O. has proved to be a cool and determined fighter pilot who always shows a calm, yet extremely resolute intention of destroying the enemy. His courage and example are admired by all ranks. He has destroyed five enemy aircraft besides damaging several others.'

On 17 February this recommendation was endorsed by Air Vice-Marshal Trafford Leigh-Mallory, commanding 11 Group of Fighter Command, and a couple of days later was approved by Air Marshal Sholto Douglas, CinC Fighter Command. Before it could be processed further, Group Captain A S W Dore DSO, at the Air Ministry in London, had to write to the Polish Embassy, from where, on 4 March, the Air Attaché replied that the Polish authorities agreed to the decoration being awarded. This then had to be submitted to the King in March, and duly approved, before the medal was given. It appears that the official citation read:

This airman has proved to be a cool, courageous and determined fighter who always shows a calm, yet resolute intention to destroy the enemy. He has shot down five enemy aircraft and damaged several others.

However, the year was mostly a quiet one for 317 Squadron, until it moved to the south-west of England in July. Operating from Exeter with its new Hurricane IIs it flew convoy patrols and the occasional bomber escort job over the Cherbourg area. There was also the odd lone raider or reconnaissance machine to chase, Miki being sent up after one on 6 December which resulted in a claim for one Ju88 destroyed off Rance Head.

This was followed on 30 December by him claiming two Me109s off Brest. Strangely, as far as my notes tell me, his log book did not record the Ju88 but did note a 109 destroyed on the 7th. In the meantime, things carried on with patrols and escorts into 1942. In May he received the *Virtuti Militari*, and the following month he was commissioned. The next bit of excitement was the Dieppe Operation on 19 August 1942.

No. 317 Squadron had moved to RAF Northolt in July and like most RAF fighter squadrons involved in the operation, flew more than one sortie on the 19th. 317, along with 303 Squadron, were over the operational area shortly after 10 am. It was 303's first trip of the day, 317's second, led by its new CO,

Squadron Leader Stanisław F Skalski VM KW DFC. There was already a fight going on between FW190s, Ju88s, Do215s and French Spitfire pilots. Maciejowski singled out a Ju88, fired, and saw it go down into the sea, then turning in behind a 190, shot this into the sea too. He also scored hits on a Dornier, although his own Spitfire received some slight damage. For his actions this day, Miki received a second Bar to his Cross of Valour, and the Distinguished Flying Cross, gazetted on September, with the following citation:

Flying Officer Micky Maciejowski DFC DFM in 1942.

Since being awarded the Distinguished Flying Medal, Pilot Officer Maciejowski has destroyed 4 enemy aircraft, probably destroyed 1 and shared in the destruction of another. He is a skilful pilot who has displayed exceptional keenness to engage the enemy.

However, the actual recommendation, dated 27 August, noted more of his achievements:

'This officer fought with an English Squadron in the "Battle of Britain" and then joined his present Squadron. Recently commissioned, he was the outstanding victor of the Polish Wing in the operations over Dieppe on 19th August 1942. In this operation he brought his personal score up to 9½ enemy aircraft destroyed and one probably destroyed, by the destruction of an enemy bomber and an enemy fighter, sharing in the destruction of a further enemy bomber.'

No sooner was this operation completed than Maciejowski was sent off on rest, becoming an instructor with No. 58 Operational Training Unit at RAF

Grangemouth, near Falkirk, Scotland. One wonders if his medal ribbons impressed his pupils as much as it impressed my ATC cadets twenty-four years later?

His next posting was to No. 316 (*City of Warsaw*) Polish Squadron in March 1943, once again finding himself back at RAF Northolt, under Squadron Leader Marian Trzebinski, who had fought in Poland and France, and knew Miki from their time together in 317 Squadron. This squadron was equipped with the Spitfire Mark IX, and its main task was bomber escort missions. On these sorties Miki claimed a probable FW190 and another damaged ten miles south of Flushing on 4 May, and then a Me109G ten miles north of Beauvais on 11 June.

Flight Lieutenant M K Manson DFC DFM VM KW, RAF Gaydon, 1966. He had now anglicised his name.

His luck finally ran out on 9 August, during a mission over France. During Ramrod 91, whilst making a turn above Montreuil, he and Flying Officer Lech Kondracki collided. Miki, although slightly injured, managed to bale out of his crippled Spitfire (BS302), but Kondracki was killed. Miki told me all about this collision and also of the treatment he received from his captors. Perhaps being Polish he was handled more harshly but he recalled being tied to a chair while a German officer interrogated him, using a lit cigarette to burn his left cheek as an inducement to talk. He did not.

Eventually he ended up in the famous Stalag Luft III, prisoner number 2021, where he remained until the end of the war. Returning to England he decided to remain in the RAF, attending a refresher course at No.16 (Polish) Service Flying Training School in June 1945 and then went to 309 Polish Squadron, part of 133 Polish Wing, flying Mustang III fighters, and commanded by Squadron Leader Henryk Pietrzak VM KW*** DFC. Miki served with 309 until its disbandment in December 1946. He finally decided to leave the RAF in January 1947.

He settled in England and was later to change his name to Manson. In 1951 he rejoined the RAF and held various appointments, including head of catering at RAF Gaydon! He retired from the RAF in October 1972 when nearing 60 years of age and lived near Liverpool with his wife and daughter. When his wife died in 1987 he went to live in Canada, to be near his daughter who had moved there, residing in Winnipeg, Manitoba, for a number of years. He died on 26 April 2001, three days before his 89th birthday.

Chapter 13

Flight Lieutenant V M M Ortmans DFC ChOL ChOC CdeG CdeE

Victor Marcel Maurice Ortmans was the son of Charles Léon Marcel Ortmans and his wife Alice Elise Jenny Ortmans, née Dartois. He was born in London on 17 April 1915, his family having been evacuated from Belgium in the First World War. They returned to Liege after the war. Vicki had two brothers, Christian and Serge, and two sisters, Marcelle and Viviane. Vicki joined the Belgian Air Force in September 1935, and once he became a pilot, served in No. 7/IIIe G.R. Squadron, which was equipped with the Fairey Fox biplane, used by the RAF in England since 1925 as a two-seat day bomber, and in Belgium mainly for army co-operation duties.

With the coming of the Second World War, his squadron moved to Liege. When the Blitzkrieg began on 10 May 1940 it was wiped out, mostly while on the ground within a few days. Ortmans made his way across to France but as France fell he and other pilots were told to remain where they were. But determined to continue the fight, he and some others, including Count Rodolphe de Hemricourt de Grunne and Leroy du Vivier, two pilots who would also see action over England in 1940, made their way to Port Vendres and then on to Gibraltar, where with the help of the British Embassy they boarded a Royal Navy destroyer and, meeting a passing convoy, were put aboard the SS *Apapa*, reaching the British port of Liverpool on 7 July 1940. Commissioned into the RAF, and having converted to fighters at No. 7 OTU, he was posted to No. 229 Squadron, flying Hawker Hurricanes at RAF Wittering on 10 August.

Ortmans achieved his first success in the Battle on 15 September, sharing in the destruction of a Dornier 17 near Cranbrook, Kent. This may have been from 9/KG2 that crashed between Goudhurst and Cranbrook, three of the crew being killed and the fourth captured. About an hour after this

Vicki Ortmans, 609 Squadron, 1940.

aeroplane had crashed, the wreckage exploded killing a member of the LDV (Local Defence Volunteers) who was trying to keep a crowd away from the danger area. Some 14 Dorniers were shot down on this day and many others damaged.

On the 27th he shot down a Heinkel, between London and Tunbridge Wells, and shared in the damaging of another near Hastings. As there were no He111s lost on this date, one must conclude it was a mistaken identification and it was possibly one of a number of Ju88s that were lost, while others came down in the Channel. Ortmans scored a probable Me109 on the 30th off Dungeness and was credited with a Dornier destroyed. The bomber was from KG3. He ended his 1940 claims with a Ju88 damaged on 18 October.

Soon afterwards, 229 Squadron were rested and sent to Northolt, then after another brief stay at Wittering in December, moved north to Speke, near Liverpool. In the spring of 1941 the squadron was told to expect an overseas deployment and Ortmans was posted to 609 Squadron. 609 had been quite successful during the Battle of Britain and was now under the command of Squadron Leader M L Robinson DFC. Just before the 'balloon went up' in 1940, Michael Robinson, serving in France with 87 Squadron, had suffered a crash and been injured. As the Germans invaded France and the Low Countries, it was touch and go whether he would be over-run by invading troops while still in hospital, but he was helped by some Belgian airmen and successfully got himself back to England. Now that the pressure of the Battle of Britain had lessened, and there were numerous foreign pilots reporting for duty with the RAF, Michael decided to help those from Belgium by suggesting his squadron adopt enough Belgians to form a Flight within 609. So in the spring of 1941, several Belgians arrived, including Vicki Ortmans.

Although he still spoke little English, Ortmans got on well with 609. His infectious grin made him very popular, together with his wit and the ability to tap dance, often on the top of the Mess piano! The squadron was based at Biggin Hill, its wing leader being Wing Commander A G Malan DSO DFC. Vicki was soon in trouble with 'Sailor' Malan as the South African watched a formation of 609 fly across the airfield. It was a perfect formation except that one Spitfire – Vicki's – was flying upside down! The WingCo asked who the pilot was, saying, 'Doesn't he know he's ruining his engine?' The squadron never officially had a Belgian Flight, but soon there were eight Belgians in one Flight, including Roger Malengreau, François de Spirlet, Bob Wilmet, 'Strop' Seghers, Willi Van Lierde and De Grunne.

The year 1941 was to see the beginning of the RAF's campaign of 'taking the war to the enemy' by mounting fighter sweeps across to northern France in order to bait the Luftwaffe fighters to come up and fight. As the RAF had found in the latter stages of 1940, there was no percentage in engaging Me109s over the south of England, for they were no threat on their own.

Vicki Ortmans (on the right) skylarking with Joe Atkinson at the pool at Biggin Hill, 1941.

So it was little wonder that the Germans tended to ignore RAF fighters; so to entice the 109 pilots to battle, Circus operations were begun, which consisted of small formations of Bristol Blenheim light bombers going for specific, if not particularly tactical targets, escorted by several squadrons of Spitfires and Hurricanes. This tactic did bring the 109 pilots into conflict but they were always able to dictate the time and place a combat might take place. Despite RAF fighter claims to the contrary, the German fighter pilots shot down far more of their antagonists than they lost Messerschmitts.

On 16 May 1941 Ortmans damaged a Me109 near Folkestone, during an enemy sweep over the southern part of Kent, and five days later shared another 109 with John Bisdee (qv), ten miles off Deal. Off Dover on 4 June Vicki and Sergeant T C Rigler each claimed a 109 destroyed, and then damaged one on the 21st. The next day, Germany invaded Russia, but the two German Jagdgeschwaders in France, JG26 and JG2, were still sufficient to cope with anything the RAF day operations could mount against them.

All during that summer, RAF Fighter Command and the Blenheims of Bomber Command's 2 Group battled on, occasionally supplemented with a small formation of Short Stirling four-engined bombers. Losses were high but the fighter pilots still thought they were inflicting equally heavy losses on the 109s.

On the last day of June Ortmans bagged another 109 near Lille during Circus 27, the target being the power station at Pont-à-Vendin, the Biggin Hill Wing flying as one of the Target Support Wings (along with the Hornchurch Wing). There were eighteen Blenheims being escorted on this occasion. Biggin's fighters, comprising 74, 92 and 609 Squadrons, headed into France stepped up from 23,000 to 28,000 feet. Many small formations of 109s were seen from St Omer to the target, and many more during the return trip, all seemingly waiting for a good moment to strike. 74 and 92 were not able to engage any of them but suddenly 609 were attacked from extreme range in what was described as 'nibbling' tactics – menacing rather than full blooded. However, a dog fight did ensue and 609 claimed four Me109s shot down with two others also hit. The Spitfire pilots could see an estimated forty enemy fighters in total.

Michael Robinson attacked one that was heading towards 74 Squadron, chasing it down to 5,000 feet over Merville aerodrome. He then turned

Group of 609 Squadron pilots, June 1941. Left to right, standing: Sgt Ken Laing, F/O Joe Atkinson, Sgt Bob Boyd, P/O Boudouin de Hemptinne, P/O Peter Mackenzie (in cockpit), F/L Paul Richey DFC, P/O Jean Offenberg, F/O Jimmy Baraldi; seated: Vicki Ortmans, Sgt Tommy Rigler, P/O Keith Ogilvie, F/L John Bisdee (qv) and P/O Bob Wilmet.

towards five others that were heading for his own Blue Section, driving them off and causing one to leave a trail of glycol. Flight Lieutenant Paul Richey DFC was engaged by several 109s, managed to hit one, and saw it half roll and dive from 1,000 feet. Sergeant J A Hughes-Rees claimed one destroyed and, of course, Ortmans claimed one. Unhappily once again claims were more numerous than German losses.

* * *

One of the Luftwaffe's major fighter aces was killed in action on 3 July 1941. This was JG2's Geschwaderkommodore Hauptmann Wilhelm Balthasar, brought down near Aire, St Omer, at 15.25 pm. Balthasar had achieved forty-seven victories, including seven during the Spanish Civil War, and had received the Knight's Cross of the Iron Cross with Oak Leaves, the Oak

Leaves just the day before his death. He was buried next to his father, killed in the First World War, in a cemetery in Flanders.

There was speculation about who might have brought him down. There were several Me109s claimed on the 3rd, and the time of his death suggests it was during Circus 31. Biggin Hill Wing flew as Target Support Wing and claimed several 109s shot down and RAF records show Vicki Ortmans as having claimed a damaged. From time to time his name is linked to the loss of Balthasar, but it is by no means certain, and in Frank Zeigler's book on 609 Squadron, it is not mentioned.

It was during July that Ortmans gained some local fame by introducing a goat into the folklore of 609 Squadron. At a nearby public house, Vicki had become a favourite with the landlady, which resulted in her giving her Belgian hero a baby goat of the Toggenberg variety. Welcomed onto a squadron that already had some animal mascots, the goat was inevitably named Billy – or William de Goat – and the pilots commissioned the animal in RAF custom. He eventually rose to the rank of Air Commodore later in the war, retiring from duty at the end of hostilities. He would eat anything in sight, and in 1944 was flown across to France when the squadron was deployed there following the invasion.

Ortmans and Sergeant A G 'Goldie' Palmer DFM got into a scrap with several enemy fighters on 17 August and had to fight desperately to survive. Reporting back at base he argued vigorously to the intelligence officer and the other pilots that one of his assailants had been 'a Me109 with a radial engine'. This went into the Wing report and it was thought perhaps the Germans were using captured Hawk 75 fighters the French had received earlier in the war. However, it emerged later that Vicki's encounter was with one of the new Focke-Wulf 190 fighters.

The next day, the 18th, in the Calais area, Vicki knocked down a real 109. This was during Circus 80 against the Shell Factory at Marquise, 609 being on rear support this time. Several formations of Me109s were seen and a battle did develop when returning over the French coast. Ortmans and fellow Belgian Pilot Officer Yves du Monceau de Bergandal each claimed one destroyed. The next day Vicki claimed a damaged on Circus 81, which was the operation that involved the dropping of artificial legs for Douglas Bader who had been brought down and captured on the 9th. Eight RAF Spitfires failed to return from this operation, one being that flown by Vicki Ortmans. 609 had engaged some 109s, claiming two damaged, one by Ortmans, but a 109 got him and he was forced to take to his parachute over the Channel, mid-way between Dover and Dunkirk. It is thought he was downed by JG2, who also had two 109s damaged, so Ortmans may have been the cause of one of them. Fortunately the Air Sea Rescue Service was on the ball and a high-speed ASR launch, HSL 123, soon had him out of the water and back in England. While he was glad to have been rescued, he lamented the loss of his favourite Spitfire, W3241, coded PR-D, Ortmans saying: 'Poor "D", she is dead.'

Ortmans had his next combat claim on 29 August, sharing a 109 damaged, on Circus 88, a raid upon Hazebrouck Marshalling Yards, Biggin in the Support Wing place. Then on 17 September his Spitfire – a new "D" – was damaged during Circus 96, but he survived unharmed. It was not the best of times for Ortmans. He had been censured by the station commander for tap-dancing, not on the piano this time, but on the green baize of the snooker table.

On the 27th, on Circus 103B, escorting eleven Blenheims to the power station at Mazingarbe, the Biggin Boys were the High Cover Wing. They were slightly delayed because they had arrived some minutes early at the rendezvous point and had to wait for the Circus to form up before heading towards France. When only about 10-15 miles inland they were engaged by 109s north-west of St Omer, and some aircraft lost position as an air fight developed. As the Spitfires headed out in rather piecemeal fashion, two Me109s attacked Ortmans, but he was saved as two other Spitfires came to his rescue. By now he was running short of fuel and headed towards the Kent coast, only to have his engine quit just five miles off Folkestone. Once again he took to his parachute and moments later splashed down into the cold Channel waters. A 'mayday' was called and before too long he was again in the arms of rescuers from the Air Sea Rescue boys, the crew of HSL 147 snatching him out the 'drink'.

Vicki Ortmans received the Distinguished Flying Cross, gazetted on 2 September:

[Pilot Officer Ortmans] *has displayed great keenness and courage in pressing home his attacks. He has destroyed at least five enemy aircraft and damaged a further two.*

Circus operations continued into the autumn. It had been a long and exhausting summer and 609 were surely due for a rest. Eventually that would come in November, but as luck would have it, Vicki's war was to be over in late October. It was the time when his brother Christian joined the squadron. He too had escaped to England, become a fighter pilot, and got a posting to 609. His first operation was scheduled for 21 October. Circus operations for 1941 had virtually come to an end: the last one for the year would be flown on 8 November. Fighter Command were now flying Rodeo missions, large fighter sweeps over France, and as the weather deteriorated, Rhubarb sorties by small sections of fighters were initiated, flying low over France hoping to surprise anything Germanic the pilots could find.

On the 21st Fighter Command mounted a large-scale Rodeo across the Pas de Calais area, numbering eighteen squadrons, in five Wings. German radar detected bombers too. There were none, but it made the German HQ send up fighters to intercept. JG26 intercepted sections of this Rodeo south of Cap Gris Nez, then Boulogne and later Étaples, and shot down nine RAF fighters. JG2 got into the action too, claiming one Spitfire but losing a pilot.

Among the claimants in JG26 were some big names. The Geschwaderkommodore Oberstleutnant Adolf Galland claimed two, his 90th and 91st victories. (He would gain his 92nd later in the day.) Hauptmann Josef 'Pips' Priller, leader of the First Gruppe, shot down two, his 54th and 55th kills. Hauptmann Johannes Schmid shot down a Spitfire for his 43rd victory, Oberleutnant Kurt Ebersberger, leader of the 4th Staffel, claimed his 15th kill, while Oberleutnant Hermann Seegatz, of 4 Staffel, got his 15th. JG26's three losses came from the 8th Staffel, one pilot killed, two baled out, one of whom was wounded.

This was 609's first major encounter with the FW190, that now JG26 had re-equipped, and lost two pilots, Ortmans and Goldie Palmer. Ortmans was hit north of Le Touquet and once again found himself in the sea. Palmer was killed. Sous-lieutenant Maurice Choron, a Frenchman with the squadron, was badly shot up but managed to get back to England where he crash-landed near Rye.

After the war Ortmans would report shooting down one FW190 and hitting two others. In the meantime he awaited the ASR lads to come to his aid once again, although this time he was in his dinghy for two days and a night, despite searches being made for him. Awaiting rescue was becoming a habit. When a rescue boat did arrive, it was German. Once in captivity he gave his name as Vicki Ogilvie, not daring to let the Germans know his real name in case of reprisals against his family in Belgium. There had been a Keith Ogilvie on the squadron earlier, who had received the DFC, but who was now a prisoner too, since 4 July 1941. As it happens, Keith had briefed Vicki about pretending to be a French/Canadian in the event of ever being captured, and Vicki had just blurted out the name Oglivie to his captors. Therefore it was some time before word got back that Ortmans was safe and a prisoner, Fighter Command not knowing who this latest Ogilvie was on the Red Cross list. In fact he was in the sickbay of Stalag VIIIC until 10 May 1942. Ortmans and Keith Ogilvie eventually met up in prison camp, both being incarcerated in the infamous Stalag Luft III, scene of the Great Escape in March 1944. Because he gave his captors the name of Ogilvie, this is how he appears in the PoW list, showing his PoW number as 706. Keith Ogilvie's number was 1409, and although he took part in the mass escape, he survived his recapture.

* * *

His brother Christian was of course devastated at the loss of Vicki, more so because of the delay in knowing he was a prisoner of war. Meanwhile he continued flying operations with 609, both with the Spitfire, and later the Typhoon, which 609 re-equipped in April 1942. In June 1942, former flight commander Paul Richey DFC returned to 609 as commanding officer. He helped set up the first Typhoon Wing. In October Richey was posted overseas and in the meantime, he and Christian had struck up a friendship and Christian often flew as Paul's wingman. When his posting to the Far East became known, Christian put in a formal application to be allowed to go too. Belgian authorities were not keen, there being no other Belgian nationals in India or Burma, but Richey made personal representations and it was finally agreed he could go.

Christian's job in India was unclear, for Richey would be working on a staff appointment. Once in India, Paul became ill for a short time and Christian was posted to a Vengeance dive-bomber squadron. However,

Richey managed to get him away from that and he ended up on a Hurricane unit, 615 Squadron in Burma. Christian's time on 615 was very unfortunate. There had been some talk that the Japanese were using captured Hurricanes and, leading a patrol of six aircraft on 11 March 1943, a lone 135 Squadron Hurricane, its pilot doing an air test, had closed in on the six Hurricanes, making a head-on approach. The pilot for some odd reason had believed the Hurricanes were Japanese and as he opened fire, Christian, thinking this must be one of those captured Hurricanes that had been rumoured, attacked him. He hit the other aircraft, which burst into flames and crashed, killing the pilot.

It must have been hard to get over this tragic event, but then on 1 April, he was leading a scramble against a Japanese bombing raid, escorted by fighters of the 64th Sentai. In the action Christian was shot down and killed.

* * *

Vicki Ortmans returned home after the war ended and was reunited with his family. Apart from the British DFC, his own country had made him a *Chevalier de L'Ordre de Léopold* (*Ridder in de Léopoldsorde*), made him a *Chevalier de L'Ordre de la Courrone* (*Ridder in de Kroonorde*), the *Croix de Guerre* and the *Croix de Évadés*.

Sadly Vicki was not to survive the peace for very long. On his release from prison camp he rejoined the new Belgian *Force Aerienne* and commanded a flight of 349 Squadron serving on occupation duties from September 1945. The following May he became a flight instructor with the Belgian Training School at Bevingen. Later he joined Sabena Airways, Belgian's national airline but was killed in a flying accident during a demonstration flight in an Auster light aircraft at Schaffen air base on 8 August 1950.

It was an Auster V (EBDT). After a normal take-off the aircraft made a low pass above the airfield, turned and began to climb to 750 feet. The engine appeared to idle and the Auster went into a left-hand spin and crashed. Pilot and passenger were killed on impact and an inspection of the wreckage found nothing wrong with either the engine or its controls. Ortmans was 35 years of age.

Chapter 14

Wing Commander P L Parrott DFC & Bar AFC

Imet Peter Parrott on three occasions. The first was at a 43 Squadron reunion at the Royal Air Force Club in London. At that time I was an officer with the Air Training Corps and, specifically, the Adjutant of No. 43F Squadron of the ATC. I was also this unit's liaison officer with the RAF Squadron, which at that time were flying McDonnell Douglas Phantom FG1 fighters at RAF Leuchars, Scotland, under the command of Wing Commander J J R Cohu, which is how I came to be invited to the reunion. No. 43 Squadron RAF have always had a strong Squadron Association.

I was fortunate on that occasion to be seated on a table which included Wing Commander Parrott, and was able to listen and soak up many stories of the squadron as he and others at the table inevitably reminisced over old times.

The second time I met him was during the period I was researching and working on a book about the RAF Fighter Command's torrid time during the 1940 Dunkirk evacuation. Using the aforementioned tenuous link I contacted the wing commander, asking if I could talk to him about his activities over Dunkirk, and he readily agreed. For reasons I did not really worry about, he preferred to meet me at a pub near his home in Surrey. We duly met up but it was difficult to record his recollections on tape with all the noise of the hostelry about us. Nevertheless, he was very generous with his memories about activities back in 1940.

The third and final time was quite by chance. I was book-signing at Brooklands and there was a do laid on by the Hurricane Association, and who should turn up but Peter Parrott. He recalled our meetings and it was nice to see him again. From memory it was not too long before he sadly left us for a higher posting.

Peter Lawrence Parrott, inevitably known in RAF circles as 'Polly', was born on 28 June 1920 in Aylesbury, Buckinghamshire, into what is described as a family of local solicitors. His schooling included a period as a boarder with the Lord Williams's Grammar School in Thame, Oxfordshire, and once concluded he joined the RAF on a short service commission in June 1938. Completing his training in March 1939 he became a staff pilot at No. 1 Air Armament School at RAF Manby, an unusual posting, but on 23 January 1940, with Britain now at war, he was sent to join 607 Squadron, Royal Auxiliary Air Force, which was in France.

His new squadron had Gloster Gladiator biplane fighters despite being in what was surely the front line, but it had been promised Hawker Hurricanes and these started to arrive in April. As Peter recalled:

'I was the only pilot in the squadron who had flown a Hurricane, and the most junior. So the squadron had only a bare four weeks with the Hurricane before we were embroiled in the most disorganised, chaotic week or ten days of action. Few, if any, of our pilots had sufficient experience on type to be classed as operational.'

Some British Press interest in the RAF in France during this 'phoney war' period led the *Daily Sketch* newspaper for 14 March to use three fighter pilots' photos made into a composite picture about the RAuxAF, under the title *Sky 'Larks' Made Them Airmen – 'Amateurs' Who Trained in their Spare Time Now Fly in France.* The three faces were those of Johnny Sample, Peter, and Willie Gore. Sample and Gore might well have been Auxiliaries, but Peter was not, having merely been posted to 607 on war duty. However, when he finally saw the spread in the paper, Peter was less than happy, as his particular face was spread all over the place at this time, especially on RAF recruitment posters. Gore was to die in the Battle of Britain, while Sample survived the Battle only to die in a flying accident in 1941.

The most well known of the posters, with Peter as the fresh-faced airman, with helmet and oxygen mask, parachute harness, and with eyes firmly fixed skywards, was entitled, VOLUNTEER FOR FLYING DUTIES, with a large RAF roundel just behind his head, and listing the ages of men needed for pilots, observers, and wireless-operators/air gunners.

Peter and his squadron were thrown into action on 10 May 1940 with the start of the German *Blitzkrieg* and he gained his first personal success on the first day, damaging a Heinkel 111, before destroying two more and damaging a fourth. These bombers were from 7./KG1 and they lost several aircraft around Albert this afternoon, although several RAF and French pilots all took part in the action. Late in the afternoon 8./KG54 lost aircraft too in similar circumstances, Peter including these in his overall claims for the day. The next day he shared another Heinkel with Willie Gore and Pilot Officer D T Jay, this one from 1./LG1 that crashed near Heist-op-den-Berg at 13.15 pm.

The portrait of Peter Parrott that adorned many RAF publicity outlets for young men to join up and fly.

On the 13th, flying Hurricane P3535, Peter was bounced by some Me109s and shot-up, bullets smashing his radio and knocking some holes in the machine, but he survived and got back to base. The attackers were from I./JG1, who shot down and killed a fellow 607 pilot in this action, so Peter had been lucky.

Attacking more enemy aircraft over the next few days, Peter shared in possibly shooting down a Dornier 17 on the 16th, but then the squadron was withdrawn from France, Peter being allowed a brief leave, but he had hardly begun to relax when he was posted to 145 Squadron. The Dunkirk evacuation was starting and every pilot was needed to help. 145 was based at Tangmere, and then at its satellite of Westhampnett, so ideally placed to send fighter patrols across to the Dunkirk beaches. On the 22nd Peter damaged a Me110, and on the 26th he engaged a Heinkel over Dunkirk and thought he had shot it down, but its rear gunner put some bullets into his fighter (N2589), hitting the cooling system which caused his engine to seize once the engine got hot. Peter told me:

'I don't think one had much time to think about the problems [of Dunkirk], we all hated flying over the sea on one engine. We really didn't have any previous experience on which to base a judgement of any sort, or reason to make any deduction. It was just that a fight was on and we were ready.

'Roy Dutton was leading the squadron and somebody spotted an aircraft and we went off after it. I was flying No.2 in the last section and was keeping a look-out and spotted another [German] off to our right which was up to the north of Dunkirk. So I called over the radio, then peeled off to go after it. I did a stern attack on it – it was a Heinkel 111 – and it very rudely shot back at me. I had just got one of its engines smoking when he put two bullets into me. One hit the wing and one hit the front water jacket on the Merlin and I immediately had a cockpit full of glycol steam so I turned round realising that the engine would run for a little while but not quite sure how long. It began to run rough, getting hot very quickly and the rest of the squadron caught me up when I was about ten or fifteen miles off the coast, having seen the trail of smoke. Somebody called up, "Who is it, what's the matter with him?" I called that it was Peter Parrott, and Roy Dutton said OK, come in on my wing.

'I was very lucky for I was losing height and I was down to about 1,500 feet when I crossed the English coast and then the engine seized absolutely solid and the prop stopped. Ahead of me were three fields all in a row on the top of a hill, so I picked those. I went sailing over the first one, and then went over the second one so decided I had to get down so just pushed the stick forward and came to a standstill pretty quickly. Unfortunately there was a flock of sheep in the field and I knocked a few off.

'I got out and being a Sunday afternoon there were a lot of people out walking. There was a crowd around pretty quickly and a policeman came up pushing a bicycle so I said can you stand by this and where is the nearest telephone. He said the farmer's house down there about half a mile, and as he was saying this, he said, "Oh! Here's the farmer coming now," and the farmer drove up in a horse and trap. As he got down the first thing he said was, "Who's going to pay for these sheep then?" So in a lordly tone I replied, "The Air Ministry!" I then asked if I could use his telephone and he said, "Yes, the 'ouse is down there!" which meant I had to walk which I did. By the time I walked down to the farmhouse, he was back at home, with his wife, having high tea, which looked pretty good to me. The 'phone was in the hall, on the wall, so I used that and then he said I could sit in the parlour which was on the other side of the hall. Eventually his wife did come over and asked if I'd like a cup of tea, but I thought the hell with you, no thanks!' He had landed at Little Mongeham, near Deal, at 19.15 pm.

Following the Dunkirk show and the period of waiting to see what the enemy had planned, 145 Squadron settled down to expect the Battle to begin. Everyone believed that if Fighter Command could stand up to the Luftwaffe it might just stave off the inevitable invasion of southern England.

Taking part in some of the Channel battles in July, Peter shared a He111 damaged on the 3rd, shared a Dornier 17 damaged on the 13th and shared yet another He111 damaged on the 18th. Finally the main assault by the enemy began in August, and on the 8th Peter shot down a Me109 and a Ju87 dive bomber. 145 were scrambled to intercept a large force of Stukas that were going to attack a Channel convoy, code-named PEEWIT, but officially Convoy CW9, consisting of around twenty ships and nine escort vessels. Squadron Leader Johnny Peel led 145's assault, actually sweeping round so as to attack with the sun behind the Hurricanes. It was a complete surprise and 145's pilots had a field day, claiming more than twenty victories during the day, although a truer score was nearer a dozen with others damaged. The Stukas were from St.G1, St.G2, St.G3 and St.G77. The fighter escort comprised Me109 and Me110 fighters from I./JG27 and V./LG1, and their pilots made a number of claims against the defending RAF aircraft from 64, 238, 257, 43 and 145 Squadrons. 145 lost five of its Hurricanes with all five pilots being killed.

Peter Parrott, 145 and 605 Squadrons in the Battle of Britain.

Peter's next claim came on 12 August, a Ju88 destroyed, but it was his last during the Battle. A number of 88s were brought down on this date, most coming from KG51. Three 145 Squadron pilots were lost in these actions, and having lost two pilots on the 11th, with two more Hurricanes lost, the squadron was rather depleted. It was withdrawn from the Battle on the 14th and the surviving pilots flew north to RAF Drem for a rest and reformation. It was not to return to 11 Group until October. By that time, however, Peter had left 145, on a posting to 605 Squadron. It was here that he received notification that he had been awarded the Distinguished Flying Cross, gazetted on 11 October:

> *This officer has been continuously engaged in operational flights against the enemy since January 1940. He has displayed great determination and keenness and has destroyed or severely damaged at least six hostile aircraft.*

Peter made his one and only claim while with 605 on 1 November, above Faversham, damaging a Me109. The pilots of Fighter Command didn't know it at the time but officially the Battle would be deemed at an end on 31 October. The fighting over southern England would continue for several weeks, and in a far more cloudier autumn sky, that proved to be extremely dangerous. The clear summer blue had gone so it was easier for enemy fighters to surprise RAF fighters. German tactics had changed. No longer were there massed ranks of their bombers heading over, but rather bomb-carrying Me109s, which forced the defending fighters to try and engage them. If they had just been fighters, there would be no point in endangering lives, as the 109 pilots on their own posed no danger unless engaged.

On the 1st, 605 had flown off with 213 Squadron late in the afternoon and met 109s from I./JG2. Both squadrons made claims and 213 lost a pilot. Other than this action, it was Peter's last combat over England. He did, however, tell me about the dangers of operating in these last weeks of 1940. One thing the German fighter pilots had learnt, even as far back as the Spanish Civil War, was that the ideal fighter grouping was the pair – leader and wingman. Two such elements would constitute something akin to the RAF's section that the Germans called a *Schwarm*, and in the event of combat, each pair could become an independent unit, the leader making any attack that presented itself, while the wingman kept a close watch on his leader's tail. The RAF fighter squadrons, however, had always flown in sections of three, referred to as a Vic, a leader and two wingmen, but in such a way that both wingmen, ordered to be tucked in tight with the leader, spent most of their time making sure they did not collide with him. Ergo, less time to watch for an attack from the rear. Some squadrons, such as 74, under Sailor Malan, had already decided to fly in sections of four, but not everyone had Malan's foresight. Sections of three prevailed in most units into 1941. Peter Parrott said:

> 'It was a measure of the discipline which existed among the pilots in a way. Flying in Vics of three never changed while I was in 145 and certainly when I later joined 605 who were at Croydon at the end of September, they were still flying in Vics and were still flying like this when I was shot down on 1st December, but by that time we had got to the stage of having two weavers, one above and one below the squadron.
>
> 'I was hit when the squadron made a turn, and baled out. The funny thing was, and this was a measure of those wretched Vics, the squadron landed back and somebody said, "Well, where's Peter?" Nobody knew where I was and no one had seen me shot down and had flown the rest of the patrol without a top weaver!'

The squadron had been scrambled at 10 am, ordered to patrol over Canterbury at 27,000 feet, in company with 253 Squadron, but were then told to head towards Brighton. One of the weavers of 253 Squadron spotted 109s and in an attack claimed strikes on one of them before they flew off. Meanwhile 605 had seen two 109s below with at least one other higher up. As they turned towards the lower two, the one 109 above dived and picked off Sergeant H N Howes, who went down and made a crash landing near Gravesend. It was then that a second 109 dived, which was obviously a second fighter that had been in company with the 'lone' Messerschmitt above. It hit Peter Parrott's Z2323 and he was quickly over the side and beneath his parachute above East Hoathly, Sussex, where he landed in a field. The reason he baled out so quickly was that he began to see flames start to appear from joints in the cowling. However, it was not that fast, as he had forgotten to release his oxygen tube and radio lead; but he quickly reached forward to do so. He was then sliding along the back of the Hurricane, hitting the tail before whirling off into space.

In the afternoon, 145 Squadron was hit again and two pilots were shot down, both men baling out safely, although one was wounded. Peter and Howes were probably the victims of Stab I./JG51, who claimed two Hurricanes, one at 11.40 the other at 11.45 am. One of the pilots was Oberleutnant Hermann-Friedrich Joppien, the unit's Kommandeur. The other claimant was Leutnant Richard Leppla, his victory timed at 11.45. Joppien was also leading the action against 145 in the afternoon, downing one Hurricane while other pilots claimed two more. One of those pilots was the leading German ace, Werner Mölders, who had over fifty kills by this date, and the Knight's Cross with Oak Leaves. Joppien had around twenty victories at this time and had been awarded the Knight's Cross in September. Leppla had about a dozen victories at this time. He would be seriously wounded over Russia in 1942, with a score of twenty-seven and a Knight's Cross award.

* * *

Peter remained with 605 until April 1941 at which time he was posted out of 605, going to the Central Flying School to attend an instructors' course. Following this he was sent to No. 9 Flying Training School at RAF Hullavington on 26 May. He stayed here for almost ten months, being posted to No. 5(P)AFU at Tern Hill on 22 March 1942 to instruct and join the Handling Squadron at Hullavington at the start of September, while also preparing pilot notes.

He was now wanting a move to front line action, and as a preliminary move was being considered he was sent to No. 57 OTU at Elshot, on 11 May 1943, in order to bring him up to speed on current thinking and tactics. His first posting was to 501 Squadron at Martlesham Heath on 1 June but the following month he was notified of an overseas posting, arriving on the island of Malta on 1 August. The massive siege of the island was well over, the Allies having invaded Sicily by this time. He was soon moved there, to join No. 72 Squadron, flying Spitfires as a supernumerary, based at Pachino.

Eight days later he moved billets at this same base, as he joined 111 Squadron as a Flight Commander.

There was less chance of air combat now but occasionally some action was encountered, and Peter bagged an Italian Mc202 fighter on 4 September. This was the day after British and Canadian troops crossed the Straits of Messina into southern Italy. 111 Squadron were also flying sweeps up along the Italian coast, using long range drop tanks, in preparation for the Salerno landings which began on the 9th.

Then, on 13 October, he was given command of 43 Squadron – The Fighting Cocks – based at Capodichino, Naples. His stay did not get off to a great start: shortly after he arrived he went into hospital with malaria. Combat again was at a premium, but when Peter recovered he managed to share in the destruction of a Ju88 on 26 November, and damage a Me109G on 17 February 1944. During his period of command the squadron was heavily involved in escort missions to British and American bombers and fighter bombers, as well as fighter sweeps. He was to lead 43 until 6 March 1944.

Becoming tour expired he was sent to Egypt and attended a course at the Air Bombing and Gunnery School at El Ballah in April, where he was appointed OC Gunnery at No. 73 OTU at Abu Sueir on 2 May. He began his third tour of operations in November with a posting back to Italy to take command of 72 Squadron at Rimini, where he remained until 15 February 1945, when he was sent to Headquarters, Desert Air Force. The award of a Bar to his DFC was announced and gazetted on 20 March. The process for this decoration began as the year of 1944 was ending, written out by the OC No. 324 Wing, Group Captain G Duncan Smith DSO DFC, and dated 1 January 1945:

Squadron Leader Peter Parrott DFC, commanding 43 Squadron in 1943.

Squadron Leader Parrott has completed many more sorties and destroyed at least 1½ enemy aircraft since being awarded the DFC. He has led his Squadron with determination and skill. During the Anzio landings he engaged and drove off numerous enemy fighter-bomber attacks with his formation and contributed materially to the honours of his Squadron. He has destroyed at least 6 enemy aircraft.

The AOC, Desert Air Force, Air Vice-Marshal R M Foster DFC, a First World War fighter ace, added on 8 January:

S/Ldr Parrott is now engaged on his second operational tour with Desert Air Force, and his third tour of the war. He proved himself a first-class Squadron Commander in his first tour, and is continuing that high standard in his second.

The deputy of the CinC, RAF Middle East, AVM G B A Baker MC, another First World War fighter pilot, added one month later:

'... despite a rather inadequate citation, and in view of the AOC's remarks, I recommend the award of a Bar to the DFC (non-immediate).'

The total operational sorties noted in the recommendation totalled 369, covering over 433 hours.

Peter Parrott saw out the war, and a short time thereafter, as Group Training Inspector, Fighters, and later Wing Commander Operations. He returned to England in June 1946.

Peter wished to continue flying, and one good and interesting, if dangerous, way to achieve this was to become a test pilot. It was an interesting time as peace returned to Europe and the world, for the jet age had begun and most aircraft companies, certainly those designing single-seat aeroplanes, were eagerly trying to get into the jet race. The RAF already had the Gloster Meteor and Peter quickly got himself into the training programme to become a test pilot, qualifying in 1948 at Farnborough.

This same year he married Mary Dunning, who had worked for the Y-Service during the war, while serving with the WAAF. The Y-Service listened into German radio transmissions picking up much valuable intelligence. They had a daughter and a son, the latter serving in the Fleet Air Arm.

For the next two years Peter tested early versions of the DH Vampire and Gloster Meteor as they became accepted into RAF service at Boscombe Down. It was really a dangerous occupation and a number of test pilots inevitably became casualties over these early years. However, he did survive and as a job well done was rewarded with the Air Force Cross in 1952.

Over the next few years he attended the RAF Staff College, served in Nicosia and Geilenkirchen, Germany, and finally retired as a Wing Commander on 10 July 1965. If he had had an interesting career thus far, it soon became even more so. Initially he worked for Autair as an airline pilot on domestic routes in the UK; then later he began flying members of the Libyan Royal Family and government officials on tours of the Middle East. During the Arab-Israeli War in 1967, he arrived at Damascus airport in a taxi, only to see his aircraft in the process of being destroyed by Israeli aircraft. Taking refuge with the British Embassy, he was asked to lead an overland convoy of British civilians escaping the war to Turkey.

In the later Arab-Israeli War of 1972, Peter, at the request of Colonel Gaddafi, flew into Uganda to collect Idi Amin, flying him to Khartoum, where the dictator was to act as mediator in the conflict. No sooner had he landed his Learjet at Entebbe, he and his co-pilot were arrested as suspected mercenaries, before Amin realised who they were.

In 1973 Peter returned to England taking work as a training advisor, a job he retained until retiring in 1983. One thing he did was to be instrumental in having a statue of Lord Dowding placed outside the RAF Church of St Clement Danes in the Strand.

Peter 'Polly' Parrott died on 27 August 2003, at the age of 83.

Chapter 15

The Rook Boys:
Wing Commander A H Rook DFC AFC
Order of Lenin Squadron Leader M Rook DFC

Tony and Micky Rook were cousins, so pretty unique in the annals of the Battle of Britain, as in addition to this family connection, they both served in 504 Squadron in 1940, and both survived the war.

Anthony Hartwell Rook was born on 4 September 1912, the son of Spencer Henry Rook and his wife Daisie, of West Hallam Hall, near Ilkeston, Nottinghamshire. Hallam Hall was a substantial residence, which had fourteen bed and dressing rooms as well as several downstairs rooms. The house stood in picturesque grounds, with stables, coach house etc, overlooking park land. Spencer Rook bought the property in about 1912. He had three sons, Philip, born in 1910, Tony and finally Christopher, born about 1917. He had interests in Messrs Skinner & Rook of Nottingham (wine merchants) and was a director of Jalland & Co, also in Nottingham. Spencer's brothers were Maurice and William Rook.

Tony had just secured an appointment in London in 1932, but tragedy struck the day following his 20th birthday. He had been at home that weekend but was not in the house on the Monday evening. Spencer Rook had been suffering from depression and had not been in good health for some time, and this evening he committed suicide by shooting himself with a revolver.

Further tragedy occurred in 1934, with the death of the eldest son Philip on 3 November. Philip was the first to get the flying bug. He had married Anne, lived in Chilwell, Nottingham and had joined the Royal Auxiliary Air Force, serving with No. 504 (County of Nottingham) Squadron, and became a pilot. On 3 November 1934, Philip and another pilot decided to fly to a friend's wedding at Attenborough. Their intention was to circle the reception and the house while showering confetti over the assembled guests. They did not fly in a Service aeroplane but chartered a biplane. As they

Pilots of 504 Squadron in 1941. F/L A H Rook is seated, 5th from the left, while F/O M Rook stands 4th from the left.

circled over nearby Chilwell Manor Golf Club the aeroplane appeared to be in trouble, then one of the wings collapsed. The machine fell like a stone, hit the ground and burst into flames. Philip and his companion, Pilot Officer Alan C Grant-Dalton, died instantly. It all happened in front of several wedding guests who had come from the house to view the display.

* * *

Tony was 25 years old when he decided, despite his brother's death, to join the RAuxAF too, going to the same local 504 (Country of Nottingham) Squadron. A year later he was joined by his cousin Micky Rook. They were close friends and enjoyed each other's company.

Tony was called to full time service on 24 August 1939, with the threat of war with Germany seemingly imminent. Completing his pilot training he was back with 504 when it went to France in May 1940, returning on the 22nd. Like his cousin he was in action against the Me110s attacking the Filton aircraft works at Bristol on 27 September, and was credited with a Me110 destroyed, and assisted in shooting down another. Three days later he was able to damage a He111. His last claim in 1940 came on 21 November, a Ju88 damaged, possibly a machine of 4(F)/122 that returned to base where it crash-landed with one crew member dead. By this time he was a flight commander.

Tony, and his cousin Micky, remained with 504 until mid-1941 having become its commanding officer in March. On 3 April he and one of his pilots engaged a He111 near Stepper Point, Padstow, Cornwall, and shot it down. The aircraft came from 1./KG27 and Leutnant Fritz Hühle and crew were lost. In July he was given command of 81 Squadron, at RAF Leconfield, which it shared with 134 Squadron. Both squadrons were being prepared for quite a new venture for RAF Fighter Command, to support Russia – in Russia!

In fact 81 Squadron had been formed from 'A' Flight of 504 and then expanded to full strength. Both squadrons were to form No. 151 Wing equipped with twelve-gun Hurricane IIs and in August the Wing took ship for northern Russia. On the morning of 18 August, the aircraft carrier HMS *Argus* was ready, having taken onboard pilots, ground crew and aircraft. In convoy, the carrier sailed via Scapa Flow towards Murmansk on the 30th. Despite foggy weather, the aircraft began flying off on 7 September, landing at Vaenga aerodrome.

It took a few days before some problems with the Hurricanes' guns were solved, and also getting to understand how the Russians worked, and so on, so it was not until the 12th that operations began. The Wing carried out fighter patrols and some escort missions, and, because their Hurricanes would be left in Russia at the end of a period of ops, they trained the Russian pilots how to fly them.

Some air combat victories were achieved, four certain kills being made on 17 September, one Me109 of JG77 being shared by Tony, Sergeant A Anson and Sergeant P Sims. Ten days later, on the 27th, he shared two Ju88s claimed as probables, one of which appears to have been confirmed later.

The Wing ended its time in Russia in December and, leaving their aircraft behind, the pilots and airmen sailed back to the UK aboard HMS *Kenya*.

Squadron Leader Tony Rook, CO of 81 Squadron in Russia, 1941.

Squadron Leader Michael Rook DFC.

Back at RAF Turnhouse, 81 Squadron re-equipped with Spitfire Vs, but in January 1942 Tony Rook left to become an instructor. He was awarded the Distinguished Flying Cross, gazetted on 3 March 1942. In addition he was one of four RAF men to be awarded the Russian *Order of Lenin* by the Russian government for services to their country.[4]

Not all awards are clear cut and in this case were further confused by the Russian awards. The Air Ministry forwarded the latest list of recommendations to the Chief of the Air Staff, Sir Archibald Sinclair, in December 1941. Twelve were for DFCs and four for DFMs, to men in the Middle East, Coastal Command, and North Russia. Item 2 of this communication noted:

'The awards recommended by Middle East and Coastal Command appear to have been earned and are submitted for approval... . As regards the 2 DFCs recommended by the C.O. of No. 151 Wing, you will be aware that just before the Wing left Russia, the Order of Lenin was conferred on the following:-

---

4. The others were W/C Ramsbottom-Isherwood, S/L A G Miller, and F/Sgt C Haw (qv).

Wing Commander Ishwerwood – C.O. of 151 Wing.
Acting Squadron Leader Rook – C.O. 81 Squadron.
Squadron Leader Miller – C.O. 134 Squadron.
Sergeant Haw.

The DFCs now recommended are for Squadron Leaders Rook and Miller but as they received what is understood to be the highest Russian Order, I am not clear that they should also be awarded the DFC and perhaps you will decide this point. I incline to the view that they should get DFC also.'

Sir Archibald Sinclair replied:

1. I agree with the recommendation for flying awards set out in 1H summarised above.
2. Although Squadron Leaders Rook and Miller have received Russian orders, I think they should also received DFCs.
3. I am of the opinion that Wing Commander Isherwood should also receive the DFC. His name does not appear, as there is no one whose business it is to recommend him, but there is no doubt that the success of that unit was to a great extent due to his leadership.'

This correspondence had been generated by Isherwood on 24 November, whilst the Wing was still in North Russia. He had recommended:

Sir,
I have the honour to bring to your notice the following officers who have served under my command in North Russia, and to recommend them strongly for the award of the Distinguished Flying Cross which I consider they had undoubtedly earned:-
                S/Ldr A.H. Rook (No. 81 (Fighter) Squadron.)

This officer has led his Squadron with great dash and skill, during a time when it destroyed more than thirteen enemy aircraft for the loss of only one of our own pilots. He has always fostered the aggressive spirit in his pilots, and his leadership is responsible for the fine record which his squadron bears in Russia.

S/Ldr A.G. Miller (No. 34 (Fighter) Squdron.)

This officer has led his Squadron with high qualities of determination and judgement. During the many escorts to Russian bomber aircraft either led by himself or provided by his Squadron, not a single Russian bomber has been lost.

I have the honour to be,
Sir,
Your obedient servant

G R Isherwood
Wing Commander
Commanding Royal Air Force, N. Russia.

* * *

Tony Rook spent most of the rest of the war as an instructor and serving with No. 55, 53 and later 57 Operational Training Units, received the Air Force Cross on 8 June 1944.

The citation for this award noted:

This officer previously commanded the training wings at Nos. 55 and 53 O.T.U and now fills a similar appointment at No. 57 O.T.U. He has a wide experience of O.T.U work which has been invaluable. Squadron Leader Rook is respected by all instructors and pupils and has the power to inspire them to overcome difficulties when these arise. He has always aimed to produce good officers and N.C.Os as well as good fighter pilots from his pupils.

He left the RAF in 1945 and returned to 504 Squadron, commanding it from May 1946 to 1948. He died in 1976, when he was 64.

* * *

Michael Rook was the second of five sons (although one died at birth) of Lieutenant-Colonel William R 'Billy' Rook OBE TD JP (formally of the 'Robin Hoods' – Sherwood Foresters) and his wife Dorothy, of Edwalton, Nottinghamshire. He received his education at Oakham School and later Uppingham School, after which he worked in the family's wine and grocery business, Skinner & Rook Ltd, of Clumber Street, Nottingham. Michael's main passion was in motor racing as well as flying. He was a large man, over six feet tall and wore size 14½ shoes. He could just about cram himself into the cockpit of an aeroplane.

He married 20-year-old Joan Leslie Corah of Queniborough, Leicestershire in November 1936 when he was 21. He followed his flying dream by joining the Royal Auxiliary Air Force in 1938, also going to 504 (Country of Nottingham) Squadron at RAF Hucknall. When war came, he completed his training at No. 6 OTU at the end of April 1940. Converting to Hurricanes he joined 504, now based at Lille in France, but before any real action came on his part, the squadron was withdrawn back to England. As the Battle started, 504 was defending northern cities until it was required to reinforce Fighter Command in the south of England in September.

His first successful combat came on the 15th, sharing a Dornier 17 south of the River Thames, one of three brought down by 504, the bombers coming from KG3. On the 27th he shot down a Me110 near Filton and probably a second. The enemy's target was the Bristol aircraft factory, and the force comprised thirty Heinkel 111s of KG55 and bomb-carrying Me110s of the specialist unit, *Erprobungsgruppe* 210, escorted by further 110s of III/ZG26.

Rook's Squadron had just recently been deployed down to Filton and met the bombers over Dorset, their attacks forcing the bombers to jettison their loads and head back towards the Channel. However EG210, as expected, forced their way through hordes of defending Spitfires and Hurricanes, losing four of their number, including its Kommander, Hauptmann Martin Lütz. ZG26 also suffered losses, with six fighters lost and another crash-landing at Cherbourg.

Michael, or Micky as he was generally known, remained with 504 into 1941, and in July he was posted to 134 Squadron which was forming at RAF Leconfield, as a flight commander. This squadron, together with 81 Squadron, were to form No 151 Fighter Wing as we read above, with Tony

Rook as 81's CO. 134 was commanded by Squadron Leader A G Miller, who had commanded 17 Squadron in the Battle of Britain. The wing leader was Wing Commander H N G Ramsbottom-Isherwood AFC. He was a New Zealander and former soldier who had joined the RAF in the mid-1930s. By 1941 he was a sector commander with 9 Group. He too would be awarded the DFC for service in Russia and the *Order of Lenin*. Sadly he was to die in a Meteor crash in April 1950, aged 44.

Once on Russian soil the Wing set up camp at Vaenga, near Murmansk and by mid-September were flying operations. On 6 October, Micky Rook destroyed a Me109. Pilots had taken off to intercept an incoming raid by Ju88s and 109s and in the course of this engagement Micky found himself detached from the others, spotted six aircraft which he decided were Hurricanes, and tagged along with them for some time until they started taking an interest in him. They were 109s of I/JG77. As one headed for him he opened fire and, according to his report, his fire blew it to pieces. The other five then chased him down to low level, and Micky only escaped by flying low over a destroyer in Murmansk Sound which caused the Germans to break off the pursuit. He was to remark later, 'The Germans must have thought me either bloody brave or bloody foolish.' After he landed he said, 'When I finally got back to the aerodrome and landed, I sat actually sweating in the cockpit for some time before I could climb out.'

Micky became famous for some of his remarks. On one occasion he had been testing his Hurricane and, arriving back in the Mess, was asked if he had made a good landing. 'Perfect, old boy! Put her down as light as a gnat's whisker.' He also became a famous egg-eater. Lots of eggs appeared in the Mess, usually served fried, three to a plate. Micky ate his three and a Russian pressed him into three more, which he also devoured. The Russian waitress then asked if he would like three more, to which Micky said, 'I can eat a Flight, but not a Squadron.'

Once back in the UK the squadron moved to Catterick to re-equip. However, Micky was then given command of No. 43 Squadron, the famed 'Fighting Cocks', in September, at Kirton-in-Lindsay. The squadron was in a state of flux as it had been warned of an overseas posting, and everyone was busy packing and preparing for a long sea journey. The number of personnel in 43 began to grow as the time for sailing approached, with extra ground people plus a contingent of RAF Regiment men, which indicated it would need some form of airfield defence. There was a delay in the movement order due to the fact that Operation Torch, the Allied landings in Algeria, had been postponed – not that the squadron were privy to that. Finally, on 19 October, seventeen pilots departed for Greenock, to board the SS *Ashland*, followed a week later by everyone else. They boarded the SS *Strathmore*, a P&O luxury liner in happier times, and after dark on 1 November she slipped away into the North Channel at the start of its journey.

The ships broke their journey at Gibraltar where the pilots were given free time but told to select Hurricane IIc machines (tropicalised) from several hundred that had been assembled there. It was not until the 7th that they were told of their destination, once Allied troops had landed and secured a beachhead at Casablanca, Oran and Algiers. The next morning they were off, but with much apprehension. Their destination was Maison Blanche but it was by no means certain that this airfield had been captured, and the pilots were told that if it had not, and without enough fuel to get back to Gib, they were to bale out over the sea near the Allied troopships off the coast.

A signal was sent to Gibraltar that the airfield had been cleared of the enemy, but nobody thought to radio 43's pilots of this helpful fact, so upon their arrival Micky took a long look at the landing ground, then with no hostile reaction from the ground, landed with 'A' Flight. Once down and safe, he called 'B' Flight, and soon all were safely on the deck. Later in the day, 81 and 242 Spitfire Squadrons arrived, all to be part of 323 Fighter Wing. The ground personnel finally sailed into Algiers on the 12th.

There was much air action with German raiders being intercepted by Wing aircraft. Micky had his own personal Hurricane, of course, HV560 FT-Z, which carried a painting of a rook on the fin. Gradually the Allied soldiers took control of the area and German and Italian forces were pushed back, making the whole operation a success. With the British troops breaking out of Egypt following the Battle of El Alamein, the Axis forces would be gradually squeezed from east and west into Tunisia, where the North African campaign would finally come to an end.

Micky was awarded the Distinguished Flying Cross in January 1943, gazetted a month later, with this citation:

This officer has rendered valuable service during an extensive period of operational flying. He served in France and later fought in the Battle of Britain when he destroyed two enemy aircraft. During operations in Russia he destroyed a Messerschmitt 109. On 8th November 1942, during the assault on Algiers, this officer led his squadron on a flight to Maison Blanche airfield before it was known that the airfield had been captured. The squadron reached the airfield at an early hour and its arrival had a most beneficial effect on the fighting and on the negotiations that were proceeding. Squadron Leader Rook's energetic leadership and splendid example have contributed to successes achieved by his squadron, which has completed a large number of hours flying since its arrival in North Africa.

Micky's Squadron continued operations, moving bases as the ground troops advanced through Algeria and into Tunisia. Finally, after Tunisia fell, 43 moved to the island of Malta on 9 June, and in July to Comiso, Sicily. One memorable event whilst on Malta was a visit by the King, 43 providing a standing fighter patrol above from dawn till dusk. At one point the King's car and his entourage arrived at Hal Far just as Micky and his section had landed. Jumping out of his cockpit he just had time to head the squadron parade as the car pulled up. A rather breathless Micky called for three rousing cheers for King George the *fifth!*

Micky left 43 Squadron on 9 August 1943 after a particularly long tour of almost a year. His new job was as a staff officer at RAF HQ in Egypt. He saw out the war behind a desk and was released from the RAF in 1946 with the rank of wing commander. However he was not done with flying, and re-joined 504 Squadron RAuxAF, although he lost his high rank in doing so, becoming a mere Flying Officer.

The squadron was based at RAF Hucknall, flying de Havilland Mosquito

Squadron Leader M Rook DFC, commanding 43 Squadron in 1943.

NF30 machines, and later Spitfire F22s. His decision to return to 504 Squadron may well have been influenced by the fact that his cousin Tony was its commanding officer. Sadly Micky was killed in an accident on Saturday, 13 March 1948. Flying a Mosquito T3 (VP345) along with Flying Officer Richard M Boyle as his navigator, they had just left the ground when at 400 feet the port engine began to lose power and smoke began to stream from it before it failed completely. Micky did not feather the propeller and the aircraft began to turn through 180 degrees, allowing the speed to drop off below the required single-engined safety speed. Continuing the turn and still losing height Micky tried to pull up over some rising ground but the Mosquito stalled and crashed inverted, catching fire and burning out. Both men were killed instantly.

Michael Rook was 32 years old and was buried in Edwalton Parish Church grounds, Nottingham. He had a daughter Suzy, 6, and a son Michael, who was 3.

Chapter 16

Group Captain E N Ryder CBE DFC & Bar,
Order of Orange Nassau

E dgar Norman Ryder (he preferred Norman) was born in Risalpur, India, on 28 November 1914, spending his early childhood in this part of the Empire. When aged ten he came to England upon his family's return, and on completion of his education, joined the Royal Fusiliers in 1931, serving with them for three years. Once free of the army he became a schoolmaster at Tredinnick School, Worcester, teaching mathematics.

This may have continued, except one evening after a reasonably social get-together at a local hostelry, he and a colleague had to work late into the night. His companion, studying a copy of the *Daily Telegraph*, noticed a recruitment notice for young men to take a short service commission in the Royal Air Force. Both thought, like many others at the time, that war with Germany would soon be coming, and having already tasted life with the army (and not liking the idea of a war at sea) thought this a good idea. Many good ideas mature after an evening drinking.

Accepted for pilot training, Norman Ryder joined the RAF in August 1936, going to Prestwick to fly Tiger Moths, before progressing to No. 9 Flying Training School at RAF Thornaby. Passing out top of his class, he asked that he could fly fighters, got his wish and in March 1937 was posted to No. 41 Squadron.

Norman Ryder DFC seated in a Spitfire.

The squadron was equipped with Hawker Fury biplanes and based at Catterick where, after accumulating a number of flying hours in his log book, he was pleased when 41 began to convert to the new Supermarine Spitfire I monoplane fighter in early 1939. It would be in these aircraft that he would go to war.

For Ryder, that war really began on 3 April 1940, by which time he was a flight commander. Radar had picked up a plot, more than likely hostile, flying in bad weather over the North Sea, and despite very poor visibility he was sent aloft to investigate. He was vectored to a spot off Whitby. There was a convoy nearby and the Luftwaffe had sent off a number of Heinkel 111 bombers on armed reconnaissance flights. Ryder, in Spitfire N3114, had been scrambled at 12.20 pm and was fortunate to find one of them, a He111H-2 from KG26, flown by the Gruppenkommandeur, Oberst Hans Helefe. It was at 400 feet, just below cloud base, less than a mile away and appeared to be having a problem with its port engine. Despite some accurate fire from the Heinkel's gunners, Ryder closed right in as he had been trained to do, aiming his fire at the bomber's starboard engine. The crippled aircraft began to head for the water, trailing smoke, and Ryder watched as it belly-flopped onto the sea where it floated for a while, during which time the four-man crew got out of it. Ryder noticed that a nearby fishing trawler was turning towards them, but he had now become aware that his own aircraft had been hit. His oil temperature was rising, so obviously his coolant tank had caught a bullet, and he knew a Spitfire wouldn't go very far before its engine would overheat and seize up. He called up control, telling them of his problem; with his cockpit becoming quite warm, he knew he would soon have to get out. He was too low to bale out and as far as he knew nobody had ever ditched a Spitfire, so this was all new territory for him, and for the RAF. The engine then caught fire and it was time to 'splash down', which he did, stalling the fighter just above the water, his cockpit hood open. The nose dug in and the aeroplane became vertical, tail up and going down. Suddenly he was under water. Undoing his harness he tried to get out but the parachute pack caught under the hood. Eventually he managed to push himself clear. He had gone down quite a way and by the time he broke to the surface his lungs were at bursting point, but he was safe.

He too was rescued by a trawler, the *Alaska*, the crew taking him below to get him a warm drink and some dry clothes. He had only been in the water a relatively short time but he was lucky to survive as his clothing had become water-logged and his Mae West did not fully inflate. The RAF took considerable interest in his experience. Ryder was right: this was the first Spitfire ditching. In his report he wrote that when he was sinking, the colour of the water changed from green to black, and this phrase stuck, so that he was often known as 'Green to Black Ryder.' The German crew were all taken into captivity, two of them being wounded by Ryder's fire. This adventure resulted in the award of the Distinguished Flying Cross for Ryder, among the first for an RAF fighter pilot. The citation in the *London Gazette* (for 19 April 1940) read:

> *During April, this officer was ordered to investigate an enemy raid at sea and took off alone in bad visibility and low cloud. He sighted an enemy aircraft and, observing that its port engine was out of action, he promptly attacked the starboard engine and after disabling it with one burst of fire the aircraft fell into the sea. Afterwards Flight Lieutenant Ryder found that his own aircraft was losing power and he was forced to come down on the sea, whereupon his aircraft immediately dived. When at a considerable depth he managed, with great difficulty, to extricate himself from the cockpit and was then picked up by a nearby trawler. His accurate flying made the interception a success and his coolness and courage materially contributed to his own rescue and the collection of much valuable information. He set a splendid example of courage and discipline to his squadron.*

* * *

The squadron remained at Catterick until the Dunkirk evacuation crisis. Down south, 11 Group of Fighter Command were battling German aircraft over the beaches of France and inland from Dunkirk and Calais. The squadrons would soon be needing a rest and reinforcements. For 41 Squadron, the call came on 28 May, by receiving an order to move to RAF Hornchurch, eighteen Spitfires heading south, under Squadron Leader H R L Hood. Ryder was one of the flight commanders, J T Webster the other.

While Ryder was involved in several sorties during this period, he claimed no definite success, and by 8 June the squadron was sent back to Catterick. The pilots were still kept busy with patrols off the English coast and out over the North Sea protecting convoys.

On 26 July it was back to Hornchurch once more. The Battle of Britain was hotting up and the squadron also used Manston as a forward base. Combats ensued and a number of pilots began to score kills over their Luftwaffe opponents. Pilots such as Benny Bennions, Tony Lovell (qv), Mac Mackenzie and Johnnie Webster were all prominent.

Ryder's chance to shine came on 15 August, claiming a Ju88 probably destroyed. While the Germans were raiding in the south, a large force of bombers headed across from Norway to attack fighter bases in the north. Two formations of bombers from KG26 and KG30, escorted by long-range Me110 fighters, were met by several RAF squadrons. Ryder was leading one section; his radio failed so he had to hand over the lead to another pilot, but he continued within the section. After the initial clash, he engaged an 88 (KG30), his fire knocking several large pieces off it, followed by an explosion and then smoke. Having used all his ammunition he broke away, last seeing the Junkers heading downwards. KG30 lost seven of its aircraft, with three more returning damaged.

It was September before he scored again, the squadron having moved down to Hornchurch on the 3rd. On the 5th, 41 Squadron suffered severely. In the morning it had a pilot shot down, and although uninjured, his Spitfire was written off. In mid-afternoon, in a fight with Dorniers and Me109s of JG54, the CO, Squadron Leader Hood, was killed, as well as Flight Lieutenant Johnnie Webster. Webster baled out but was dead by the time he reached the ground. It later transpired that they had collided during an attack on a bomber, and Webster's parachute either failed or became detached. Two other pilots were wounded, one landing with a leg wound, while Flying Officer A D J Lovell baled out near Benfleet, landing safely.

During the first encounter, Ryder's section was covering two other sections and engaging the fighters. He got behind a 109 and opened fire at 200 yards, which caused an explosion, followed by steam from its radiator. As the 109 began a gliding turn he was engaged himself and lost sight of his opponent.

Pilots of 41 Squadron in 1940. S/Ldr H R L Hood is seated in the middle of the first row; Norman Ryder is third from the right; Tony Lovell (qv) stands third from the right middle row.

The second scrap that afternoon began with a scramble, Ryder leading A Flight, and acting as rear guard to the others. The battle began over the Thames estuary when B Flight was bounced by 109s. Ryder picked out a 109 that was attacking another Spitfire, firing five bursts into it. Trailing smoke, the 109 began to lose height, exploded and caught fire at about 7,000 feet, falling in a mass of flames.

Norman Ryder had now to take temporary command of the squadron, and led it into combat the next day. The first scramble did not result in a combat and then Ryder led the pilots down to Rochford, from where they were sent off in the later afternoon. In the air they had just identified friendly fighters below but then ran into several Me109s, being covered by more higher up. Ryder went after one Messerschmitt, snapping off bursts as the German pilot took evasive action. Smoke eventually spewed back from the 109, and it went down and blew up before falling into the sea off Southend Pier. The squadron had in fact tangled with JG27 and JG53, and Ryder's victim was

Hauptmann Joachim Schlichting, commander of Stab/III of JG27. He baled out, seriously wounded, and was captured.

Schlichting was an experienced fighter pilot, having seen action during the Spanish Civil War. He was credited with eight kills (five in Spain) and reported afterwards that he had been having problems with his rudder and supercharger, losing a certain amount of manoeuvrability. This 26-year-old from Kassel was later awarded the *Ritterkreuz* (Knight's Cross of the Iron Cross) in December 1940 for his leadership of the 3rd Gruppen of JG27.

Ryder led the squadron on several sorties on the 7th, the day the Luftwaffe began its attack on London. On the last patrol, they encountered Dornier 17s being escorted by an estimated fifty Me109s a few miles south of Whitstable. They went for the bombers first. After damaging a Dornier Ryder became embroiled with 109s, firing at one but without seeing any result. He then went after another 109, causing black and blue smoke to emit from its engine as it began to half-roll. He was credited with a probable.

On the 8th it was announced that Squadron Leader R C F Lister DFC was to take command of 41, an announcement that dismayed many of the pilots, for they thought that Ryder was the logical successor to Squadron Leader Hood. Robert Lister had been in the RAF for some time and had won his DFC for actions in Waziristan in 1937. Tony Lovell (qv) became the other flight commander.

Two days later Ryder was in a fight with more 109s. Several Messerschmitts were claimed in a late afternoon scramble, Ryder credited with one shot down near Maidstone. He then damaged a Ju88 on the 10th and shared a Dornier on the 15th. By this date Ryder was back in command, Robert Lister having been shot down on the 14th. Flying at the rear of the formation Lister had been bounced from out of the sun by a 109, wounded in the arm, then forced to bale out of his burning Spitfire. Lister survived and when he returned to ops, was attached to 92 Squadron and later took command of it. In the meantime Ryder became acting CO.

Ryder led the second scramble, on the afternoon of the 15th, warned of a large formation of German Dorniers and 109s. In his combat report he said:

'I dived through [the] fighter escort expecting to be engaged but was not attacked, so carried out a diving approach on a single Dornier; this aircraft was engaged before I got into firing range, but I circled once and fired a burst of approx 5-6 secs from astern as E/A entered cloud tops. I felt certain my burst was hitting (tracer) but I could see no results due to cloud. I followed the aircraft with 3 or 4 other friendly fighters until it force landed on Sheppey Isle.' [actually at Allhallows on the Isle of Grain.]

This bomber, from 4./KG3, had both its engines damaged. Sergeant S Fejfar of 310 Czech Squadron had also fired into it, and so had Pilot Officer Ras Berry (qv) of 603 Squadron, as well as 41's Flying Officer J G Boyle. On the ground the Dornier caught fire and was burnt out at Lower Stoke, its four crewmen taken prisoner, three of whom had been wounded. Its pilot was Feldwebel Manfred von Görtz. John Boyle would be killed on the 28th.

* * *

Ryder was again overlooked as squadron commander with the arrival of Squadron Leader D O Finlay. Don Finlay was 31-years-old and, like Lister, a pre-war airman with considerable experience. A former aircraft apprentice since 1925, he re-mustered to become a pilot, and once this had been achieved he was commissioned, in 1935. The following year he represented Britain in the 1936 Olympic Games, as a hurdler, winning a silver medal in this event. A month before being given command of 41, he had been made CO of 54 Squadron but had been shot down by a 109 and wounded after two days. Not long after joining 41, Finlay was shot up by a 109 and had to make a forced landing.

On the 27th, Ryder was shot down. 41 had already suffered two losses in the morning, but the pilots had survived. In the afternoon, operating again from Rochester, he was flying R6755 and got on the wrong end of a 109. He managed to bale out without injury, his Spitfire crashing at East Malling. He gained entry into the prestigious 'Caterpillar Club', receiving the small gold silk worm emblem with a small ruby eye, from the Irvin Parachute Company, because of his safe descent by parachute.

Norman Ryder claimed two victories during October, in what had become dangerous autumn skies. The only good news was that the squadron received the first of their Spitfire Mark IIs. On the 25th he was credited with a probable Me109. The squadron was in company with 603 Squadron against a large formation of Me109s south of Maidstone. Ryder led 41 against a group of four 109s and the 109 he attacked began to trail smoke, half rolled and began making aileron turns. Another burst on target caused the smoke to thicken and darken and he could see coolant smoke streaming back too. The German pilot then stopped evading and began a dive, but Ryder lost it at 6,000 feet as it disappeared into cloud. There is a good chance that this 109 was from 5./JG54, flown by Oberleutnant Joachim Schypek, escorting bomb-carrying 109s to London. Before taking off he had been with the Staffel medical officer and told not to fly, but he ran to his aircraft and flew off anyway. Later Schypek wrote:

'We were attacked when the bombers had reached the London Docks and I yelled an alarm, "Indians at six o'clock." The warning was received and the bombers released their bombs and started a 180 degree turn. Seconds later I had an Indian in my rear view mirror and guessed it was a Spitfire.

'The Indian was right on my tail in my steep dive and opened fire. I could see bullets hitting my wings and from the white trails on both sides I knew he had hit my radiator. I throttled back as I knew it would soon seize. My Indian drew alongside and the aircraft appeared strange to me as I had never been so close to a live Spitfire before. I was rather relieved that he recognised I did not have any chance of getting home and that he did not insist he completed his kill.'

The story with the squadron was that the German pilot, who came down at Scotney Court Farm, Lydd, East Sussex, was taken prisoner and insisted his Iron Cross 1st Class, should be sent to his victor with an accompanying letter of congratulations. These two items duly arrived and were later used in displays to admiring customers in their local Upminster pub. Norman would enjoy drinks on the house when this occurred. It is odd if this story is true, that Ryder did not appear to have his claim confirmed as destroyed.

However, he did receive credit for one destroyed on the 30th. The squadron was scrambled and joined up with 222 Squadron over Tilbury. Ryder and B Flight turned to engage as he later reported:

'I was Red 1 and led the squadron into attack on 6 Me109s acting as rear guard at approx 12.15 hours. I fired at enemy A/C and saw smoke and light vapour.

'Followed E/A down and gave another long burst when the E/A burst into flames and [the] starboard wing broke in half. The pilot was not seen to abandon A/C. I saw the 109 entering cloud in a spin, burning furiously.'

The 109 was being flown by Unteroffizier Kurt Topfer of 7./JG26, and reported shot down over Marden. It crashed at Brook Farm, and it was assumed Topfer was already dead when it hit the ground.

Ryder's last victory came on 27 November. 41 Squadron engaged a formation of Me109s between Maidstone and Ashford at 21,000 feet. Ryder got behind one 109 as it was turning left to fire a deflection bust at Red Section. He closed right it and fired a short burst which caused light and dark smoke to trail back, and then the 109 was going down. It crash-landed south of Ashford with engine stopped. As Ryder circled he saw the German pilot climb out of the cockpit as a couple of civilians ran towards him.

The squadron claimed eight 109s, all from JG51, but this unit only lost six. The pilot Ryder watched was probably Feldwebel Wilhelm Erdniss of 3./JG51 who came down at Horton Court, Monks Horton, three miles north of Hythe, Kent. When I met John Mackenzie, who flew with 41 during 1940, he remembered this action and told me:

'In November we had our day. We went up on this occasion and everything was perfect. On our way home I suddenly saw a squadron of 109s. Two of us were flying out at the back, and they were on our port side, slightly below only about 150 feet. I yelled to Norman, who was leading, and the boys turned round and there they were. We went straight into them. I had the best of all targets - he never budged an inch. I followed as he went down in flames and he actually hit a hayrick or shed on a farm near Folkestone. I circled around but being low on fuel by then had to head off and land at Hawkinge.'

Early in the new year of 1941, Norman Ryder finally achieved squadron commander, being posted to lead No. 56 Squadron. He had been with 41 for three years and nine months, so it was undoubtedly something of a wrench. He had been well thought of by both fellow pilots and ground crew.

No. 56 Squadron were based at North Weald and equipped with Hurricanes – something of a change from Spitfires as any pilot making this sort of transition will testify only too well. They too had seen considerable action during the summer of 1940, but the winter weather curtailed much operational flying until February. This was the time the period of taking the war to the enemy was just beginning, with fighter sweeps and Circus Operations beginning over France.

Ryder took part in the first of these Circuses but by June Norm Ryder became tour-expired, and as a 'reward' was posted to No. 53 Operational Training Unit as an instructor, for a so called rest! He was however, awarded a Bar to his DFC, gazetted on 29 July 1941:

This officer has been on operations continually since the outbreak of war and has shown extraordinary powers of endurance. He has set a splendid example by his leadership and determination, and has destroyed at least five and damaged other enemy aircraft.

In fact his tally was seven and one shared destroyed, three probables and two damaged.

Later in the year he was promoted to Wing Commander and given the job of Wing Commander Flying to the Kenley Wing. Although fighter wings had been instigated during the Battle of Britain, it was the wrong time to do so, and the wrong fight, but with Fighter Command operating in large numbers in support of Circus missions over Northern France, it needed experienced fighter pilots who could lead in the air and remain aware of all that was going on around them, to lead wings from two, three or even four squadrons, in escort and support sorties as well as fighter sweeps in support of such operations.

While a good deal of air-to-air combat continued to take place during such sorties, it was just as important for leaders to escort and protect the small formations of bombers that were the 'bait' for German fighters, so that they could be engaged and shot down. Fighter Command overall thought they were hurting the Luftwaffe fighters but as it was to prove later on, the German fighter pilots shot down more RAF pilots than they lost.

Nevertheless, Wing Commander Ryder led his Wing during the summer of 1941. He did so well enough until his luck ran out on 31 October. On this day Ryder led two squadrons, 485 New Zealand and 602 Squadrons, as close escort to Hurricane II bombers attacking barges along the Bourboug Canal, just inland from Dunkirk. This was a low ramrod operation, also listed as Circus 109. The 12 Hurri-bombers came from 607 and 615 Squadrons. The operation was completed but Ryder's Spitfire V, W3579 (a presentation aircraft named *Southland II*) was hit by ground fire and he was forced to

Wing Commander Norman Ryder's Spitfire in which he force-landed in France on 31 October 1941, to be taken prisoner. This was on Circus 109 in W3579 OU-Q *Southland II*, a 485 Squadron machine.

Ryder's smashed Spitfire after it had been taken to a German dump.

crash-land. 607 Squadron also lost a Hurricane to flak while 615 had one pilot wounded.

Unable to evade capture Ryder eventually found himself at the infamous Stalag Luft III (his prisoner of war number being 658), the scene of the Great Escape, in March 1944. After six months captivity he went to Oflag XXIB at Schubin, from where Ryder managed to escape in 1943 by hiding in a heavy box on the back of a truck, only to be recaptured two days later when he was discovered trying to find a suitable aeroplane to steal. Sent back to Luft III, he continued to make a nuisance of himself to his captors and after his return to England at the end of the war his name was Mentioned in Despatches for his service while a prisoner. His final five months had been spent at Stalag IIIA at Luckenwald.

Remaining in the Service he was later awarded the Order of Orange Nassau by the Dutch, and in June 1958 became a Commander of the Order of the British Empire (CBE). In July 1959 he took part in the London to Paris Air Race, celebrating the 50th anniversary of Bleriot's first flight across the Channel in 1909; the prize was £5,000. Flying a Hawker Hunter T7 jet fighter-trainer he was placed third, in 42 minutes and 6 seconds, slowed by having injured a leg in a motorcycle accident in Paris.

He retired from the RAF the following year with the rank of Group Captain, his last post being that of station commander at RAF Duxford. He spent his retirement in Arizona, USA, and died in October 1995. He was just short of his 81st birthday.

Chapter 17

Wing Commander J G Sanders DFC

James Gilbert Sanders was a regular RAF pilot, having taken a short service commission in late 1935. I met James on several occasions in his later life. He lived in Wimbledon, not far from my home, and it was always a pleasure to be in his company, and that of his friendly little Jack Russell that he named Elliott.

James had an unusual background and upbringing, for although he was born in Richmond, Surrey, on 19 June 1914 he spent most of his early years in Italy until he was aged 19. I learnt from him that in his late teens he was convinced there would be a war coming, and that Mussolini's fascist Italy would be involved, and not on the Allied side. Having come to this conclusion he felt certain that he would much rather fight in a war in the comparative comfort of a fighter aeroplane, than in the mud and grime of the trenches.

Having returned to England, being able to speak perfect Italian as might be imagined, his successful application to join the RAF was easily and quickly achieved, thus finding himself posted to No. 10 Flying Training School at RAF Ternhill, near Market Drayton, Shropshire. This had opened on 1 January 1936 and James arrived exactly one month later. Here he had his first piloting experience in those silver biplanes of the 1930s, the school having Hawker Hart, Hawker Audax and Avro Tutor training machines for its instructors to impart their wisdom and experience to the embryonic would-be airmen in their charge. Ternhill became an RAF training centre for the next forty years.

To know James, even in his later years, one was impressed by his forthright stance on all matters, and there can be no doubt that he quickly became a dedicated and very professional pilot. There would have been no flippancy in his work, which would be accomplished with keen efficiency and precision. By August he had won his RAF 'wings', whereupon he received his first

Pilots of 111 Squadron in 1937. Sgts Mortimer, Smith, W L Dymond, F/O M L Robinson, P/O J G Sanders, P/O R G Dutton, S/L J Gillan, P/O R P R Powell, F/O S Darwood and P/O S D P Connors.

posting, to No. 111 Squadron at RAF Northolt, his CO being Squadron Leader I E Brodie. 111, or Treble One as they were normally referred to, were flying Gloster Gauntlet fighters, Marks I and II. Over the next couple of years he honed his flying skills and built up a pleasing number of flying hours in his Pilot's Log Book.

By the late 1930s James was not the only one feeling strongly that war was fast approaching. Fortunately, aircraft designers such as Reginald Mitchell and Sydney Camm were convinced of this too and had pushed ahead their ideas for a more modern design, certainly away from biplanes. Their creations, the Supermarine Spitfire and the Hawker Hurricane were fast becoming a reality, and in December 1937 Treble One became the first RAF fighter squadron to receive the Hurricane. As far as James Sanders was concerned, this was the future, and an aeroplane that could be used to great effect against an enemy.

The task given to Treble One was to fly and fly and fly the new type, in order to find all the wrinkles and have the engineers at Hawkers iron them out. For James it seemed he was always in the air at this stage, bringing the Hurricane up to a real world-beater and ready for any conflict that occurred. The squadron also had a new commanding officer, John Gillan. James told me:

> 'We took to them like ducks to water, finding them much easier than expected. We had John Gillan as our CO who was a magnificent man and liked publicity. As a fighter squadron commander he was remarkable. He made us so enthusiastic about flying this new monoplane which at the time we all knew to be quite special.
>
> 'We had been flying Gauntlets and even with them we were quite a well known squadron because we did all the flight aerobatics; but John expressed the new concept in fighter aircraft, in spite of some inadequacies. For instance, it was quite slow taking off and took time to gain height with its fixed two-bladed propeller. But we coped with that very well and all the pilots took to it at once. To begin with, I admit, we may have kept the cockpit hood open a little longer than was necessary, but we had been used to open cockpits for a long time.
>
> 'The two test pilots at Brooklands, where we collected the first Hurricanes, were George Bulman and Philip Lucas and they were marvellous and enthusiastic, but we did find it difficult to get them off from the airfield and could only just about clear the old high-banked racing track.'

Gillan was always on the lookout for publicity for his squadron and with this new fast fighter, he found the chance. He decided to see what the new fighter could do flat-out so on 10 February 1938 took off for Turnhouse, in Scotland. He had something of a head-wind to contend with but after refuelling in Scotland, headed back to London, now taking advantage of the tail-wind. His speed was recorded at an average of 408.75 mph covering the 327 miles in just 48 minutes. Gillan got the publicity he sought.

By the time war started in September 1939 James was a very experienced Hurricane pilot, with a lot of hours to prove it. But in October, his skill became his downfall. He had perfected a technique, when nobody senior was around, of taking off, then pulling up sharply, making a slow roll and getting into level flight quickly at height. One Saturday morning, believing everyone was busy elsewhere, he took off for a flight and went into his restricted and unauthorised manoeuvre. Unfortunately, the station commander had arrived unannounced – to him anyway – and James was seen and quickly hauled up before him. Being a senior pilot on the squadron did not save him and he was posted out as an example to others. One might have thought that with his vast experience on Hurricanes, his knowledge and talents would have been of use to another Hurricane squadron, but of course the RAF being the RAF, he was posted to 615 Squadron, Royal Auxiliary Air Force, which was equipped with Gloster Gladiator biplanes!

His new squadron was based at Croydon, south of London, and in November it was ordered to take off for France. Four Hurricane squadrons had already been sent off to France shortly after war had been declared, but it seems a little strange that a biplane squadron would now be sent to help out in case the 'phoney war' ended. 615 was accompanied by another Gladiator Auxiliary unit, 607 Squadron, both being sent to Merville. On 29 December, James flew a weather test and sighted a German He111 bomber. He chased it, all the while the German climbing away from him. He fired when he felt he had a chance of hitting, or at least of deterring the enemy pilot from continuing to fly away, but by the time it had reached 23,000 feet James had gained little in the chase and all his ammunition had gone. What he might have done if he was in a Hurricane. His fire, he hoped, had caused some damage, but the reconnaissance Heinkel, from Wekusta (Wettererkundungsstaffel) 26, was, sadly, not harmed.

No.615 Squadron was commanded by Squadron Leader J R Kayll and it began to exchange its Gladiators for Hurricanes in April 1940. James and his fellow flight commanders began to convert their pilots onto the new fighter, so his experience and knowledge finally found a home. The German invasion began at dawn on 10 May and at last the 'phoney war' was at an end. The French and British air forces were soon faced with the might of the Luftwaffe and quickly found themselves up against a formidable foe.

James' first real encounter with the enemy came on 17 May, fortunately now back in a Hurricane. Operating from Moorsele, he attacked and shot down a Ju88 bomber from 7/LG1 near Lille at 10.20 am. However, its rear gunner got in a telling burst at the Hurricane and James had to make a hurried force landing. He was not hurt and his machine could be repaired. The Junkers crashed at Flines-lez-Raches, north-east of Douai. Three of the crew were killed, a fourth died later in hospital, one being the Staffelkapitän, Oberleutnant Ernst Schwarz.

On the 18th James and the others returned to England and he was ordered to lead a Flight of old Gladiators from Manston during the period of the Dunkirk evacuation. Sadly little is recorded about this detachment, other than to say he operated patrols over the little ships and survived for several days doing this dangerous job.

I should say at this point that of the many flying log books I have seen over the years, James Sanders' is about the poorest I have ever gone through. Most pilots make some interesting comments, especially on the right-hand page, even some personal observation or a note of what they experienced, what they did, and any possible results of an air action. His log book records little more than time up and time down. It wasn't in his nature to make comment or to try to show how well his actions had gone. He was every bit the professional regular air force pilot, and knowing it was good enough for him.

So it is not easy to make any clear comments about his combat successes. Moreover some combat reports from the French campaign appear to have been lost, destroyed in the evacuation, or misplaced. However, records do show that he shot down a Me110 on 22 June, over Rouen, and damaged a second. 615 had returned to England, based at RAF Kenley, but were flying missions over France prior to the final surrender of the French. He had been on one of these patrols, and returning from it had run short of petrol and was forced to land on the Isle of Wight. Neither he nor his Hurricane was harmed. On another patrol over France on 30 June he claimed a Me109, although he was unable to have it confirmed.

Flight Lieutenant J G Sanders DFC, 615 Squadron, 1940.

For his actions over France, James was awarded the Distinguished Flying Cross, the brief citation for which appeared in *London Gazette* on 4 June:

This officer has led his Flight well and has personally shot down three enemy aircraft.

He was presented with his DFC by HM King George VI at RAF Kenley on 27 June.

His squadron, while based at Kenley, was also using RAF Manston as a forward base. The Battle of Britain began and James' first successful participation in it, as far as one can tell, was on 16 August. South of Brighton the squadron intercepted Heinkel III bombers, and he damaged two, while other pilots were credited with two destroyed, also damaging at least three more, all from KG27 and III/KG55.

Two days later, on the 18th, he bagged one He111, one Ju88 and shared another Junkers. The Heinkel possibly came from III/KG53, attacked south of Kenley at around 13.30 pm. The target had been Kenley aerodrome itself and several RAF squadrons were involved in combats with the attackers and there was, no doubt, some over-claiming. Several Heinkels and Ju88s came down, or failed to make it back across the Channel.

The squadron was sent away from the south for a rest, moving to Prestwick, but James managed to remain in the battle area and, borrowing a Hurricane that 615 had left behind, attached himself to 253 Squadron at Kenley. As well as wanting to continue the fight, he was seeing a young lady who lived nearby, whom he later married and they were to have two children. He also managed to get himself off after dark to intercept night raiders. On the night of 24/25 August, near Hastings on the south coast, he shot down a Ju88 and damaged a He111. The 88 came from II/KG51, and crashed into the sea at 01.20 am.

One month later, during another nocturnal sortie on the night of 23/24 September, James bagged another Heinkel, over Chobham, this time in a 253 Squadron Hurricane that had also been left for the squadron by 615. His victim came from the 6th Staffel of KG26 during its mission to bomb London. It seems it may have been already hit by AA fire, but James, attracted by the gunfire, also intercepted it and helped finish it off, the bomber falling in flames near Gordon Boys Home, West End, Chobham, Surrey, at 01.37 am. Unteroffizier Karl Niemeyer and his crew all baled out and were taken into captivity.

In October he was given command of 422 Flight and attached to F.I.U. (Fighter Interception Unit), operating night patrols from RAF Shoreham on the south coast. On 18 December, the Flight became No. 96 Squadron and began to operate from Cranage, south of Manchester, mainly for the defence of Liverpool and the surrounding area. It also had a detachment at Squires Gate, near Blackpool. Obviously James' night-fighting achievements had impressed 'higher authority', who were actively seeking out people to fly night operations, something that was lacking in Fighter Command's defence locker. Airborne radar was still being developed and in the interim Hurricanes were being used on nights that were not completely black. The pilots were directed by radio to where bombers were known to be in the hope the fighter pilot would somehow pick up the bomber, perhaps from its glowing exhausts, or the raider being caught in searchlight beams and/or exploding anti-aircraft fire.

Wing Commander James Sanders DFC with a Spitfire IXB (MH819) on the occasion when three Spitfires were presented to the RAF at Squires Gate by the Lancashire Constabulary.

James was still a flight commander, his CO being Squadron Leader R G Kellett DSO DFC VM. While the Hurricane did valiant service in the night fighter role, Blenheim and then Beaufighter aircraft stood a better chance of a successful interception once night radar sets were carried in them and operated by a radar operator, who would direct his pilot to the target aircraft. In the interim, the Boulton Paul Defiant was pressed into night operations, but without radar, or front firing guns. If the crew found a raider it could only be engaged by a gunner who had four .303 machine guns in a turret behind the pilot.

The Defiant did not look dissimilar to the Hurricane at first glance, and this 'first glance' fooled a number of German fighter pilots on the occasion they first began meeting them over Dunkirk in May 1940. A closer look, however, revealed something very different behind the cockpit area: the turret. Coming in behind one of these, thinking it was a normal day fighter, surprised several enemy pilots, who were suddenly faced with return fire from four guns. After this they did not attack from behind, and in consequence the Defiant crews suffered grave losses. The fact that the pilot did not have any forward armament did not improve matters either. Just two forward firing .303 guns in the wing would have made quite a difference.

Now, however, the Defiant had been withdrawn from day fighter ops, and relegated to other areas. Some became eyes for Air-Sea Rescue units, others were used as target-towing for air gunner training, and now for night-fighting. Provided the two-man crew were able to locate a night raider, the pilot should be able to creep up alongside it, or below, allowing his gunner to turn the turret and open fire.

No. 96 Squadron now began to acquire Defiants for this purpose, in March 1941. However, James was then sent to command a Flight of No. 255 Squadron at Kirton-in-Lindsey, roughly between Hull and Sheffield. His CO was Squadron Leader R L Smith, who had been with 151 Squadron in 1940. Operating on the night of 12/13 March, in a Defiant, James and his gunner found and attacked a He111 over base and claimed it as 'probably destroyed'. This may have been the aircraft from III/KG26 that force-landed at Amiens after receiving damage from an RAF night-fighter. On the night of 7/8 May he and his gunner located a Ju88 over Brigg and claimed to have damaged it too.

* * *

In September 1941 Sanders was posted as a squadron leader to East Fortune, Scotland, as officer commander of its No. 60 Operational Training Unit. This was a night-fighter outfit but it was about to start going from Defiants to Blenheim and Beaufighters, and be re-designated as a twin-engined night-fighter OTU.

His time as an instructor was enhanced in the summer of 1943, being promoted to Wing Commander Flying at Llandow and later Rednal, flying North American Mustang fighters. He then had spells as station commander at RAF Hunsden, then Zeals and finally Hutton Cranswick. He then attended a senior commanders' course at RAF Cranwell, and followed this with a posting to the SHAEF (Supreme Headquarters Allied Expeditionary Force) mission to the Netherlands. The war ended while he was engaged in this work, based in the Belgian capital of Brussels. Later in 1945, following the Japanese surrender, he was posted out to Java, and later to Burma, to become Wing Commander Flying at Mingaladon, Rangoon.

Returning to England in 1947, he discovered his wife had been having an affair with a fellow RAF officer, in fact a highly successful fighter ace, and former friend. They had earlier been in the same squadron together, but were now working at the Air Ministry. James once told me of his great anger, so much so that he took his service revolver and was about to walk into the man's office; but common sense prevailed. He returned home and destroyed the gun.

He retired from the RAF in 1947, spending the rest of his working life in the insurance business. His first marriage having been dissolved, he remarried a lady that had lost two fiancés during the war, a situation that made it virtually impossible for him to have any contact with historians about his war time experiences, or even attend RAF reunions. When she died he at last was able to attend certain reunions and feel able to speak to people about his RAF service. Several times he attended 615's get-togethers at Kenley. The marriage had produced a daughter.

His mother had, for many years, been the owner of a rather well-positioned box at the Royal Albert Hall in London. After her death he had continued with it, and even helped to manage the box adjacent to it. They both had a wonderful view of the stage, and just along from the Royal Box. I have to say that my wife and I were often invited to take advantage of using his box, sometimes with some of his friends and former RAF pals. Wine and snacks during the intervals were simply splendid. We would meet him at his Wimbledon home and he would drive us up to town, as he had, being a box owner, a personal car parking spot. His driving was never dull!

One of his pals in 111 Squadron pre-war was Peter Powell (later Group Captain R P R Powell DFC & Bar). He married James' sister Joan during the war. James Sanders died on 12 August 2002, at the age of 88.

Chapter 18

Wing Commander H M Stephen CBE DSO DFC & Bar AE

I met and interviewed H M Stephen when I was working on a biography of Group Captain A G 'Sailor' Malan, and wanted his views on Malan which he was only too pleased to provide, having flown with him in 74 Squadron in 1940. At that time he was still managing director of the *Daily* and *Sunday Telegraph* newspapers, so he invited me to his very nice office at the *Telegraph* building in Fleet Street. From memory it was either late afternoon or early evening, and while I was given a gin and tonic, he was still talking to people and disappearing for several minutes at a time, obviously making certain everything was progressing with that day's edition. Once that had been sorted, we sat in a couple of easy chairs and talked. I saw him a second time while researching a book about the RAF over Dunkirk, and he was just as welcoming and charming. He had a pretty solid build, and even in his wartime pictures he appears less like the slim, debonair fighter pilot of popular image, but more like the sort of pilot you would like to see captaining your Boeing airliner as you were about to fly off on holiday. Firm and dependable.

Harbourne Mackay Stephen was born in Elgin, Scotland on 18 April 1916, the son of a banker. In the Service he was always referred to as 'Steve', which was not only usual for someone with a surname like his, but was probably much easier than calling him by his given first name. He received his education at local schools in Elgin, Edinburgh, and finally Shrewsbury, but left the latter at the age of 15 and got himself a job as a copy boy with Allied Newspapers in London, later moving to the London *Evening Standard*, in 1936, working in the advertising department.

Considering his future life, he still had time to do what so many other young men did in the 1930s, prepare for a world conflict which seemed not too far off. He chose flying as his way of meeting such a future, and learnt to fly at

No. 13 E&RFTS, at White Waltham, near Maidenhead, and joining the Royal Air Force Volunteer Reserve. Apparently he was well suited to flying and went solo after nine hours of dual instruction. He continued with his newspaper career, but at weekends progressed onto Hawker Hart biplanes, thereby almost assuring himself the role of a fighter pilot. He also had the opportunity to take a course on the Hawker Hurricane, one of Britain's new monoplane fighters, and he was given leave of absence to do so by the general manager of the paper, Mr T Blackburn. However, by the time he had completed the course, war was virtually on Britain's doorstep, and the RAF retained all trainee pilots because of the likelihood of immediate hostilities. Sergeant Stephen was sent to join 605 (County of Warwick) Squadron, RAuxAF, so he was on active service from the start. He remained with 605 all through the bad winter of 1939-40, and was in the air, part of Yellow Section, on 28 March, the day the squadron engaged and shot down its first enemy aircraft, a He111.

In April, Stephen was commissioned and posted to 74 Squadron at RAF Hornchurch, just in time to take part in Operation Dynamo, the evacuation of British forces from Dunkirk. Steve was now flying the Spitfire. The official date of the start of this operation was 26 May, but there had already been a number of encounters with the Luftwaffe, as the retreat to the Channel beaches progressed. Therefore it was on the 24th that Steve had his first successful combat, sharing in the destruction of a Hs126 observation machine as well as a Dornier 17. There were a number of these Henschel aircraft in the air at this time, keeping an eye on the progress of German troops and the retreating Allied soldiers. The one engaged by 74's Flight Lieutenant W P F Treacy, Flying Officer J C Mungo-Park and Steve, came from 4.(H)/31, crashing between Bissezeele and Esquelbecq at 7 am. Both of the crew were killed. The Dornier is not so easily identified: 1./KG77 lost one over Dunkirk, and there were several others that got home damaged.

Two days later he and two other pilots attacked another Hs126 over Bergues but it was not a confirmed victory. He had better luck on the 27th. Mid-morning, 74 were in action along with the Defiants of 264 Squadron, against a force of Me109s from I Gruppe of JG1, two 109s being shot down. In the afternoon, Steve and Paddy Treacy attacked a Do17z of 3./KG3, shooting it down over Hondschoote, south-east of Dunkirk. It crashed and burned out south-west of Fruges, although the crew managed to escape from the blaze. However, Treacy's Spitfire was hit by return fire and had to force-land near Gravelines where he was taken prisoner by advancing German soldiers. Treacy managed to escape a short while later only to be recaptured. Later in 1940 he escaped again, this time returning to England via Spain and Eire.

I asked Steve about developing tactics over Dunkirk and he told me:

Flying Officer H M Stephen DFC, 74 Squadron in the Battle of Britain.

'What Dunkirk did for air fighting was, that it moved the fighting, which we had always thought we would do from around 7-10,000 feet, straight up to over 20,000 feet in about four days. For every time we went over we said, right we must be higher than the Germans were, so we'd go up another 4,000 feet and when we got there they would be about 2,000 feet above us. In no time at all air fighting changed from the traditional pattern were one could see the ground, to right up top where you couldn't see it at all. This is one of the reasons I'm sure the army has often said, "Where are these fighter boys?" They were there all right but they couldn't see them.'

At the end of the Dunkirk episode, 74 Squadron – known as the Tigers – went north to Leconfield for a brief rest before heading back south, this time to Rochford in June, then across to Hornchurch once more before the month was out. It took part in some of the Channel skirmishes, during which Steve damaged a 109 over Dover on 28 July. 74 Squadron engaged a number of fighters from JG51, claiming seven of them. It appears JG51 in fact only lost three, but it had others damaged. One of those damaged was the Messerschmitt flown by Major Werner Mölders, the Geschwaderkommodore, who was wounded. Once the Battle of Britain got into its stride, the Tigers were in action almost daily.

Steve's big day came on 11 August, over Dover and the eastern end of the Channel, during the battles fought over the convoy BOOTY. Although he was only credited with a single victory, over a Me109, in several combats he had two others unconfirmed, and one damaged. Against Me110s he had another two unconfirmed victories and a damaged, so seven German aircraft hit during the day. 74 lost three Spitfires, with two pilots killed. The 110s came from I/ZG26, the 109s from III/JG26. Several RAF squadrons were involved in the day's actions and invariably over-claiming of victories took place. It is difficult to keep an eye on a probable victim as the fighter pilot needs to constantly keep looking around in case an enemy is sneaking in for an attack. Looking back at a machine he had just fired at, all too often there was a splash in the sea which the pilot thought was his kill, where in fact someone else had just shot it down, and the intended victim may have recovered and flown off. Two days later Steve knocked lumps off a Dornier but could only claim a probable.

For his actions over recent weeks, Steve was awarded the Distinguished Flying Cross, the following citation appearing in the *London Gazette* of 27 August:

Since May, 1940, Pilot Officer Stephen has flown continuously with his squadron on offensive patrols, and taken part in numerous engagements against the enemy throughout the Dunkirk operations. He has also been engaged protecting shipping in the Channel and has taken part in intensive operations over the Kentish coast. During one day in August, in company with his squadron, Pilot Officer Stephen participated in four successive combats against large formations of enemy aircraft over the Thames Estuary and Channel and during these engagements he shot down five enemy aircraft. He has now destroyed a total of twelve enemy aircraft and has always displayed great coolness and determination in pressing home his attacks against the enemy.

No. 74 Squadron was on the move again, relocating at RAF Wittering, and then Kirton-in-Lindsay for a break. In September it moved to Coltishall, near Norwich. It was from here that Steve had his next combat, on the 11th – over London. He put in claims for a Ju88 destroyed and a 109 damaged, but the problem is that the Germans do not list any Ju88s as lost on the 11th, so either Steve was a trifle over-optimistic about his claim, or in the heat of action, he misidentified the twin-engined bomber as a Ju88 rather than a He111. The Germans lost at least ten Heinkels this day and half a dozen Me110s, although Steve would surely have identified the twin-rudders of the 110s.

The Tigers moved yet again to Biggin Hill in October, but not before Steve had two final claims from Coltishall, a He111 damaged on October 1st, south-east of Cromer, and a Dornier shared with others on the 5th. The Dornier went down thirty miles off Harwich, according to 74's pilots, but yet again there is no Dornier lost this date that matches the action.

74 Squadron would remain at Biggin on the Bump till February 1941, and the good news was that it now had Spitfire Mark IIs on strength. Steve was in action on the afternoon of 20 October, claiming a 109 destroyed and another probably so between Sevenoaks and Dungeness. 74 were engaged with 3./LG2 who lost one fighter and had two others damaged, one being written off following a crash-landing at its base. A week later, the 27th, the Tigers were in combat with Me109s of 3./JG52 in the morning, that were escorting bomb-carrying 109s to London. Two were brought down, one being flown by Oberleutnant Ulrich Steinhilper, who came down near Canterbury, and whose story was told many years later in a book *Spitfire on my Tail.* He gained some fame through his escape attempts after being sent to prisoner of war camp in Canada.

Fighter Command had now entered the most dangerous phase of the 1940 fighting, in the cloudy skies over southern England, trying to thwart bomb-carrying Me109 fighters, escorted by other 109s, all eager to engage the Spitfires and Hurricanes, in conditions that were advantageous to the Germans. The Germans, taking advantage of these weather conditions, began to re-employ Stuka dive bombers. They had proved vulnerable to RAF fighters as the Battle started in July, in clear blue and sunny skies, especially when they began to pull out of their bombing dives. In November they were sent across to England once again.

In the early afternoon of 14 November, 40 Ju87s from StG.1 were launched to attack shipping off Dover, escorted by Me109s from JG26. 74 and 66 Squadrons were sent off from Biggin Hill and a short time later more fighters from 46, 249 and 603 were scrambled. A huge battle took place and the Biggin squadrons claimed a total of sixteen dive-bombers destroyed with numerous others probably destroyed and damaged. Steve was credited with three, one of which he said had crashed into another one following his attack. These days it is understood that over-claiming combat kills was prevalent during the Second World War – and the First World War come to that – but in this action only two Ju87s were lost and one got home badly damaged – all the rest got home safely.

By this date Steve had already been notified of the award of a Bar to his DFC, and it was published in the *London Gazette* of 15 November:

> *One day in October, 1940, this officer was on patrol with his squadron when enemy fighters were sighted and attacked. Pilot Officer Stephen fought four Messerschmitt 109s at 29,000 feet, causing the tail of one to break off, and destroying a second. He has destroyed at least 13 enemy aircraft, and his courage and skill as a fighter pilot have been a great incentive to other pilots in his squadron.*

On this same day Steve damaged a 109 off Bognor Regis, but it was another day of exaggerated claims, 74 claiming to have shot down two destroyed, one probably so, and Steve's damaged, but only one was actually lost, a 109 from JG2 whose pilot baled out off the Sussex coast. On the 17th results were more positive for 74. In the afternoon the Spitfire pilots were scrambled, and engaged 109s of JG27 near Brighton and chased them towards the west. Flight Lieutenant J C Freeborn DFC and Steve each claimed hits on one which fell into the sea. This, it would seem, was Unteroffizier Willi Grotum, who baled out before the aeroplane hit the water, and was taken prisoner.

On the final day of November, Steve was in action again, and again the result was positive and also historical. All fighter squadrons are keen to record the number of enemy aircraft their pilots have shot down and been credited with, even if some, on examination, prove to be in error. RAF stations also keep a running total of victories achieved by squadrons operating from them. During the height and clamour of the summer battles, it had not been realised that Biggin's war total of victories had reached and passed the 500 mark. Indeed it was fast approaching 600. A sweepstake was organised and the person who picked the name of the pilot who would eventually achieve the 600th, would receive the prize. On a boozy Mess night the total appeared to be 599 and tension ran high to see who might be lucky enough to down the next victim.

On the morning of the 30th there was thick fog, so no early missions were contemplated, but around 8 am, operations telephoned to say that a small convoy in the Channel was being attacked. With Biggin being on a hill, the fog was less dense and the suspicion was that once off the ground blue sky would be found. So 74 sent off a two-man section of fighters, Johnny Mungo-Park and Steve. Once over the Channel the two pilots saw a large gaggle of Me109s heading in. The sky was a deep blue, as Steve recalled it, in a most beautiful autumn day, with crystal clear visibility. As the 109s swept in across southern England, the two Spitfire pilots headed out to sea in order to come back above them as they returned across the coast, heading back to France. Surely, they thought, they should be able to bag one!

As they closed in they carefully selected a 109 flying on the edge of a formation which was flying at 34,000 feet. Steve opened fire with a short burst from the starboard beam, which was followed by another by Mungo-Park, while Steve swung round to come in again. Pieces began to fly off the 109 and then it rolled over and started down. Steve followed, closed to about 20 yards and gave it another three-second burst, whereupon it went into cloud, and inverted, at a speed that was estimated at around 450 mph.

The 109 pilot was hit as well as his fighter which fell at Ham Street, Kent. The pilot was Unteroffizier Fritz Wägelein of 5./JG53, who managed to bale out, but his parachute had been damaged and he fell heavily; he was taken prisoner but subsequently died of his injuries. Biggin Hill had its 600th victory. The story of this action gained a lot of publicity and both men were interviewed by the media and the RAF's publicity boys. As Steve was to record:

'Mungo-Park made for one of the two higher aircraft with me close behind. The German turned to the right when he eventually spotted us. As he swung to the right I went straight across and gave him a deflection shot. Mungo-Park, by now dead astern of the enemy, gave him a three-second burst. Our first shot caused him trouble. We saw

H M Stephen, with his flight commander, J C Mungo Park DFC, on the occasion they shared in the destruction of Biggin Hill's 600th enemy aircraft in October 1940.

him try to climb but fail in the attempt. Then in turn we each gave him some more bursts. Smoke began to pour from his aircraft and he dived away.

'I was doing more than 500 mph, and when I was down to 6,000 feet I straightened out. Meanwhile the German pilot had baled out; his machine crashed near Dungeness and he was taken prisoner.

'We both returned to the aerodrome where pilots from other squadrons were disappointed that they had not got the 600th victim, for naturally we were desperately keen to claim him. Yet they will join in the party we are giving to celebrate the victory.'

* * *

December continued in much the same vein. On the 2nd Steve claimed a 109 probable south-east of Dungeness, and on the 5th a 109 destroyed and a second shared. Although only credited with a probable kill on the

2nd, it appears that the unit they were in action with was JG53 who lost two fighters. One had been shot down by Sailor Malan in company with Sergeant N Morrison, and then Steve and Sergeant J N Glendinning had hit the other but did not see it crash. However, the 'Y' Service later reported that two 109s had crashed into the sea, one at 12.27 the other at 12.46. Malan and his wingman shot down Leutnant Siegfried Fischer, who was killed; Steve and Morrison had sent Farhrich Wolfgang Hauffe into the Channel, but he was later rescued.

The action on the 5th involved another German fighter sweep by JG26, which crossed the English coast at Dover. Several RAF squadrons were sent aloft, but 74 got the lion's share of the claims. Steve attacked a 109 and claimed its destruction near Folkestone, confirmed by his No.2, Sergeant J Murray. Steve and James Murray then combined their fire-power to down another 109 six miles off Dungeness. Other Tigers made claims too, but JG26 only lost two fighters and had another badly damaged. One problem with claims against Me109s was that the German pilots' natural defensive manoeuvre to an attack from behind was to half roll and dive at full boost, which threw out a burst of black exhaust smoke. This looked very similar to an engine catching fire whilst under attack, and at this stage neither Spitfire nor Hurricane could emulate the roll over and dive without starving the engine of petrol for a few seconds; the difference was that the 109 had fuel injection, the Merlin a float carburettor. It was easier to assume a hit on the opponent and hope it had gone down.

Steve Stephen was now decorated for a third time, the latest award being an Immediate Distinguished Service Order gazetted 24 December 1940. It was the first ever Immediate award for an RAF pilot. It means the recommendation did not go through several layers of commanders to get their approval. Most awards for gallantry were non-immediate, that is to say they had recommendations written up by someone like a commanding officer, who then had to have it passed through, say a wing leader, or station commander, then on to a group commander, and sometimes to even a more senior officer. It was more prestigious to get an Immediate award than one that came 'through with the rations'. The recommendation was completed and signed by Biggin's station commander, First World War fighter ace, now Group Captain F O Soden DFC, and dated 2 December 1940:

Particulars of Meritorious Service for which recommendation is made.

On 14.11.40, this officer led a section of No. 74 Squadron on an offensive patrol in the vicinity of Dover, when an enemy formation of Junkers 87s, escorted by Me.109s, was encountered.

Owing to his skill and determination as a pilot he succeeded in destroying three Junkers 87s.

On 30.11.40, this officer accompanied by his Flight Commander went on a voluntary patrol. These officers, before volunteering knew that the station had been responsible for the destruction of 599 German aircraft and their object was on the last day of November to make it 600.

They took off and patrolled the Dover area and when in the vicinity of 30,000 feet encountered many large enemy patrols which they avoided. They climbed to a height of 34,000 feet where a weaver squadron of Me.109 was selected as the victim, and P/O Stephen succeeded in destroying it.

P/O Stephen has always displayed exceptional courage and skill in the face of the enemy, and his devotion to his squadron, station, and the Service, inspired him and his Flight Commander to take off and create a record to the station concerned. This, I consider, a spirit to be encouraged and admired in all fighter pilots.

P/O Stephen due to his courage and determination his succeeded in destroying nineteen enemy aircraft.

Group Captain Soden recommended Stephen be awarded a Second Bar to his DFC. This recommendation then passed to Headquarters 11 Group, and onto the desk of its commander, Air Vice-Marshal K R Park MC DFC, another First World War fighter pilot veteran. He wrote the following on 8 December:

REMARKS OF THE AIR OFFICER COMMANDING.

P/O. H. M. STEPHEN.
On two occasions in particular this outstanding gallant young officer scored a magnificent success.

On 14.11.40 when leading a section of his Squadron, he attacked a formation of enemy bombers escorted by fighters and personally destroyed three enemy bombers.

On 30.11.40 he volunteered with his flight commander to bring before the end of the month, the total of enemy aircraft destroyed by his Station up to a record of 600, this he succeeded in doing by destroying an enemy fighter at 34,000 feet.

He has shown exceptional courage and skill in the face of the enemy combined with great devotion to duty and his magnificent spirit has been an encouragement to all ranks.

He has himself destroyed 19 enemy aircraft.

I very strongly recommend him for the award of the DISTINGUISHED SERVICE ORDER.

3rd December 1940. K R Park
Air Vice-Marshal
Commanding No. 11 Group

REMARKS OF THE AIR OFFICER COMMANDING IN CHIEF.

Approved

DATE 8/12/40W S Douglas
Air Marshal
HEADQUARTERS FIGHTER COMMAND.

* * *

Air fighting during the Battle of Britain had certainly changed from the early days. Several thinking sort of leaders were moving away from the Vics of three aircraft, to flying in pairs. They had noticed the Germans used this basic element and it seemed to work. Steve highlighted this, as his CO, Sailor Malan, had changed over to pairs and fours. Steve said:

'We were all learning how things should be handled and those who were senior were also learning the art of leading. I could see the very beginning of the two-by-two formation. It was all just sheer endeavour, professionalism and hard work, disciplined into us youngsters; we were all in our twenties. It shows what an extremely high standard the professional RAF was. Men like Paddy Treacy, Sailor Malan, Tink Measures, in 74 showed the way. After that they had all the amateurs coming through, the VRs etc, to instil how it should all be done. How to survive in combat.'

H M Stephen left 74 Squadron and was posted to RAF Turnhouse in Scotland, to take up an appointment with No. 59 Operational Training Unit and became later its Chief Flying Instructor. In June 1941 he helped to form 130 Squadron at Portreath and one month later he was given command of 234 Squadron at RAF Warmwell, soon to be re-equipped with Spitfires Mark V. On a 12 Group operation over Holland on 12 August, he and one of his pilots, Sergeant J B Shepherd, engaged a couple of Ju88s near Antwerp and claimed their probable destruction. However, it seems that the 88 hit by Steve was a night fighter of I./NJG2 on a daylight flight and it was destroyed.

His last combat occurred on 15 October, leading 234 over Le Havre. His squadron had now moved back to Warmwell within 10 Group, and on this date became part of a 10 Group Ramrod, escorting a dozen Blenheims to attack a tanker in Le Havre at around noon. Several 109Fs were encountered and after the fight the RAF fighters claimed several enemy fighters shot down. Steve shared one with the CO of 118 Squadron, Squadron Leader F J Howell DFC.

Steve's days in England were now numbered. He was tour-expired in January 1942 and had a period as an instructor, also working for RAE, for which he received the Air Efficiency award. However, he was soon on his way east with an overseas posting, to India. The Japanese war had started and the problems in the Far East were mounting.

Once in India, Steve was made Wing Commander Flying at Dum Dum airfield, and later at Jessore. Later still he took command of No. 166 Fighter Wing on the Burma front and eventually took up a post at 224 Group Headquarters in charge of Fighter Operations. He continued in these command roles, until finally he was made Operations 'A' at Air Command, South East Asia Command (SEAC).

On his arrival in India he found there were few aeroplanes to fly, but he and two engineers collected lots of parts and together they put them together, with Steve test flying them himself, feeling it was too dangerous an occupation for anyone else to contemplate. There was one occasion on which he was shot down into enemy-held territory while commanding 166 Wing at Chittagong on the Arakan coast. He managed to trek back through dense jungle to safety, something that a number of RAF airmen failed to do during the course of the Burma war. He also told me that on one occasion he flew a lone reconnaissance patrol in a Hurricane up the Chindwin River, trying to locate where Japanese troops might be.

Once the war was over he returned to England, took his leave from the RAF and soon joined the Beaverbrook Newspaper Group, working on the *Scottish Daily Express, Scottish Sunday Express* and *Glasgow Evening Citizen,* until 1955. Meantime he had married, in 1947, Miss Erica Palmer, whom he'd met in Ceylon, where she worked with the Women's Royal Naval Service. They were to have two children.

During this time he returned to flying, joining the Royal Auxiliary Air Force, commanding 602 Squadron from 1950-52. In 1958 he became general manager of the *Sunday Express,* followed in 1960 by the *Sunday Graphic.* Four years later he moved to the Thompson Newspaper Group as general manager, then managing director of the *Daily Telegraph* and *Sunday Telegraph* until retiring in 1986. The previous year he had been made a CBE. Steve was a keen fisherman in his spare time, having learnt the art whilst living in the vicinity of the Spey and the Dee. The year before he died he was still fishing on the Kennett. Steve died on 20 August 2001 at the age of 85.

Chapter 19

Squadron Leader D W A Stones DFC & Bar

I met Donald Stones on several occasions and we got on. It was around the time of Desert Storm, and the name of note in the papers was General Norman Schwarzkopf Jr, who was in charge of American forces in the Iraq war. Having the same first name, Don quickly began referring to me in the same way the media was referring to Schwarzkopf – *Stormin' Norman*. I took it in good part, after all, here was a man who had lived with a nickname of his own, *Dimsie* Stones.

Donald William Alfred Stones was born in Norwich on 19 June 1921 and completed his education at Ipswich Grammar School. Upon leaving, he applied for an RAF short service commission, becoming a pilot officer in May 1939. His parents had other plans for their son, in the world of insurance, but his mind was fully focused on flying. His initial training took place at a civilian flying school at White Waltham, Maidenhead, Berkshire, flying Tiger Moths. However, he had already been exposed to aviation, having met Percy Sherren MC & Bar, a Canadian who had served in the RAF in the First World War and continued to do so until 1936. It was Sherren who encouraged Dimsie to try for the RAF when he was old enough. Sadly, Sherren was killed in the King's Cup Air Race in 1937, but the seed had been well and truly planted. It was Sherren's wife Joyce who later persuaded Dimsie's parents to sign the consent forms for the Service.

Once war began, Dimsie completed his training at Pehrhos, North Wales before being sent to 11 Group's Pilot Pool, to fly Hurricanes, in December. Once he had completed a course on these fighters he received a posting to join No. 32 Squadron at RAF Biggin Hill in January 1940, his flight commander being Michael 'Red Knight' Crossley. It was not long before Dimsie and the squadron were flying convoy patrols for ships taking men and supplies to the British Expeditionary Force in France. It was while with 32 that he received his nickname. Mike Crossley and another pilot spotted a book sticking out

Squadron Leader D W A Stones DFC.

of Don's coat pocket, entitled *Dimsie goes to School*, by Dorita Bruce. From such little things do lasting nicknames flourish.

The name went with him when he was sent across to join 79 Squadron, also at Biggin. They were short a pilot and Don, being the latest arrival, was the easiest to send. All was well until the morning of 10 May. At 8 am his flight commander, Bob Edwards, burst into his room and told Dimsie to get up, the squadron was heading for France! This news, once conveyed to his family back home, could not have been welcomed, knowing that in the First World War Dimsie had lost three uncles and two more badly wounded. The pilots flew off shortly before noon and landed at Merville, where they were billeted in civilian houses while using the Hotel Sarafand as their Mess. Over the radio they gathered that the Germans had broken through at Sedan and were fast approaching.

Contact with enemy aircraft was slow in coming, but finally on the 14th, during a three-man patrol between Louvain and Namur, they met three Ju88s in a wide 'V' formation. In the initial attack, Dimsie hit one of the 88s and it began to turn. Leaving it to one of his companions, he chased after the leading bomber, closed in and set its port engine on fire. As he overshot, then turned, he saw the Junkers spin down and crash onto the river bank of the Maas. Returning to base, he found his companion had finished off the first 88, but that their section leader was missing.

The bombers came from II./LG1 and were in fact Heinkel 111s. The fight had taken place south of Antwerp, Dimsie's second attack forcing one to crash-land at Broom. Two of the crew were killed, two captured. The first bomber, which he shared with Sergeant H Cartwright, came down at Wetteren, south of Gent, one crewman killed and three captured. Dimsie's Hurricane, L1716, was damaged by return fire from the bombers but was repairable.

Pilots of 79 Squadron in France, 1940. Left to right: Pilot Officer L L Appleton (KIA 14 May), Pilot Officer J E R Wood (KIA 7 July), Don Stones, Flight Lieutenant J W E Davies DFC (KIA 27 June), with some French pilots.

There was no let up. Patrols and air fights happened almost every day now, often several times a day. In the late afternoon of the18th, having been made a section leader, Dimsie scrambled alone in a new Hurricane with no radio crystals, as raiders were bombing nearby Vitry-en-Artois. Over the area he could see several Hurricanes burning on the ground and looking up saw what he thought were other friendly aircraft. Pulling up to join them, they materialised into Me110s, one of which he quickly fired at. He scored hits but the other 110s were now coming down on him. Diving to ground level, he pulled up to find one had followed him down, but it overshot right in front of him. Opening fire with several short bursts whilst chasing it around a small village, until his guns fell silent, he found he had been hit by the 110's gunner, setting his engine smoking. Dimsie crunched into the ground, hitting his face on the gun-sight but quickly leapt out and ran for cover, then fired the six rounds of his Webley pistol as a 110 zoomed by.

Rescued by an army despatch rider, they quickly looked over the Hurricane finding just one bullet hole, the bullet having gone into the oil tank. The soldier took him to the nearest aerodrome, Vitry, carrying his parachute. All was confusion there, the RAF people there rapidly leaving. He asked for a lift, but the squadron CO there ordered him to return first to his Hurricane and set it on fire. Having done this, with some difficulty, he returned to the aerodrome, jumped into the last lorry and headed west.

The Hurricane had been P3451 and his opponents had been 110s of 5./ ZG76, one of which had crashed near Douai, its crew being killed. Dimsie also claimed another 110 as damaged.

The next day he was back in action, claiming a Henschal 126 destroyed, one of several that Allied aircraft encountered over the front, as the Germans tried to find where the British and French armies were. On the 20th he helped bag another one near Arras. The luckless German crew from 3./ (H)41 crash-landed near Neuville-St-Vaast, north of Arras, following the unfriendly attentions of Dimsie and his two wingmen, plus five pilots of 213 Squadron. In the afternoon, 79 Squadron were also sent out to ground strafe advancing enemy troops and armour, but lost two pilots and had several Hurricanes damaged by ground fire, Dimsie's being one of them. Back at base the order came to evacuate back to England, some pilots flying the last remaining serviceable aircraft, whilst the others were torched. The pilots that were left went with the ground crew and returned by ship. Dimsie was able to fly back. After landing at Northolt they headed for Biggin once more, then were sent on a 48-hour leave.

On the 27th, having had a brief rest and the squadron having received new Hurricanes, operations began again, escorting bombers to France to attack Germans still heading west. Between Gravelines and Veurne they encountered a number of Me110s, Dimsie shooting down two, but only one was confirmed.

In early June Dimsie was awarded the Distinguished Flying Cross, with the following citation appearing in the *London Gazette* on the 4th:

This officer has shot down five enemy aircraft during recent operations. He was indefatigable in his search for enemy aircraft, and during one day he was in the air for eight hours.

Biggin Hill, 27 June 1940, HM King George VI invests a number of pilots. About to be decorated is Pilot Officer V G Daw of 32 Squadron, while Pilot Officer D H Grice, also of 32, and Don Stones, Sgts A Whitby and H Cartwright of 79 Squadron, wait in line.

For the rest of June the Biggin Hill squadrons, along with others, were kept busy flying fighter sweeps across to France, or escorting Blenheims. The only light relief came during a celebration of his 19th birthday, on the 19th. However, he did claim a Me109 near Abbeville on the 7th, but it was not officially confirmed, although it appears it was a machine from 8./JG3, whose pilot, Leutnant W Schmidt, baled out wounded. The next day he shared a He111 south east of Le Tréport.

On the 23rd he ran into trouble during some night flying practice, being told to get back to Biggin as fog was expected. This he did, but he did not beat the fog. Gingerly feeling his way down, he suddenly spotted the runway and got down quickly, but despite braking quickly he ran the Hurricane into an anti-aircraft gun position, much to the alarm of the gun's crew. P2698 became a write-off.

* * *

Some of 79 Squadron at Biggin Hill, early July 1940. From left to right: Sgt Henry Cartwright DFM (KIA 4 July), Pilot Officer T C Parker, Squadron Leader J D C Joslin (KIA 7 July), Don Stones, Pilot Officer Murray and Flying Officer Edwards, squadron intelligence officer.

Dimsie and 79 remained at Biggin during June and July, with just a small break at RAF Digby, and also used Hawkinge, before moving to Sealand. He received his DFC from the King during an award ceremony at Biggin.

His first action during the Battle of Britain came on 4 July. Attacking some Dorniers off the coast, they were engaged by 109s and although he managed to damage one, he received some holes in his Hurricane. The sad part was that his long-time wingman, Sergeant Harry Cartwright DFM, did not return. Three days later, during a convoy patrol, they were suddenly attacked in error by some Spitfires and lost their CO. On the 9th he claimed a 109 but it was not confirmed.

The squadron then went to Sealand for a break, not returning to Biggin till 27 August, relieving 32 Squadron. On the 30th Dimsie survived a bomb raid on the airfield but some ground crew personnel were killed. He got his revenge the next day. The Germans attacked RAF Hornchurch and were engaged by fighters on their way home. Dimsie got behind one Dornier 17z. His fire was damaging it but an attacking 109 forced him to break away. Then he went for another bomber, getting in two good bursts, which sent bits flying off. The Dornier began to go down, and another burst from the Hurricane set the port engine smoking. Putting the last of his ammunition into the starboard engine, Dimsie watched agonisingly as the bomber continued to fly across Kent; but it eventually came down in a field near Newchurch, north of Dungeness, and was immediately surrounded by farm workers. The bomber came from 2./KG76, and Dimsie later received the pilot's flying goggles as a souvenir.

Another Dornier got away from him on 1 September, but not before his fire had caused damage to it. On the 4th he got a probable Me110, and it appears this may have later been confirmed. Dimsie reported that this 110 had a red dragon painted on its nose.

Three days later, on the 7th, Dimsie claimed a Dornier probably destroyed and shared a probable Ju88, both in a fight above Biggin Hill. 79 were ordered to patrol above the airfield at 24,000 feet that afternoon, but after a while, fuel was running low so Dimsie and another pilot remained above while the rest went down to refuel. Suddenly they were told the enemy were on their way in. Both Hurricanes made attacks against Junkers, Dorniers and Me110s, Dimsie going for them head-on. He fired as he went through the 88s and Dorniers, feeling he must have hit something, and coming out found a 110 in front of him, but he had only just opened fire when his Hurricane was hit from tail to cockpit by a 109 he had not seen. Diving steeply, he found a hole in the side of the cockpit, while the rear-view mirror picture showed him a tattered tail-plane. Luckily he spotted an airfield below, which turned out to be West Malling, and despite the damage to his fighter, he got it down. Any thought of baling out had vanished after trying to slide open the hood, and finding it damaged and jammed.

He had also been wounded in the right leg and woke up in Preston Hall Hospital near Maidstone. He was not seriously hurt but remained there for a few days and was soon back at Biggin. His final claim during the Battle was on 29 September, sharing in the destruction of a He111 forty miles north-west of St David's Head.

Nine Heinkels of KG55 had flown an evening sortie to attack targets at Merseyside, flying up the Irish Sea, initially hugging the neutral coast of Eire. Radar picked them up and eleven Hurricanes of 79 were scrambled. One bomber attacked by Pilot Officer P F Mayhew, G H Nelson-Edwards and Dimsie came down in the sea, its crew lost, while two others were shot up and returned damaged to make forced landings on the Brittany coast.

The unescorted bombers must have put all their best gunners on this mission, for their cross-fire hit three of the Hurricanes. Flying Officer G C B Peters was killed, while Mayhew and Nelson-Edwards also went down, Mayhew force-landing in Ireland unhurt, but his fighter became impounded. George Nelson-Edwards baled out and was rescued by a ship.

* * *

In December Dimsie went to the Central Flying School to become an instructor and in the new year went to No. 8 EFTS, and then to 59 OTU in March. After this he returned to 79 Squadron but in July he volunteered to go out to Malta, where he joined 249 Squadron. He and several others flew out to Gibraltar where they boarded a Wellington, landing at Luqa, Malta in mid-July. Malta was in the midst of its famous siege and it took time to get used to the conditions. It was a very dangerous place, with German and Italian air raids a daily occurrence. Food was scarce, equipment limited, petrol on strict ration, as were shells for the anti-aircraft guns. The food problem created internal problems too, and 'Malta Dog' was a malady most people suffered from at one time or another. For the pilots it was equally as dangerous on the ground as in the air. However, the defence of the island had to be maintained at all costs.

Dimsie's first action came on the 25th. A lone Italian reconnaissance aircraft came on radar, a Cant Z.1007bis, heavily escorted by Maachi MC200 fighters. No fewer than twenty-two Hurricanes of 249 and 185 Squadrons were sent aloft, believing there were more aircraft than reported; the pilots also misidentified it as either a BR20 or a SM79. Several pilots attacked the Cant. It had an escort but it really had no chance. It was hit sufficiently by six pilots and it crashed into the sea. Each pilot, including Dimsie, received credit for one sixth of a kill. A couple of the escorting fighters were also shot down. When I interviewed Dimsie he recalled this incident vividly. As he had made his attack he saw something detach from the enemy machine:

'As we closed in something flew off and whizzed past me and I thought at first it was a bomb. After we attacked it began to go down in a ball of fire. Later, after we had landed our Intelligence Officer asked us to go down to a hospital at Kalafrana to have a word with the rear gunner of the bomber. I said I thought all the crew had been killed but he insisted the gunner had survived and baled out. Apparently it was this gunner I had seen falling from the bomber. We went down with an interpreter and asked the gunner, "Did you tell your pilot you were abandoning ship?" To this he replied with a typical shrug of the shoulders, "No. I saw seex Hurricanes, so I go. It's nota my war." "But your crew were all killed," we said. "Si, but I am alive."'

Things were about to change for Dimsie, as he explained:

'It was at this time that Malta's AOC, Hugh Pugh Lloyd, got us to form a night fighter flight of Hurricane IICs, into the MNFU (Malta Night Fighter Unit) later 1435 Flight, which later still became 605 Squadron for a while.

'George Powell-Shedden commanded it, while Ernie Cassidy had A Flight and myself B Flight. We painted our Hurricanes black and did night interception and then started intruder operations sitting over German and Italian airfields on Sicily and usually shut them up for the night. It could be a bit of a bore just flying round and around, but on 4/5 September, David Barnwell and I shared an Italian Cant Z.1007 which was illuminated by searchlights. Over Sicily we'd also shoot up trucks and staff cars.'

The Cant on 4/5 September was one of several Cants from 9° Stormo that attacked Hal Far airfield shortly before dawn. Two of the crew were thought to have baled out but only the wounded pilot was found and rescued. These night ops and the intruder sorties took up much of Dimsie's time, and caused him a problem on 9 November:

'I was taking off on a night interception from Takali when my engine blew up at 400 feet. I had no way of putting it down because the fields on Malta were all the size of tennis courts, and everywhere else was rocky, so I baled out – just in time.

'The Hurricane was burning nicely in the next field as I was accosted by some Maltese who thought I was a German until I stripped off my flying overalls. Getting to a telephone I rang ops and spoke to Cassidy who said he couldn't speak to me at the moment as the B Flight commander had just gone in. I said, "It's me you oaf."'

On intruder sorties over Sicilian airfields, their presence caused the Italians to turn out all the lights, while the Hurricanes stooged about, either keeping them in the dark, or waiting in case the lights came on again. One night, in the pitch black:

'Jackie Grant, a New Zealander, called up in his quaint nasally accent, "Dimsie, I can't see the airfield." "OK," I said, "I'll show you where it is." I dived down and flew low across the airfield which caused the Italians to open fire with everything they had. Unfortunately, Jackie, unknowingly, was much nearer the airfield than he thought. "You bloody bastard!" he yelled. "Can you see it now, Jackie?" I asked.'

Dimsie had a couple of frustrating interceptions at night, lining up enemy bombers and then having his guns refuse to fire. But on 2 February 1942, during an intruder sortie, he spotted a military car near Modica, setting it on fire with his cannons. An unusual mission at this time was when he was asked to drop a message bag to an agent on Sicily, which he accomplished, dropping it at a spot half-way up Mount Etna.

He then went back to day flying, using a Hurricane IIC, with 605 Squadron. He had two of the four cannons taken out in order to deal with the faster turning 109s. It helped but he missed the fire-power. He was flying this Hurricane during a scrap with fighters over Kalafrana Bay and was heading for the airfield when he was told over the R/T that someone had gone into the drink, was in a dinghy and was being molested by a 109. He found the 109, had a bit of a whirl round with it, as he was out of ammunition, and then the 109 headed off towards Sicily. Landing at Takali, he saw everyone running and, looking up, saw a formation of Ju88s just beginning a bombing run. Jumping out of his machine he managed to dive into a slit trench in the nick of time: his Hurricane got a direct hit and was blown apart.

Dimsie engaged a Ju88 towards the end of February, which he caused to jettison its bombs that unfortunately fell on a farm house, injuring its occupants. However, on Sunday, 1 March, 605 were part of an interception of three Ju88s of 8./KG77 and escorting 109s. Dimsie and Flight Sergeant D J Howe managed to evade the 109s and both pilots inflicted much damage on a couple of the bombers. They could only put in claims for these being 'damaged', but in fact they were so badly hit they both crash-landed on their return to Sicily, and were destroyed, with casualties among their crews.

On the 6th he shot down a 109. Up with aircraft of 185 Squadron, he engaged this fighter, getting in a long burst, raking it from nose to tail, but then lost sight of it. Not long afterwards a parachute was spotted, so Dimsie, who was now acting CO of 605, was credited with a kill. Dimsie told me:

'He had been attacking me but overshot, and the man who confirmed this victory for me was Group Captain Woodlall, our chief controller.'

Three days later he shot up another Messerschmitt but could only claim a probable, having already had a burst at a Ju88 without visible results. On the 18th he got some hits on a couple of Ju88s but again without visible results.

Dimsie was now due for a rest and got a posting to Middle East HQ, but before he could board the Sunderland that would fly him there, it was shot up in Kalafrana Bay, so Hugh Lloyd gave him the job of visual operations, reporting any sightings from a high vantage point, while he waited for another ride. However, Dimsie blotted his copy book on 1 April. He called the Ops Room on his field telephone telling them that 30+ enemy aircraft were heading in over St Paul's Bay.

'I was expecting someone to say they couldn't see them on radar, but instead the man just slammed down the 'phone and then all the air raid sirens began. I was trying desperately to get back to them and eventually Group Captain Woodlall picked up the receiver, and I said,

"April Fool, for God's sake. Don't scramble!" After a moment Woody replied, "Come and see me at five o'clock this afternoon!" He really tore a hell of a strip off me.'

Finally he got his flight to Egypt, becoming an instructor at an OTU, but he did receive a Bar to his DFC for his work on Malta. The citation said:

Since being awarded the Distinguished Flying Cross, this officer has destroyed at least 6 enemy aircraft besides damaging many more. By his exceptional ability and complete disregard of danger, Flight Lieutenant Stones has set an example worthy of the highest praise.

* * *

Most fighter pilots would probably have felt that fighting in three major campaigns, the Battle of France, the Battle of Britain and the Battle for Malta, was enough to be going on with, but in Egypt, Dimsie kept pestering HQ saying that Hugh Lloyd had recommended him to lead a squadron, but they insisted he take a break. Finally he got his wish, and was given command of 155 Squadron, which was forming – in India.

Once in India he found his new squadron was to equip with Curtis Mohawks, but it was some months before they were ready to be collected from Karachi, and then not until September before they began flying convoy patrols and a few scrambles in defence of Madras. In January 1943 he managed to escape back to Hurricanes by being posted to join 67 Squadron at Alipore, as a supernumerary to Squadron Leader J H Bachmann, and leading B Flight. The real reason for the move was that Dimsie had had a run-in with a provost officer and was relieved of his command, but it got him back to Hurricanes.

In April the squadron moved to the Arakan coast, based at Chittagong. The Japanese were keen to push the British and Indian troops north in order to be able to reach the Indian border, but it faced stiff resistance, supported by the RAF. Japanese Army Air Force aircraft began raiding RAF airstrips, RAF pilots having many combats at this time. On 1 April, exactly one year after his April Fool joke on Malta, Bachmann was killed in combat, Dimsie finding himself running the squadron. Three days later he led ten Hurricanes up to engage a Japanese raid on Dohazari, estimated at 30+. He and one of his pilots attacked the bombers (Ki-51s, code-named Lilly) despite some very hostile Jap fighters, and they managed to damage one.

In the meantime, RAF squadrons were also heavily involved in ground attack sorties, strafing Jap troops on the move north. It was difficult and dangerous work, with heavy jungle inland from the coastal areas where the enemy were easily able to secrete themselves. On 15 May he led eight pilots to attack a Japanese landing strip at Kamgaung, a satellite of the big aerodrome and base at Meiktila, which was some distance inland, across both the Chindwin and Irrawaddy Rivers. As they approached they dropped their long-range tanks and dived to the attack. At first the airfield seemed deserted but the Hurricane pilots strafed and blasted buildings, sheds and huts until they spotted several Oscars (Nakajima Ki-43) at the far end, props turning. One was actually taking off but was shot down by two of the Hurricane pilots, while others were shot up and destroyed on the ground, including one by Dimsie. However, his fighter was hit by ground fire, wounding him in the left arm and leg. Despite being in great pain he extricated himself from the action and flew home to land safely. The wound ended his war. Dimsie recalled:

'The Japs had inertia starters for their fighters and they were actually trying to start up their aircraft, so we caught them with their pants down for a change. Unfortunately we did a third run, by which time the ground gunners were getting their eye in. They got me in the cockpit, tail and armour plate and I was wounded. I managed to fly the old Hurricane back but ended up in hospital. As it turned out this was my last operation.'

While in hospital he went down with dysentery, which kept him off flying for three months, and then went into two more hospitals. Once recovered he was sent to Bombay to do some test flying, after which he became an instructor at Drigh Road, Karachi, where he remained for a year. Returning to the UK he was loaned to Vickers-Armstrong as a test pilot. There was the occasional horseplay among the pilots and one day someone was fitting a detonator in the engine of someone else's car when it exploded and Dimsie lost his left eye. Recovering, he was given a staff job, but being unable to fly, he left the RAF in August 1946. From then on he wore a black eye-patch, making him look particularly piratical.

In 1945 he married Betty Thompson, and had a son. When that marriage failed he married Caroline Crawford in 1952, and that produced two daughters and a son, the latter serving with the Army in the Falklands war. His third wife was a Dutch lady in 1965 and his last wife, Beryl Thompson, he married in 1984.

Once out of the RAF he joined the Colonial Service and had quite a career, serving in Kenya, Tanganyika and Malaya as both district officer and magistrate. During the Malayan emergency Dimsie would fly a light aeroplane to various plantations in order to drop sacks full of cash so the owners could pay their workers. After this phase, he took up farming in the late 1950s in the West Country of England, but returned to Africa where he established an agency for British and European aviation companies. He worked as a salesman as well as demonstrator, the loss of his eye not affecting seriously his flying ability. He finally came back to England in the mid-1970s, retiring to Hampshire.

He gave up flying but took up sailing, often crewing for a yacht delivery syndicate. Dimsie died on 22 October 2002, at the age of 86. Once when he was asked if he was a good shot, he replied that he was. "Birds or buck?" was the next question. "Neither," he replied, "Men."

Chapter 20

Wing Commander J E Storrar DFC & Bar AFC AE BSc MRCVS

I met James Storrar twice, or to be more correct, was in the same room with him once and later met him at his veterinary office in Chester. The first occasion was during a fighter pilot symposium in London and among the dignitaries on the top table were Douglas Bader, Lord Balfour, Johnnie Johnson, Jeremy Howard-Williams and Philip Lucas, plus Jack Bruce of the RAF Museum. At one stage, Douglas Bader was waxing lyrical about the need for height in a battle and in response, a fairly big man a few seats from me stood up to give his views, which were somewhat in contrast to Bader's. There followed some lively but good humoured banter between Bader and this man, whom I noted Bader calling him Jas. It was only later that I asked someone if he knew who the man was, and was told Jas Storrar. I knew the name, of course, realising this was quite a famous Second World War fighter pilot who among other things, had fought during the Battle of Britain. Later I decided to talk to him, only to discover he had left, obviously having been in London on other matters and having to depart earlier than the rest of us.

I have to admit that it took me a few years before I was able to find an excuse to contact James Storrar but in September 1982 an excuse arose, so I contacted him and he was only too pleased to have me visit. I was told to call in the late afternoon, as, being a busy vet, he had several cases to attend to. I duly arrived around 4.30 pm and was asked to sit in a waiting room till he was free. In due course, the man I remembered at that London meeting strolled in – not in a white coat as I half expected, but in slacks and shirtsleeves. He was holding something in his hands which he then proceeded to show me. 'A dog's gallbladder', he announced, holding the item towards me. 'James Storrar,' he continued, 'pleased to meet you.' Fortunately the hand he offered in friendship had not been the one holding the former part of the dog's anatomy.

He was certainly an interesting man to talk to, and having recently interviewed another former RAF pilot he knew, I seemed to be accepted quickly and we got down to talking about his RAF career, especially about the Hawker Hurricane, a book about which I was then engaged in writing.

I see from my old diary that I was having a very interesting time in mid-1982, for that same month I had met John Mackenzie DFC, over from New Zealand, also a Battle of Britain man, who had flown with Tony Lovell (qv), Paul Richey DFC, of *Fighter Pilot* fame, Sir Harold Maguire, who had commanded 229 Squadron at the time of Dunkirk, and H M Stephen DSO DFC (qv), 74 Squadron in 1940, and then editor of the Daily Telegraph – but I digress.

James Eric Storrar was born in Ormskirk, Lancashire, on 24 July 1921, into a family of veterinary surgeons, established back in 1848. However, James (the IV – as all male first born were named James) decided he wanted to fly before possibly settling down in the family business, so once free of school (Chester City and County School, captaining the swimming team and also a member of the Chester Swimming Club) joined the RAF on a short service commission in October 1938. Once he had gained his 'wings' he attended a Blenheim Conversion Course in August 1939, and when war came moved to 145 Squadron. This squadron soon exchanged its Blenheims for Hurricanes, otherwise the Storrar story might well have been very different.

The squadron moved down to Croydon as its war station and, for the convenience of getting into London, he and a couple of pals bought an old Packard car between them. Little did he know that it was going to be his sole property within a few days after the commencement of the Dunkirk period! At this time he was the most junior member of the squadron, being only 18 years and ten months old.

When the 'phoney war' ended on 10 May 1940, 145 Squadron, along with many other fighter squadrons in England, were quickly needed to support the RAF in France, by ferrying aircraft there and flying patrols in support of the retreating British army. The squadron was quickly in the thick of the fighting and Jas (his mother always called him Jimmie, but his RAF pals shortened James to Jas) shot down his first enemy aircraft, a Me110, on 23 May whilst operating over France. Next day he downed a Dornier

17 near Gravelines. Two days later the Dunkirk evacuation began, and Jas shot down two Me110s on the 27th. Jas told me:

Squadron Leader James Storrar DFC.

> 'Once we got to Dunkirk, squadron operated individually and continued to do so. There was no wing leader only squadron commanders and they did what they liked and one would detach sections. Once you saw something you started to act on your own.
>
> 'Over the beaches we never went very low, for the people on the ground whenever they saw an aeroplane, thought it was a Jerry and let fly. Understandably, I guess, because there were not many of us around. Therefore we usually stayed between 8 to 10,000 feet to keep out of the range of light flak. The average length of a sortie was about an hour and a half or three-quarters, which meant that you used pretty well all your fuel, at even normal throttle opening, without bashing it around a bit.
>
> 'At that stage we were in vics, and if anyone yelled "109s!" there were 12 Hurricanes travelling in opposite directions as fast as possible, and looking round all over the place. We kept by the book, in vics, right through Dunkirk and then the Battle of Britain. In August 145 Squadron was virtually destroyed and had to be reformed up at Drem.'

The squadron had been operating from Tangmere, but then moved to nearby Westhampnett as the Battle of Britain began. On 11 July Jas shot down a Heinkel 111 south of St Catherine's Point, and by the end of July he had added four more victims to his tally, a Dornier on the 15th, another Heinkel shared on the 18th, a Me109 on the 27th and a Ju88 shared on the 29th, all over the Channel.

The 8th of August was a disastrous day for 145, losing five pilots killed, two in the morning and three others in the late afternoon. The squadron were heavily engaged over a Channel convoy code-name "Peewit". For his part, Jas shot down two Ju87s and damaged one other. Jas Storrar later recorded this following an attack on a Stuka:

'As I finished my ammunition with little obvious effect I suddenly became aware that there was a flame around his right undercarriage leg. I came up alongside. There was no sign of the rear gunner but the pilot was looking at me and I was no more than twenty or thirty yards away. I could see his face clearly and could virtually see his hand on the stick. The flame suddenly burst over the top of the wing. We both looked at it for what seemed like seconds when the Stuka's wing suddenly buckled – the aircraft turned over, smashed into the sea and exploded.

'I circled the smoke a couple of times, and was then joined by another Hurricane from 145 Squadron which headed back with me towards the Sussex coast. I could see as we pulled back our hoods he was giving me the thumbs-up and that it was Sub. Lt. F A Smith, a pilot who had joined our squadron from the Fleet Air Arm. I then had a sudden urge to look back over my other shoulder and saw two Messerschmitt 109s pulling in behind us. I yelled "Break!" over the R/T and turned in hard towards them. As I got round to engage I pressed the button and it just hissed – of course, no ammunition. So I kept turning to avoid them and they eventually disappeared. Sub. Lt. Smith didn't come back and was never found. I was the last person to see him alive.'

Both 145 and 43 Squadrons claimed a number of Stuka dive-bombers destroyed, more than were actually lost, but I/St.G3 and II/St.G77 suffered severe losses, with others returning home badly knocked about. 145 also claimed a couple of fighters.

On 12 August Jas got a probable Me110 south-west of Selsey Bill, but then the squadron was pulled out of the Battle and flew up to Drem.

On 8 September, Jas and another pilot were sent off to engage a Dornier east of Montrose. They both attacked in and it appeared to be mortally hit but then lost it in cloud, so could only claim a probable victory. Storrar had received the DFC by this time, this citation appearing in the *London Gazette* on 30 August:

This officer took part in the intensive fighting over Dunkirk last May, and has since been engaged in numerous successful actions. His squadron was responsible for the destruction of twenty-one enemy aircraft in one day; he personally destroyed two of these. Pilot Officer Storrar has displayed an unfailing desire to engage the enemy at all times and has shot down eight enemy aircraft.

Storrar now moved to another unit, No. 421 Flight, which later became 91 Squadron. In the autumn of 1940 it had an interesting role to play, as he explained to me. They were the first unit to have Hurricane II, which were lightened aircraft with a two-stage blower:

'We used them to patrol on what we called Jim Crow flights over the French coast and just inland, to look for raids coming in which the radar couldn't pick up and give the people back home the number and direction of these raiders. 421 had lost a couple of aircraft when they were doing solo patrols so we decided to patrol in pairs. The first occasion we went up in pairs I was with a chap who later became quite well known, Billy Drake.[5]

'We were patrolling, and con-trailing, which is what we aimed to do, so that if anyone came up to our height we would spot their con-trails, and see them from a long way away. We were flying abreast, about 2-300 yards apart, over the St Omer region I should think, when we saw some trails come up from inland, but which went down again, so we returned back along the coast. Suddenly we realised we were being attacked from behind. We saw cannon shells exploding around us and took immediate evasive action. However, Billy had been hit in the radiator by one of the shells and he began to stream glycol, but we managed to get away back to England. He forced landed in a field, ending up in a hedge. I waved to him to see if he was alright and he got out of the cockpit, so I flew back to base.

---

5. Later Group Captain B Drake DSO DFC & Bar, DFC (US), who saw action in France 1940 and was a successful fighter ace in North Africa in 1942.

'We worked out that the reason we'd been able to be surprised was because when we looked back at our con-trails we had not realised that the enemy fighters had actually climbed up into our con-trails and closed in along them. This is why we hadn't seen them and why they hadn't been able to take a very good shot at us. We discovered later that they were specially modified Me109s for the job. The Hurricane was a bit slow at height, and these 109s were considerably faster. I suppose we were flying at about 34,000 feet at the time.

'When I got back I was told I had been posted to 73 Squadron. The squadron was being sent overseas by way of the aircraft carrier HMS *Furious*, from Gladstone Docks, Liverpool, from where we left on 12 November. We flew off the carrier on 29 November and landed at Takoradi, on Africa's Gold Coast. These were the first Hurricanes of what finally became a stream of aircraft which eventually arrived at Takoradi before flying across to replenish aircraft in North Africa. We lost one chap who took off from the carrier in coarse pitch and his Hurricane dropped down in front of the *Furious*. He was later picked up by a cruiser which was with us, HMS *Naiad*. The captain of *Furious* sent a message to *Naiad* I remember, saying: "Well fielded, Naiad."

'Having landed at Takoradi we later flew up the route on 3 December, arriving at Heliopolis on the 9th. Then we went into the desert and did a number of odd trips including a very long range trip over Benghazi from back near Gazala, just to impress the Germans of the range of the Hurricane.'

For a short period in February, Jas and two other pilots were attached to 3 RAAF Squadron at Benina to augment the Australian's defence at Tobruk. At the end of the month, he and two more pilots boosted 3 RAAF again for a few days.

'Finally, after moving up as far as Benghazi and being stationed there, we came back very rapidly in front of Rommel and got shut up in Tobruk. I was actually shot down and walked into Tobruk just before they closed up on 9 April and the siege began. I finally flew out on 25 December, with a Hurricane that had an internal glycol leak, rather than leave it to be destroyed. So I flew it back and landed at the first available airfield, and had it fitted with a new radiator so that it could be used again.'

Prior to all this, Storrar had been in action over the desert. Operating from Gazala West, 73 Squadron flew single aircraft patrols over both Gambut and Tobruk, whilst also escorting Blenheim bombers. On one of these patrols Storrar came into contract with Italian CR42 fighters, shooting down that flown by S/Tenenti Leopoldo Marangoni of the 75ª Squadriglia, 23° Gruppo, who did not survive. It was a strange encounter. Jas and Sergeant R I Laing spotted CR42s near Ras-el-Meheta, Jas reporting:

'I saw two CR42s which appeared to be playfully dog-fighting another – the CR42s observed me just before I opened fire but one 3-second burst in the engine was enough. The e/a fell on the beach. The second CR42 made a head-on attack then dived away fast.'

There were also a good deal of ground attack sorties flown, against both Axis forces, their transport, and their airfields. 73 sent a detachment to El Adem on 1 February and then sent six Hurricanes to strafe the airfield at Appollonia, near Barce. The CO, Squadron Leader A D Murray DFC, Pilot Officer M P Wareham and Storrar each claimed one Caproni Ghibli Ca310 destroyed on the ground, while the other section strafed MT on a nearby road. The next day was less than glorious for Jas Storrar. He had had a liquid lunch at El Adem and returning to base on a very warm afternoon, forgot to lower his wheels and flaps, finishing up with his Hurricane on its belly. As he himself recorded:

'Yes, of course, there had been the odd beer at lunch, but it must be remembered that we had been flying long hours for some considerable time, and fatigue played its part. I remembered it well enough – it cost me a small fortune in drinks for everyone for three days.'

On the 5th, Murray, Storrar and Sergeant Marshall went out and strafed the airfield at Benina, and destroyed some eight Italian bombers on the ground between them. It is thought they were Savoia S-79s and 81s and a Breda Ba88. One of those that Storrar went for blew up. On the 19th Jas engaged several Me110s over Benghazi and damaged one. These were aircraft from III/ZG26, fifteen miles out to sea off Benghazi. Log book entry:

Scrambled over Benghazi, caught by six 110s, got one damaged.

The next bit of excitement came on 8 April, as 73 and 6 Squadrons withdrew into Tobruk's fortified area. Storrar was asked to take a message bag to be dropped to troops in the Bomba area. Having completed this task, he was on the way back, and ran into a lone Ju87 of II/StG2 near Derna. He shot this down, but then noticed a Lockheed Lodestar aircraft which had force-landed in the desert. A Very light was fired so he landed alongside it, finding the aircraft was the personal aircraft belonging to General Sir Archibald Wavell, CinC Middle East and North Africa, forced down due to loss of oil pressure. He helped get the aircraft working, transferring oil from his fighter, and it took off, but then Storrar was unable to get his own engine started, so was forced to walk back to Tobruk on foot. It was over thirty miles and took him two nights, cursing his flying boots all the way as they kept filling with sand. Reaching the perimeter he was met by some Aussie troops and soon Jas was driving back again, in a lorry, with oil, and got his fighter (V7550) going, allowing him to fly back safely. The Lodestar did not fare much better, for the pilot was forced to land again twenty minutes after getting off, ripping off a wing in the process. They were rescued by armoured car. Jas recorded the following regarding this adventure:

'I knew that I was just about due south of Tobruk, and was faced with a 30-mile walk back to the squadron. It took me two nights, and I was grateful for my Boy Scout training as I headed directly at the Pole Star. The worst part of the trip was that I was wearing flying boots which kept filling with sand and did my feet no good at all. Just before dawn on the second night I heard voices – Aussie voices – from troops guarding the Tobruk perimeter. We took a truck down to V7550 with some oil, and I flew it back to base.'

His pals on the squadron did not spread the story to the CO, for they knew he would not have been happy about what had happened. Jas of course should have flown over the downed aircraft so that they knew they had been seen, then returned to base and organised someone to drive out and rescue them.

*   *   *

Storrar left 73 Squadron in May and was posted to No.1 Test Flight where he remained until December. He then returned to England, taking a position at No. 55 OTU at RAF Annan until January 1943, being promoted to squadron leader, and given command of No. 65 Squadron, flying Spitfires Vs at Drem. In the spring it moved to Perranporth, Cornwall, then to Fairlop, before finally settling at Selsey, but it continued to move about during this year.

The squadron was engaged in numerous operations over France and Jas was once more in air combat situations, probably destroying a FW190 on 29 June off Le Havre. In the summer they changed their Mark Vs for Mark IXs. On 18 August Jas shot down a 109G near St Omer, damaged another 190 on 31 August, and his last wartime victory came on 18 September: another Focke-Wulf north of Rouen. His Spit IX carried the squadron code of YT while his individual letter was 'J', to which he added in small letters, 'as' so as to read Jas. His leadership and combat success brought him the award of a Bar to his DFC, gazetted on 29 October 1943. The recommendation had been endorsed by two well-known fighter pilots, Wing Commander H A C Bird-Wilson DFC, and the commander of the wing, Group Captain Jamie Rankin DSO DFC, both of whom signed it on 17 September 1943. The final endorsement was made by Air Marshal Trafford Leigh Mallory, AOCinC of Fighter Command, on 8 October:

Since the award of the D.F.C. in August 1940, Squadron Leader Storrar has destroyed 5 enemy aircraft, probably destroyed 2 and damaged 4 in the air, and has destroyed 9 enemy aircraft on the ground. He has now made more than 300 operational sorties[6] and has destroyed 12½ enemy aircraft in the air and 9 on the ground, and has probably destroyed and damaged a

---

6. In fact 326 sorties with a total operation flying time of 628 hours.

further 12. Squadron Leader Storrar has led his Squadron with skill and determination and has always shown keenness to engage the enemy.

* * *

Jas left 65 in November and was given an unusual assignment, as CO of No. 1697 ADLS Flight, which stood for Air Delivery Letter Service, at RAF Northolt. With the invasion on the horizon, it would be their job to fly secret mail and later secret equipment, into the Normandy beachhead. He began flights in May 1944, starting by delivering secret and sensitive mail to various landing grounds along the south coast of England. They were equipped with the Hurricane IIc, specially modified with an increased range. All the armour had been taken out.

Once the invasion started, Jas got his first trip into Normandy on 9 June, just three days after the landings, and from then on it was almost a daily routine, where messages were too sensitive to be given over the radio. Twice he landed in Vichy French territory and on 12 August was instructed to fly to Paris, as he told me:

'I landed at an airfield right in the centre of Paris. There was practically no one there to meet me at all, until then a chap came out from what looked like a porter's office. When he gave me, for want of a better expression, the pass-word, I handed over what I was carrying and stayed there for two days. It was then I gathered that where I'd landed was virtually next door to what a few hours beforehand had been the Gestapo Headquarters, and that the Germans were still at nearby Le Bourget, which was only a few miles away. It was the 25th, thirteen days after I landed in Paris before General deGaulle and his men finally entered Paris and took the German commander's surrender. The Free French fighters had received the information I'd flown in, that told them not to expect the General and to make sure that a battle wouldn't start inside Paris itself. Later, when we began to fly in more equipment we started to use Dakotas and Ansons but it was then I left the outfit as it wasn't very exciting after that. I went back to Fighter Command.'

Tiny Millist & I on patrol south of El Adem

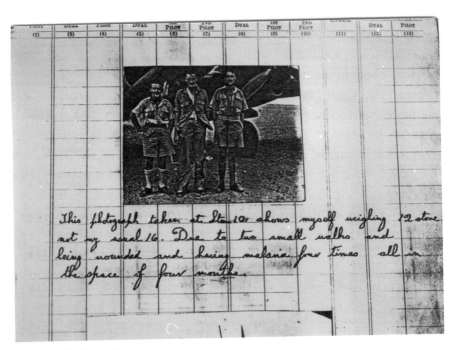

This photograph taken at St. 100 shows myself weighing 12 stone not my usual 16. Due to two small walks and being wounded and having malaria four times all in the space of four months.

Pages from Jas Storrar's log-book.

Storrar converted to the North American Mustang, and commanded 234 Squadron in early 1945, becoming wing leader at Hunsden between March and May, then at Digby during May to July. During this period his Wing escorted Mosquito aircraft against the Gestapo headquarters in Copenhagen, Denmark, on 21 March.

Immediately after the war, Jas took a staff appointment at 12 Group HQ, during which time he was able to fly a Meteor jet fighter. In early 1946 he commanded 239 Wing at Treviso, in Italy, flying Mustangs again. They also managed to get their hands on a Russian Yak 9 fighter, no doubt one used by the Bulgarians. Jas managed to fly it on occasions, and there is some discussion about him having JAS marked on the fuselage. Early in 1947 he decided to leave the Service, and resigned his commission in April 1947.

Immediately after his return home he went to the University of Edinburgh to do a BSc course and a five year course to become a veterinary surgeon. He returned to the family veterinary business in Chester, completed his exams, and eventually became head of the practice, a position his son then held, followed by his grandson. He could not, however, stay away from flying so in 1949 joined No. 603 Squadron RAuxAF, flying Spitfire F22s, which he later commanded, and later still commanded 610 (County of Chester) Auxiliary Squadron in the mid-1950s, again flying the Meteor. He was awarded the Air Force Cross in the 1955 New Year's Honours List.

Married with three sons and a daughter, Jas Storrar often appeared larger than life in his six-foot frame, always portraying the flamboyant style of the wartime fighter pilot, having, for instance, his jackets lined with red silk. When his son Andrew also became a vet, this made it five generations of Storrar veterinarians. Jas was also a keen motorist in car rallies, including Monte Carlo and the RAC Rally. He also navigated and completed a course in the Round Britain Power Boat Race. Jas died in April 1995, at the comparatively young age of 74.

Chapter 21

Wing Commander H Szczęsny VM KW &
3 Bars DFC

I met Henryk Szczęsny in a bar in Folkestone, during one of those flying days the town puts on. There were a number of illustrious airmen taking a lunch break and I was sitting with, among others, Colonel Jim Goodson, a former 8th Air Force pilot, who resided in Kent. Another was Paddy Barthropp DFC who I persuaded to sign a piece of paper so I could stick it in a copy of his biography that I had on my shelves. We had a chat too.

I knew Szczęsny, for we had corresponded at the time I was writing a biography of Sailor Malan, and he had been most helpful. Szczęsny had a mass of white hair I remember, but he was still the big man I had seen in photographs, and he still had that huge infectious smile. He was pleased to have finally met up.

He had been born in Ruszkowo, 80 km north of Warsaw, what today is Mazovia, on 27 March 1909, son of Stanisalw and Marianna Szczęsny (née Werc). When he eventually came to England and joined the Royal Air Force, he fitted the image of the older pilot, which most Poles were, when compared to the younger British men who were generally much more tender in years in 1940.

He had attended primary and secondary school in Pułtusk, and in 1931, having completed his final certificate examinations, followed general training and practice with a Polish infantry regiment. In 1933 he was promoted to pilot officer and sent to No. 5 Air Wing at Lida. He was then posted to the Air Force Officers' Training School at Dęblin, to start his flying training. At the end of the course he became a pilot with No. 3 Air Wing in Poznań. He became a proficient and outstanding aviator, which brought him to the Air Force Air Cadet Officers' School, back at Dęblin, as a chief instructor and lecturer on gunnery theory, at Grudziadz, near East Prussia. In April the school was transferred to Dęblin.

Henryk married Angela in 1936 and would have two sons, Cezary Henryk in 1937, and a year later Zdzisław Andrzej, both born in Posnań.

When, on 1 September 1939, Germany invaded Poland, the airmen at Dęblin formed themselves into an *ad hoc* fighter unit in order to defend the town and the airfield at Wielick. Henryk first flew a PZL P-7, claiming two Dornier 17s damaged on the 2nd. Later, flying a PZL P-11, he destroyed Heinkel 111s on 14 and 15 September, receiving a slight wound in his left leg. Henryk confirmed to me that over Poland he had shot down two and damaged two more in total. He also said he had flown against the Germans on the eastern border in a P-24 *Korbus*, with four machine guns, while attached to two Polish bomber squadrons, at Wielicko. In fact, Henryk told me he was the only Polish pilot in the Polish Air Force to fight against the Germans in one. However, when Poland fell, like hundreds of others he decided to escape in order to continue the fight against the Nazis from another country. In his case he got away by aeroplane to Romania, although he needed some hospital attention in Bucharest. His leg wound had not been attended to very well in the rush to get away and gangrene was about to set in. He then managed to escape aboard a Greek ship – the *Patris* – which took him to Malta under an English flag. From here he got into France and finally reached England in February 1940. He found himself at Eastchurch, where he began to be taught some English. In May, along with several other Polish airmen who were formed into a platoon at RAF Manston, he was told to be in command. In July he was moved to Blackpool, then to an OTU at Old Sarum near Salisbury.

Following a five-day conversion course at No. 5 Operational Training Unit at RAF Aston Down, he was posted to No. 74 Squadron at Hornchurch, Essex, on 6 August, as a Flying Officer. At this same time another Pole, Stanisław Brzezina, five years older than Henryk, arrived on 74 Squadron. They had been together at Dęblin. The British pilots in 74 Squadron, like all RAF pilots with a penchant for nick-names, and being unable to do justice to the Polish pronunciation, dubbed them 'Sneezy' and 'Breezy'. [Szczęsny is pronounced Chesney] Henryk was also known as 'Henry the Pole'. As he once told me: 'I was happy to be in the air once again and on Spitfire I – superior to Me109, in Tiger Squadron and like Tiger, to kill.'

Flying Officer Henryk Szczęsny (in Mae West) opposite Johnny Freeborn, 74 Squadron, 1940. On the left is Flying Officer Roger Boulding and standing to the right is Flying Officer H M Stephen DFC (qv).

A week after his arrival, Henryk claimed his first victory with the 'Tigers', shooting down a Dornier 17 on the 13th. The fight was with KG2 over the Thames estuary. In his combat report he wrote the following, although considering his poor English one has to suspect the Intelligence Officer did the writing, Henryk merely signing it:

'I saw three Do17s in front of me. I went to attack No.3 of the formation when he swung round to the right. I broke away to the left and came round behind the Dorniers and on their tails. One of the machines was out of formation and I attacked it from astern. At this point the Dornier dropped several bombs into the sea.

'I got a good burst in from very close range and the Dornier started to dive towards the sea. He tried to land there, but as he flattened out he burst into flames and toppled straight into the water. This must have been somewhere in the Estuary east of the Isle of Sheppey. I did not know where I was and managed to force-land at Manston with my undercarriage up, as I could not get it down.'

Actually it was West Malling and the Spitfire, K9871, tipped up.

In this action Flight Lieutenant Brzezina's Spitfire was hit and he was forced to take to his parachute, but he landed safely. He'd been hit by cross fire from the bombers.

On 11 September Henryk claimed a Messerschmitt near London. His report noted:

> 'I sighted two bombers and delivered a stern attack at 100 yards, giving 3x1 second bursts, but observed no apparent damage. I then saw two Me109s attacking two Spitfires and closed to the attack. I fired at one from 200 yards, closing in to 100 yards, and the 109 dived steeply, apparently out of control. I then sighted one Me109 and closed to attack from astern, giving 5x1 second bursts from 300-150 yards range. The 109 dived and crashed to the ground in flames. I then returned home.'

His next claim was a third share in the destruction of a Dornier 17 on 5 October, east of Harwich. His section leader was Flight Lieutenant H M Stephen (qv), and after he and his number two had made passes, Henryk got behind the bomber and expended all his ammunition, only pulling away when down to 1,000 feet, the German diving with its port engine in flames and heading for the sea.

Shortly after the Battle, 74 Squadron began to receive Spitfire IIs and Henryk claimed his first victory on this type on 1 December. 74 and 92 Squadrons were on patrol along the south coast, in bright clear weather. South of Dover, Henryk spotted a lone Me109 which he attacked and shot down some ten miles from the English coast. The next day he damaged another 109 of JG53 and on the 5th

Sketch of Squadron Leader Henryk Szczęsny VM KW DFC.

claimed another one destroyed over the Channel. 74, 64 and 92 were again in the action, against JG26 near Dover. Between them the 74 and 92 squadrons claimed twelve destroyed, but JG26 only lost one with two others damaged.

Henryk left the Tigers on the 12th, going to 257 Squadron – and Hurricanes! It was at a time when all Polish airmen with RAF squadrons were being directed into Polish squadrons. He did not want to move, and had often flown as Malan's wingman, as he told me:

'I am very proud I was his Number Two on many, many occasions and defending his tail, because he told me what to do and to follow blindly his orders. He was shooting down Jerries and I was very close to him – defending his tail. Order is order.

'Once Malan told me by radio to put "Pipsqueak" on. Of course, I could not hear him; my radio was always off – my English was practically nil, so why bother to listen to it? So, poor Operations Room at Biggin Hill, interpreted our 74 Squadron as bandits 12 plus, with Hurricane squadron over Kent. Then Sailor shows me two fingers up, so I did also show him my two fingers up. He laughed and laughed – after pancake.

'He also introduced me to Winston Churchill, when he was passing to Chartwell, near Westerham, Kent. At Biggin Hill, at dispersal of B Flight, when we came to readiness. He smiled and shook hands with me and asked in his usual deep voice, "Henry the Pole, how many today?" I replied shyly, "Only one Me109, Sir." He said, "Good, many more to come." Then in my broken pidgin English, standing to attention, saluting in Polish way, two fingers closed together, said, "Sir, please remember Poland, is and forever will be the Bastion and the wall of Christianity of Western Europe, so make her great, free and independent." My flight commander, Mungo-Park, translated to Mr Churchill in perfect English. Churchill smiled at me once more and bubbled, "We will see on Victory day," and showed me his "V" sign and drove off.

'Sailor did not want me to leave, and fought like Tiger to keep me in his squadron, offering me B Flight commander because my English was improving rapidly, but no luck – I had to go. Later I was decorated by AOC 12 Group with Distinguished Flying Cross for all my battles in the air with 74 Tiger Squadron under Sailor Malan. He wrote about me, "Henry the Pole – pilot second to none and so on ..." Motto of our Tiger Squadron was, 'I Fear No Man', but I did add, 'Only God and Women'.

'Sailor Malan was and always will be in my eyes and in my heart, the greatest pilot and ace number one of the Second World War.'

He did not stay with 257 Squadron very long before being posted to 302 Polish Squadron on 19 December. On 1 February 1941 he received the Polish Cross of Valour and Bar (the *Krzyżem Walecznych*). He also received the British Distinguished Flying Cross, approved on 12 February, with this citation:

This officer has shown remarkable skill in adapting to the Royal Air Force flying technique. He is a courageous and determined pilot and has destroyed at least four enemy aircraft whilst operating in this country.

Then on the 24 February he was moved again, this time to 317 Polish Squadron, at Ackilington, where, on 1 April, he was awarded a second Bar to his Cross of Valour. He was put in command of B Flight. On 10 July, the squadron now operating in the south-west's 10 Group area, he shared a 109 destroyed with his No.2, Sergeant Stanislaw Brzeski, near Le Havre during a 10 Group bomber escort mission to Brest. Four days later he and another pilot operating over the sea south of Tenby, he and Sergeant Brzeski engaged and shot down a Ju88 at 4.20 in the afternoon.[7] His Spitfire during these operations was W9272 with squadron code letters JH. The individual aircraft letter was 'S' – for Szczęsny.

Henryk was given command of 317 Squadron on 18 August, which he led until 17 March 1942. The previous CO had been his old pal Stan Brzezina, who now took over the Wing Leader job of the 2nd Polish Fighter Wing.

---

7. Brzeski had also seen action over Poland and with the RAF saw considerable service, winning the DFC, VM and KW with 4 Bars.

The downside was that 317 was still a Hurricane unit, but at least Spitfire Vb aircraft began to arrive in October. By the cockpit of his personal Hurricane was the Polish badge and above it the name 'HESIO' – the diminutive of Henryk.

Henryk received the Silver Cross of the Virtuti Militari War Order on 15 September. However it was now time for a break from operations. On 7 March 1942 he became a liaison officer to 10 Fight Group Headquarters, at RAF Colerne, followed on 12 May by a similar appointment with 12 Group at Watnal.

He finally got back to operations shortly after Christmas, being appointed deputy leader of No. 1 Polish Fighter Wing at RAF Northolt on 28 December. This brought forth a number of operations over France, escorting bombers or flying fighter sweeps in the early weeks of 1943. One such operation occurred on 12 February. A large ship had been spotted in Boulogne Harbour and became the attention of Circus 262 three days later. Several Polish squadrons provided fighter escort, including 303 and 315 Squadrons, led by Henryk, as target support wing. Combats took place with FW190s, the Poles coming out on top.

His luck ran out on 4 April. On this day he was leading the Wing escorting American bombers in an attack on the Renault Works factory near Paris, in a Spitfire IX – BS514 PK-U. The operation was billed as Ramrod 51, with 95 Flying Fortress bombers of the 91st, 303rd, 305th and 306th Bombardment Squadrons from the 1st Bombardment Wing being the raiding force. Two Polish Squadrons, 315 and 316, acted as withdrawal cover and got into a fight with FW190s. Two of the pilots collided near Rouen and both were killed. Henryk led an attack on the Focke-Wulfs, shooting down one, with another pilot claiming one. But in the whirl of battle, Henryk collided with another 190 and had to bale out. Two other pilots were also lost in the combat. The enemy group was an old enemy, JG26, led by Hauptmann Wilhelm-Ferdinand Galland, brother of the famous Adolf Galland. In this major battle, W-F Galland, leader of the Geschwader's Second Gruppe, shot down one Spitfire and two Boeings for his 35th, 36th and 37th kills. Adolf Glunz scored his 31st with another Spitfire. Six more were claimed by other JG26 pilots. JG26 had one fighter shot down by B17 gunners and another wounded. It also lost one pilot killed. JG54 were also in this fight and also lost one pilot.

Parachuting from his crippled Spitfire Henryk was quickly taken into captivity by German soldiers who had seen him coming down in his parachute and were waiting for him. After the usual moves via Dulag, Frankfurt, where he was interrogated, he ended up in the famous Stalag Luft III prisoner of war camp at Sagan, prisoner number 1229, where he saw out the war. He also helped with the work on the tunnels that led to The Great Escape in March 1944.

He returned to Britain after the German surrender and once more became a liaison officer with 12 Group HQ at Coltishall. In 1946 he completed an accountancy and administration course with the Service and became a British citizen in March 1950. He had already arranged for his wife and sons to join him in Fenland. He remained in the RAF until he retired on 27 March 1965, working with the Fighter Control Branch as Operations Officer at RAF Northolt.

He was divorced from Angela in 1957 and married that same year, Margaret, who came from Ireland. When I was corresponding with Henryk in 1979, he was living in Monasterevan, County Kildare, Eire. His eldest son was living in Los Angeles with his mother, wife and three daughters. His other son was an airline pilot with Saudi Arabian Air Lines. He had one son with his first wife, and a daughter with his second.

He often visited his native Poland, where he had family; on one occasion, in 1988, for a Meeting of Air Generations, in celebration of the 60th Anniversary of the 1st promotion in the School of Eagles, and again in 1992 in a Worldwide Rally of Polish Airmen.

Henryk remained a man with a wide grin, full of energy and with a wonderful sense of humour. He lived in West London in his later years until his death on 25 July 1996, aged 87.

Henryk Szczęny.

Chapter 22

Group Captain P S Turner DSO DFC & Bar, Czech War Cross, Czech Medal for Bravery

P ercival Stanley (Stan) Turner is generally known as a Canadian, but was actually born in Ivybridge, Devon, England, on 3 September 1913 – so when the Second World War was declared, it occurred on his 26th birthday.

When still a child his family emigrated to Canada, settling in Toronto, Ontario. As a young man he began studying engineering at Toronto University, but also joined the Royal Canadian Air Force Auxiliary as an airman with No.110 (Auxiliary) Squadron. At the age of 25, his appetite duly whetted, he decided to join the Royal Air Force. He was one of more than a dozen hopefuls accepted for a short service commission, in October

Stan Turner during his training. Note the ring–and–bead gun sight.

1938. Completing his training in England just as World War Two began he was posted to No. 242 Squadron, a unit being formed mainly manned by Canadians serving in the RAF, so he fitted right in, and, it must be assumed, his age made him something of a father figure to most of the pilots who were much younger than him. His nickname was 'The Bull' due to his stocky build and aggressive nature.

If any of the pilots hoped to become fighter pilots, they were initially to be disappointed as their first aeroplanes were Bristol Blenheim 1f, twin-engined fighters, which were far removed from the Hurricanes and Spitfires of their dreams. The Blenheims began to arrive in December 1939, but in the same month they at least began to fly single-engined machines, even if they were Fairey Battle day bombers. They had been told that they would be flying regular fighters back in November, and finally, after much wrangling, which was ended by Air Ministry's desire to have more single-seat squadrons made available, this came about. Thus in February 1940, Hawker Hurricanes began to be shipped. The pilots might have wished for Spitfires, but there was a strong suggestion that 242 might be sent to France to support a Canadian army force there, and nobody wanted to send Spitfires to France at this stage, only Hurricanes. In the meantime, 242 remained in the north of England, helping to defend the naval base at Scapa Flow while they trained on their new aeroplanes. Not that the arrival of the Hurricane went off smoothly. The squadron CO and five other pilots, including Turner, proceeded to St Athan in South Wales to collect the initial batch, but bad weather caused an upset. One pilot was killed whilst having to force-land, and later other pilots were also forced down. Stan Turner had to make his landing at RAF Finningly, in Yorkshire.

In April 1940, 242 was preparing to replace 85 Squadron in France but when the Germans invaded Denmark and Norway, events changed. However, as the Germans turned their attention to Holland, France and Belgium on 10 May, things began to look very different again, so much so that 242 were ordered to France on the 15 May. Stan had already been sent over on the 10th, to help reinforce 607 and 615 Squadrons, but soon rejoined a Flight of 242 once it arrived. Fighter Command was only sending half squadrons across, the thinking being that if things went badly it was better to lose parts of squadrons rather than whole units. 242 were engaged in several actions, but Turner does not appear to have achieved any successes. Most of the time the squadron was desperately trying to give air cover to retreating Allied forces that were being pushed back towards the Atlantic coast. 242 got out, headed back to England, and began operating, as a temporary measure, from Manston.

However, Turner and the others eventually managed to become involved with enemy aircraft during the evacuation from Dunkirk and on 25 May he became embroiled with a number of Me109s, claiming three shot down, one of which was not confirmed. On the 28th he claimed another between Dunkirk and Nieuport, followed by more 109s on the 29th, a damaged and an unconfirmed kill,

Flight Lieutenant P S Turner DFC, 242 Squadron, 1940.

but then a confirmed victory over yet another Messerschmitt on the 31st that he saw dive into the sea off the French coast. There was no let up on 1 June, Turner bagging two more 109s, one being unconfirmed. Thus during this intense period, Turner had gained four confirmed victories, another four unconfirmed (probables) and one damaged.

During the Dunkirk operation, 242 lost six pilots killed, two became prisoners of war, and another was wounded. It had been credited with twenty-one enemy aircraft shot down, seven probably so and eight damaged. Turner had nearly become a casualty on the 29th having suffered oxygen failure at 20,000 feet. He had spun down and recovered his senses in the nick of time before hitting the ground. During the whole of the recent fighting, fifteen pilots had been killed, made prisoners, or been wounded. However, some new pilots were posted in, ready to continue the fighting.

Dunkirk may have ended, but British troops and RAF elements were still in France – and still retreating. On 8 June 242, together with Hurricanes of 17 Squadron, flew to Le Mans, to help support 1, 73 and 501 Squadrons still operating from there. Later that day, 242 moved to Châteaudun, north-west of Orléans, with 67 Wing, where the men slept in bell tents. They were quickly on the move, flying first to Marigny and then Reims. In the first action by the squadron, on the afternoon of the 9th, they were attacked by 15 Me109s of JG52, one of which shot down fellow pilot D G MacQueen. Moments later Turner was able to exact revenge by shooting down this fighter, then attacked and destroyed a second. That evening they returned to Châteaudun. (There seems to be some confusion of these dates, Turner being credited with two victories on the 8th but none on the 9th).

It was now the beginning of more retreating as the Germans advanced. Pilots and ground crew were constantly falling back, and eventually were told to get to St Nazaire and board a ship back to England. They almost boarded the *Lancastria*, a liner already crammed full with some 5,000 military and civilian personnel. In the crossing she was sunk with the loss of several thousand men. The 242 Squadron boys eventually got away on a Polish liner, the *Sobieski*, which set sail during an air raid, reaching Falmouth on the 18th. They gathered at RAF Coltishall, in 12 Group, later that month. Their CO, Squadron Leader F M Gobeil, ended his period of command. They were about to receive an altogether different man in charge.

* * *

Anyone who has seen the film *Reach for the Sky* will be familiar with the arrival of 242's new Boss – Squadron Leader D R S Bader. How accurate was the scene that showed Bader's arrival is unclear. Certainly the pilots had just returned from a very trying time in France, including losing much of their personal equipment due to a tent fire, but one would have thought the arrival of a new boss, whatever his apparent disabilities, would have brought everyone to their feet.

However Turner's character in the film, played by Lee Patterson, did not instantly rise to his feet, and was distinctly surly. There followed a demonstration of what Bader could do in the air, and there followed a very quick appreciation that this man with no legs was no slouch – on the ground or in the air. As Patterson's script read, this was a real god-damned fireball.

The squadron received a number of replacement pilots, not specifically Canadians, and soon Bader had the unit operational. Down south, in

11 Group, the Battle of Britain had started and Bader and his men were keen to become involved, but they had to wait. There is also the matter of the 12 Group Wing, that Bader was persuading the Group Commander, Sir Trafford Leigh Mallory, to instigate, whereby Bader could lead three or even five squadrons, thereby having more fighters to attack the large enemy formations 11 Group were meeting. The tactic, of course, had some merit, but not in this fight. It took too long to form them all up, by which time the Germans were on their way home. Fighter Wings in 1941 were fine, but not in 1940.

Stan Turner had become an acting flight commander, still with the rank of Flying Officer, and then he was attached to the Air Fighting Development Unit from 1 August for a fighter course. Gradually 242 began to see some action, some against lone raiders as July began, and in August 12 Group had better chances of joining battle. Duxford of course was the parent station, Coltishall, where 242 resided, was a satellite airfield. The squadron only moved to Duxford permanently in mid-October.

Turner returned from his course to find several pilots had shot down enemy aircraft. His own turn came on 7 September, the day the Luftwaffe made its first daylight raid upon London. His share in the day's activities was in damaging yet another Me109. This was also the first time the Duxford Wing took to the air, 242 in company with 19 and 310 Squadrons. However, on the 15th – the day that became Battle of Britain Day – Turner knocked down two Dornier 17 bombers south-west of London in the first action shortly after midday (KG2), some of its crew seen to bale out, the other, also from KG2, later in the afternoon. He also blew pieces off a 109 but could only claim a probable. The second Dornier crashed on the north bank of the Thames between two houses. During the action his Hurricane was hit, throwing him into a spin but he recovered.

These were the only tangible results for Stan Turner in the Battle, but his contribution as a flight commander and leader were outstanding. When several decorations were announced towards the end of the month, Turner was among them. His DFC appeared in the *London Gazette* on 8 October:

On September 15th, 1940, Pilot Officer Turner succeeded in shooting down one enemy aircraft, when his own aircraft was hit by a cannon shell which put it temporarily out of control. On recovery, he saw and attacked a further enemy aircraft which he destroyed, afterwards bringing his own damaged aircraft safely back to its base. This officer has personally destroyed a total of ten hostile aircraft during engagements over Dunkirk and England. He has proved himself a most courageous and capable leader, displaying coolness and initiative in the face of the enemy.

* * *

His next fighter action came on 8 February 1941, forty miles to the east of Clacton on Sea.

Turner, along with Flying Officer Denis Crowley-Milling and L E Cryderman, from Ontario, were scrambled to intercept a raider near a convoy approaching Felixstowe. Despite a lot of cloud they located the raider which was described as an all-black Dornier 17, and attacked. Turner closed in, ignoring the rear gunner's fire, and his bullets smashed into the starboard wing and fuselage, setting the engine in fire. Then the bomber entered cloud but Turner twice heard Lawrence Cryderman calling over the radio that he was returning to base. Moments later Cryderman's calm voice said he was going into the sea. Despite searches, he was never found.

His last two bits of excitement came on 14 March, sighting a Me110 during a morning patrol, but he lost it; he was then subjected to British anti-aircraft fire during another patrol near Felixstowe, fortunately without damage. Turner also went on the first Squadron Rhubarb operation in company with Bader, shooting up a German E-boat and a drifter in the Channel.

Turner's time with 242 Squadron ended on 13 April 1941. He was promoted to Squadron Leader and given command of 145 Squadron at RAF Tangmere. They were equipped with Spitfire IIb fighters. This was the time of Fighter Sweeps and later Circus Operations over France, taking the war to the enemy after the previous summer of 'taking it' during the Battle of Britain. Wing Leaders now began to come into their own, and the Tangmere WingCo was – Douglas Bader DSO DFC.

Turner began to lead his squadron as part of the Wing during the spring of 1941. To entice enemy fighters to come up and fight, small formations of Blenheim bombers would attack small targets, such as power stations, aerodromes, factories, etc. They would be escorted by anything up to three fighter wings, with other wings escorting them home as the previous escorting fighters began to run short of petrol.

In March, Turner was sketched by Captain Cuthbert Orde, who wrote of him:

'When I made this drawing he was one of Bader's Flight Commanders. I admire very much a particular quality he has got – mental resilience. Bader's enthusiasm and ideas were not always immediately clear to everyone, and his occasional acid retorts to any who did not agree at once were not easy to bear. But Stan took them well with an amazing outward imperturbability. He must have minded; but no trace of resentment did I ever see. He was a great friend of Bader and absolutely loyal, and I suppose understood him and had the power of separating the important from the unimportant. I couldn't write about Stan without mentioning this because I think it a clue to his character: he's tough all right in every way.'

He had a few successes in combat during the year, damaging a 109 near Le Touquet on 26 June and another south-west of Calais on 14 July. On 29 July he destroyed a 109 to the east of Dunkirk. On 9 August Bader was brought down over France and taken prisoner, but his own time was coming to an end, for in October he was posted overseas. Before this, however, two things of interest happened. Once it was known that Bader was a prisoner, but had lost one of his tin legs, Turner led his squadron as part of the escort to a force of Blenheims which, apart from going for a target, also carried a box with the replacement leg, which was parachuted into enemy territory. Then he was awarded a Bar to his DFC, gazetted on 5 August:

This officer has led his squadron on all sweeps over France and set a splendid example by his quiet coolness in the face of the enemy. He has been responsible for the destruction of at least twelve enemy aircraft.

Despite the wording of this citation, it is difficult to reconcile his victory tally, even if that matters. During the war he lost two log-books and post war would say that he lost count of how many Germans he shot down. From those records that can be found, he appears to have shot down ten for certain, one shared, three more unconfirmed, a probable and eight damaged. However, his value came in his leadership and this would come to the fore in the Middle East. Firstly he had to leave 145, handing over command to Squadron Leader A D J Lovell DFC (qv).

Prior to going overseas Turner was posted to No. 82 Group HQ in Northern Ireland but within two months had been given command of 411 Squadron RCAF in October. They saw little in the way of combat, but when in February his overseas posting came along, the squadron diarist recorded the impact of that news on the unit:

'Information received that Squadron Leader Turner DFC & Bar is to be posted overseas shortly. The squadron are feeling extremely 'blue' as a result and a rush of applications was received from the pilots as well as the Adjutant and M.O., to proceed overseas [too]. 'The powers that be' only laughed. However, one pilot, Pilot Officer McNair, is now extremely jubilant as he was selected to go along. The rest of the lads are more down at the heel than ever. Being with us for only two months, as a Squadron Commander in every way and a great improvement in efficiency and discipline, both on the ground and in the air has resulted.'

Malta was the destination for Turner and Buck McNair, the latter destined to be a high-scoring fighter pilot and winner of the DSO, DFC & 2 Bars, gaining fame over Malta and later over northern Europe. Both men flew into Malta in a Sunderland. Others on that flight were Flight Lieutenant P B Lucas, Flying Officer R Daddo-Langlois, Pilot Officer G A F Buchanan and Pilot Officer Jeff West DFM, who had been Bader's wingman in 1941. All would do well on Malta.

Arriving on Malta, Turner took command of 249 Squadron, which meant a return to Hurricanes. On 22 February 1942 he was involved with enemy aircraft and scored hits on a 109 of JG3, part of the escort for three Ju88s. However, on the 24th he and another pilot vectored onto a raid. They could not see the opposition; but the opposition, Me109s of JG53, saw them, and bounced them. His wingman was shot down into the sea. Turner's fighter took hits in the engine, which caught fire; one bullet actually clipped his goggles, and he was also slightly wounded. He was unable to release the canopy so had to ride the Hurricane down, which fortunately put out the fire, and he succeeded in making a wheels-up landing at Luqa.

It was about this time that Stan Turner met with the AOC on the island, Sir Hugh Pugh Lloyd, and the senior controller, Group Captain Woodall, giving them his blunt and frank appraisal of the fighter defences on Malta. Spitfires had been promised but had still not been delivered. He is reputed to have said: "Either Sir, we get the Spitfires here within days, not weeks, or we're done. That's it."

Spitfires began arriving in early March and 249 began operating with them. On 22 March Turner and McNair engaged Me109s, each claiming one damaged. In April he was promoted to acting wing commander and assigned staff duties, but he at least had managed to convert his squadron on to Spitfires. Shortly after this he left the island for the Middle East HQ. In September there was an attack being planned against Tobruk which needed an RAF officer to coordinate sea and air operations. Turner was assigned to the light cruiser HMS *Coventry*. In the event, the raid, on the night of 13/14 September, was a fiasco; enemy gunfire sank two destroyers and bombs and shells hit and sank the *Coventry*. Turner managed to dive overboard and was rescued by another ship.

Turner was then given another seaborne job, as air controller aboard HMS *Orion*, escorting a convoy running supplies from Alexandria to Malta. They were attacked by Italian torpedo aircraft that badly damaged one ship and, as Turner watched, he saw how close another torpedo came to hitting his ship.

Turner then took command of 134 Squadron, in Tunisia, so back on Hurricanes. This unit was experimenting with napalm bombs. One day he made a practice run on a tank in the practice area, but came in so low that he hit the vehicle forcing him to crash land. He got out OK and saw the tank was ablaze, but with all the dust and smoke his men did not see him, so he was forced to walk towards home. Fortunately a British armoured car crew found him and saved him a long walk.

He was now given command of 417 Squadron RCAF, a unit in need of a strong leader. Turner turned the squadron around in short time and he and his men were flying almost constantly over Sicily and Italy in mid-1943. Air combat had lessened but enemy AA fire was a constant danger. But it was a land mine that nearly got him on 3 August. He and another pilot were driving along in a truck but ran over the mine, blowing his fellow pilot out, who was uninjured, but Turner was trapped in the wreckage. People got him out but he was off ops for ten days.

Turner returned to wing commander rank in November 1943, taking command of 244 Fighter Wing. He managed to get into a couple of air fights over Anzio on 8 February 1944, damaging two FW190s flying a Spitfire VIII, but that was the last of his successes in air combat. He is also supposed to have accounted for two more probable victories but totally forgot to put in claims.

Finally, in May, he became a staff officer again, but his recent actions brought him the award of the Distinguished Service Order, gazetted on 23 May 1944:

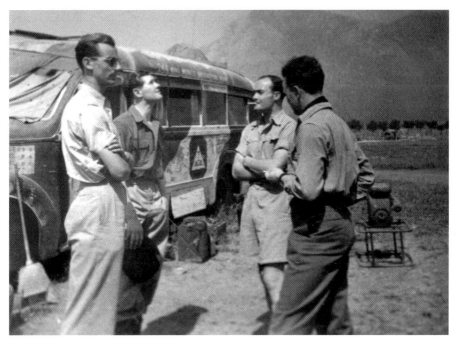

With 224 Fighter Wing in Italy in 1944. Left to right: Squadron Leader N F Duke DFC, Squadron Leader G Cox DFC, Wing Commander B F Kingcome DFC, and Stan Turner.

This distinguished fighter pilot has flown nearly 900 operational hours in single-engined fighters. Since November 1943 he has taken part in all the more important air operations during the invasion of Sicily and Italy and in the Sangro and Anzio battles. He has destroyed fourteen enemy aircraft and has always shown the utmost gallantry, enthusiasm and leadership.

Stan Turner returned to England in November 1944 and in the new year took command of No. 127 (RCAF) Wing, part of the 2nd Tactical Air Force, at Evere, Belgium, with the rank of group captain. His Wing Commander Flying was J E Johnson DSO DFC. He commanded this unit until July 1945. On 16 September 1945 he was part of the twelve-strong Spitfire pilots, all having fought in the Battle of Britain, who flew across London to celebrate the fifth anniversary of the Battle. It was led by Group Captain Douglas Bader.

In 1948, twenty-one Canadian airmen were decorated by the Czechs, recognising the co-operation between Canadian and Czechoslovakian flyers during the war. Stan Turner was among them, being awarded the Czech War Cross, and the Czech Medal for Bravery.

Post war he remained in the RCAF in a number of interesting jobs until he retired in 1965. At that time he became an executive with the planning staff of Expo '67, and later was involved with 'Son of Expo', Man and his World. His last years were spent living quietly in Chambly, Quebec. He died from a heart attack in Ottawa on 23 July 1985, aged 71. At the time he was teaching children to swim at the downtown YMCA. He had been a swimming instructor in 'an earlier life'.

He is credited with being the Canadian with the most operational sorties to his name: 500.

Chapter 23

Squadron Leader J R Urwin-Mann DSO DFC & Bar

John Ronald Urwin-Mann I did not meet, but I did meet his daughter Jacqueline, spending a couple of pleasant hours chatting with her about her father. There has sometimes been some confusion over his nationality, having been born in Victoria, British Columbia, Canada on 29 July 1920 to English parents, John Urwin Mann and Josephine Ronald, living in Canada. However, within two years his parents returned to England and resided in Hove, East Sussex for the remainder of his childhood. He went to Xaverian College in nearby Brighton and at the age of 18 decided to enlist into the Royal Air Force on a short service commission in March 1939. Sadly his father had died the year before, but his mother continued to live in Hove.

Squadron Leader J Urwin-Mann DSO DFC.

He received his commission with effect from 1 May and by the time war began he was well advanced in his training to become a pilot. Indeed, by December he was posted to 11 Group, Fighter Command's Fighter Pool at St Athan and, once converted onto Hawker Hurricane fighters, was sent to No. 253 Squadron on 26 January 1940. 253 were at Manston but in May he was moved to 238 Squadron at Tangmere, two days after the German invasion of France and the Low Countries. In June, 238 moved to Middle Wallop, where it would remain until August.

As the Battle of Britain began, 238 were in the forefront of the action, and John's first air battle came on 11 July. 238 in company with 601 Squadron, also from Tangmere, engaged enemy aircraft – Stukas of III/StG2 – over the south coast, and several escorting Me110s of III Gruppe of ZG76 were brought to combat. 238's Green Section, including John, attacked one that was later harried by a pilot of 87 Squadron and another from 601. The German finally force-landed near Lulworth Cove, its crew of Oberleutnant Gerhard Kadow, the Staffelkapitän (9th Staffel), and Gefreiter Helmut Schollz, becoming

Jack Urwin-Mann at the beginning of the war.

prisoners. Kadow was shot and wounded on the ground while attempting to burn his papers. Another 110 from ZG76 lost this day was flown by Hermann Göring's nephew Oberleutnant Hans-Joachim Göring, and his gunner, Unteroffizier Albert Zimmermann, who both perished.

Two days later John claimed a 110 as probably destroyed, and shared another, whilst battling V/LG1 over a Channel convoy.

It was a completely different type of enemy aircraft he was involved with on the 20th, a Heinkel 59 seaplane. Still operating over the Channel, again a section of 238 became involved in combat, and chased and shot down this seaplane some three miles off Cherbourg at 14.10 pm. The machine was from *Seenotflugkommando 4*. Although these were air-sea rescue aircraft, they had recently become legitimate targets for RAF fighters. 601 Squadron also shot down a He59 off Selsey Bill three hours or so later.

There was no let up in August, and John (he was invariably known as Jack) was able to claim Me109 fighters destroyed on the 11th and 13th. The German unit involved on the 11th was JG27, late morning, over the Swanage area. On the 13th it was probably JG53 near Lyme Regis.

238 Squadron now moved down to St Eval, Cornwall, as the Germans were taking more interest in targets in the West Country. He signalled his arrival

by shooting down a Ju88 on the 21st, one of two 88s lost from *Kampfgruppe 806* (KGr.806). This unit was originally a coastal bomber-reconnaissance unit but then became part of *Luftlotte 3* as an orthodox bomber outfit. John's victim was engaged off Trevose Head, Cornwall, at 17.30 pm. By mid-month 238 were back at Middle Wallop.

The RAF's big day, 15 September, saw John claim a He111 bomber shot down and another probably so. Of several Heinkels brought down this day, all came from KG53 or KG55, and both claims were for bombers attacked south of London.

Ten days later he accounted for two more Heinkel bombers. These were again aircraft of KG53 and KG55 raiding the Bristol Aero Works, that were also engaged by 152 Squadron. His first went down south of Yeovil at 11.50, the second over the Dorset coast, twenty minutes later.

Next day it was back to Me110s, Urwin-Mann knocking down an aircraft of III Gruppe of ZG26 over Southampton at 16.35 pm.

He was in action again on the 27th claiming damage to a 110 over the Bristol area. Again it was ZG26 that several RAF squadrons engaged, including 238, shortly after noon.

Hurricanes of 238 Squadron, on patrol.

His final victory for 1940 came on 7 October, a Ju88 west of Portland. No doubt from KG51, part of the Luftwaffe's last major bombing raid of the Battle.

Soon after the Battle ended, Irwin-Mann was awarded the Distinguished Flying Cross, gazetted on 26 November 1940:

This officer has displayed initiative and dash in his many engagements against the enemy. He has led his section in an excellent manner and has destroyed at least eight enemy aircraft.

Not long after John received his DFC, he was drawn by the famous war artist, Cuthbert Orde, one of many RAF airmen he sketched, having been commissioned by the Air Ministry to capture images of famous pilots and aircrew. A book was produced in 1942 with sixty-four of these charcoal drawings, Jack Urwin-Mann being one of them. He was number 20 in the book, and Orde wrote a short note about each man. About Jack he said:

'I went to a camp near Andover to do this drawing – the muddiest and most windswept place I was ever in. The Mess was a torn, dark, and draughty marquee, and the only buildings then were two Nissen huts, one for the squadron office and the other for 'dispersal'.

'We worked in the squadron office to the clicking of typewriters, and the incessant opening and shutting of the door, not to mention an endless argument about a cap that someone had lost. We both survived, and it was rather an amusing experience.

'Urwin-Mann is a particularly good pilot and was terrific at Hurricane aerobatics. He, like Hugo [Flt Lt P H Hugo DFC, 615 Sqdn], was the best of his course at the Air-Fighting School, and is a very good leader. He definitely comes in the category of "inherently tough", I think. Physically he is of the Norman Ryder, Butler, Burnell-Phillips type – good straight line from the neck to the shoulder-blades, a sign of strength. He was very quick and I should think quite imperturbable. There was another very nice chap there called Davis [Fg Off C T Davis] whom I drew too. They were extremely kind hosts to me each day I went over there. Those little things stick in one's mind!'

* * *

In 238 Squadron Urwin-Mann had rubbed shoulders with several successful pilots during the summer, Mindy Blake (qv) of course, and Bob Doe, Charles Davis and David Hughes. The squadron had moved to Chilbolton although it returned to Middle Wallop in the new year. It was back to Chilbolton in February, and then to Pembrey in April, then back yet again to Chilbolton. However, things were happening in other parts of the world and as it did not seem as if the Germans were going to continue major air assaults on Britain in 1941, interest (prior to Russia in June) had turned to the Middle East, including the island of Malta and North Africa.

In May, 238 were slated to go to North Africa and quickly found themselves aboard ship en-route to Egypt, arriving in June. In July 1941 it was at El Firden in the Canal Zone, its pilots being attached to 274 Squadron to gain operational experience in this new desert environment. Air fighting did not occur with the regularity of the previous summer and it struggled on with Hurricane IIa machines until mid-September, at which time pilots were sent to Takoradi on the African west coast, to collect Hurricane IIB machines that were being landed there by ship from England.

Once re-equipped, 238 Squadron became part of 258 Fighter Wing, and along with the Hurricanes of 1 Squadron, South African Air Force (SAAF) it moved to Landing Ground 109 (LG109) in the Western Desert, in October, which is almost due south of the coastal town of Sidi Barrani. From here the Wing's tasks were of escorting Blenheim bombers on raids or flying fighter sweeps. This continued until mid-November, at which time they moved to LG123 at Fort Maddelena No.3, just inside the Libyan border. Operating from this base the squadron became part of Operation Crusader, planned to aid the relief of Tobruk, continuing fighter sweeps and engaging enemy aircraft on a regular basis.

On 23 November, 238 in company with Hurricanes of 229 Squadron, Hurricanes of the Royal Navy and Tomahawks of 250 Squadron, they escorted nine Blenheims on a raid on Sidi Rezegh and were harried all the way to the target by German fighters, mostly 109s of JG27, a unit Urwin-Mann had tangled with during the Battle of Britain. During the combat John's fighter was hit and he was slightly wounded, but he managed to fly himself home to base some sixty-odd miles away. He was back in action the following day.

Leading his Flight almost daily, he was not blessed with much combat success, but was always in the forefront of any actions, and he did attack and damage one of a small formation of Me109Fs of JG27 during a sweep south-west of El Adem on 9 December. He also damaged a Me110 on 28 December. Then, on 14 January 1942, he was promoted to squadron leader and given command of 80 Squadron. Towards the end of January 80 Squadron moved to LG109, where John had earlier been with 238. 80 were having trouble with their cannons at this time in their Hurricane IIC machines.

On 10 February the squadron were on the move once more, moving to LG102 at Helwan, south of Maaten Bangush, part of 243 Wing. British forces had been pushed back into Egypt. In March it took up residence at Gambut, back into Libya, the tide having swung back westwards. From here operations were flown back over the Tobruk area, and again fighting was almost a daily event. However, John became tour-expired on 4 April and was posted. He did, however, receive a Bar to his DFC, announced in the *London Gazette* on 7 April 1942. The citation to this award read:

> *In November 1941 this officer led a formation of aircraft in combat against a superior force of Messerschmitt 109s. Although he was wounded in the back and later his aircraft was badly damaged, Flight Lieutenant Urwin-Mann flew it safely back to base. Next day this officer was again leading his flight. He has been engaged on operational flying almost continuously since June 1940, both in England and the Middle East. He has led his flight, squadron or wing on some 40 sorties, often in adverse weather conditions. Many successes have been achieved in which Flight Lieutenant Urwin-Mann played a prominent part. He has destroyed at least eight enemy aircraft.*

This citation was only slightly amended from the recommendation by Royal Air Force Headquarters, sent to Air Ministry in London on 24 February. To quote from this:

> 'On 23 November 1941, Flight Lieutenant Urwin-Mann was leading a formation of four fighters which was engaged by a much superior force of Messerschmitt 109s. During the combat, he was wounded in the back and later had his aircraft badly damaged. Nevertheless he managed to

bring his aircraft over 60 miles across the desert to his base, and was leading his flight again the following day. This officer has been engaged on operations with his squadron almost continuously since June 1940, both in England and the Middle East, and has destroyed eight enemy aircraft, and probably destroyed or damaged four more. During the present campaign he has led his flight, squadron [and] wing on more than 40 operational sorties, sometimes in extremely bad weather and it is due to his unflagging keenness that formations led by him have successfully engaged and destroyed numerous enemy aircraft.'

* * *

John Urwin-Mann was sent to fly a desk at Headquarters, Middle East until October, at which time there was a vacancy to command 126 Squadron on Malta. This squadron's CO, Squadron Leader B J Wicks DFC, a veteran of the fighting over France and the Battle of Britain, had been killed in action on 12 October. John had to make a quick – but easy – conversion to Spitfires as he took command of his new unit.

The desperate days of the Malta siege were coming to an end and offensive actions were to replace the island's defensive strategy in 1943, by flying sweeps and bomber escorts towards Sicily prior to that island's invasion. John took part in several of these operations until 13 April. On this date his Spitfire was in collision with a Photographic Reconnaissance Unit aircraft on the runway, resulting in John suffering burns to his arms and face, and he was evacuated back to England for treatment. However, it did not apparently slow him down on the romantic front, for he was married on 22 May to Dorothy Sarah Short. This union produced, in due time, four children, three girls and a boy.

Eight days before the wedding, on 14 May, the award of the Distinguished Service Order was promulgated in the *London Gazette*. The citation for this award reads:

Within the past six months whilst operating from Malta, this officer has completed a large number of sorties, involving attacks on factories, warehouses, port installations, power stations and airfields in Sicily and nearby enemy islands. On one occasion he led a formation which attacked an airfield and destroyed many aircraft on the ground. Squadron Leader Urwin-Mann also obtained a hit on a petrol installation, causing a violent explosion and a large fire. Another of his successes was the destruction of a portion of the main railway line during a sortie to Gela in January 1943 [the 28th]. During the same operations Squadron Leader Urwin-Mann engaged a Messerschmitt 210, shooting away its starboard engine. By his great skill and inspiring leadership, this officer has raised his squadron to a high pitch of fighting efficiency.

Eventually released from hospital he spent six months at Fighter Command Headquarters, before, in January 1944, he was posted to No. 53 Operational Training Unit as an instructor. In June, at the time of the Normandy Invasion, he joined No. 85 GSU (Group Support Unit) responsible for providing replacement aircraft to front line squadrons, in their case mainly Mustangs and Tempests. As this unit became redundant in August, he moved to No. 61 OTU at Rednal and at the end of the war, served at the Central Flying Establishment at RAF Tangmere until August 1945. He spent the next two years with the Operations Air Defence office at Air Ministry, although with the post-war policy, he had to take a lower rank, being reduced to flight lieutenant. From August 1947 to October 1948 he was with the Day Fighter Leaders' School at RAF West Raynham before taking a post at the Instrument Training School (ITS) back at Tangmere.

In July 1949 he was posted to No. 1 Squadron, at a time when the American Air Force ace, Major Robin Olds, on an exchange posting, had command of this squadron. The squadron was flying Gloster Meteor jets. A return to ITS in November till August 1950 when he moved to the Instrument Landing School (ILS) at Digby, was followed by a conversion course onto Canberra bombers. In 1952 he led the last formation flight of Hawker Hurricane fighters over Britain for the film *Angels One-Five*. He retired from the Service in April 1959 with the rank of squadron leader.

He became sales manager with Randalls Ladders, and had a number of sales jobs over the next eleven years, and finally worked for the National Westminster Bank before retiring. In early 1999 he was diagnosed with cancer and died in St Barnabas Hospice, Dallington, on 7 March of that year. He was 78.

Chapter 24

Squadron Leader T S Wade DFC AFC

Trevor Sidney Wade was a London lad, born in the borough of Wandsworth, south London, on 27 January 1920. After leaving Yardley Court School, Tonbridge, aged 18 in April 1938, he joined the Royal Air Force Volunteer Reserve as an airman under training, at No. 19 E&RFTS, at Gatwick. Called to full time service upon the outbreak of war, he completed his training and was commissioned in late April 1940.

On 21 May, just prior to the start of the Dunkirk operation, Wade was posted to No. 92 Squadron at Croydon. By this time he had gained the nickname of 'Wimpy', taken from the American cartoon character of *Popeye* fame. 92 was a Spitfire squadron, no doubt to his delight, and he arrived on the 26th, driving his Packard convertible. The squadron had seen some action over Dunkirk and lost their CO, Roger Bushell, and the new 'boss', Squadron Leader Sanders, arrived at the same time. According to Tony Bartley, already a veteran with 92, the pilots were at fever pitch over recent achievements, and replacement pilots needed to fit it. On his first day, Wimpy borrowed Bartley's Spitfire in order to get in a few more flying hours on type, and straightaway rolled it at zero feet, so was immediately accepted.

On 28 July, the squadron having moved and now operating from RAF Pembrey, sent Wimpy off on a night patrol over Swansea Bay – not an easy task with the Spitfire – and in deteriorating weather and having his radio fail, he was forced to take to his parachute over Exeter, his Spitfire crashing two miles from Chudleigh.

Still at Pembrey, within Fighter Command's 10 Group, he was in action for the first time on 19 August, sharing the destruction of a Ju88, although his Spitfire was hit by return fire from the bomber, and he was forced to make a crash-landing. The fighter (R6703) came down at Norton, Selsey, Wade managing to run clear before it blew up. The Junkers came from III/KG51 and went down off the Solent, following a raid on Bibery. Its four-man crew were reported missing. The victory was shared with Flight Lieutenant J A Paterson, a New Zealander from Dunedin. James Paterson was one of many bomber pilots who heeded the call by Fighter Command to become fighter pilots, having flown several raids in France in Fairey battles. He was to be killed in action on 27 September, and in the New Year's Honours List his services in France were rewarded by being made a MBE.

Despite further combats, Wade did not officially score again until 12 October, claiming a Me109 destroyed and probably another, with a third damaged. Their opponents were from LG1. He got another 109 probable on the 26th (JG53), a Me110 probable on the 29th, another probable – this time a Dornier – on 26 November, and finally a 109 destroyed on 2 December. The 'Do17' on 29 November was probably a Me110 of III/ZG76, flown

Group of 92 Squadron pilots at a party at Biggin Hill, celebrating the Station's 600th victory claim. Front, left to right: Squadron Leader Johnny Kent DFC, Flying Officer Tony Bartley DFC, Mrs Josephine Wade, Flying Officer Bob Holland, Wimpy Wade. At the rear are Seb Maitland-Thompson, Tom Weise (intelligence officer) and Geoff Wellum.

by Unteroffizier Walter Vockhardt, who failed to return from a mission at this time. Four Spitfires of 92 had been vectored towards the Thames estuary, locating an aircraft north of Eastchurch. On 2 December he had engaged 109s from II/JG51, and although they did not lose anyone, one 109 did in fact crash-land at Denain, having received combat damage, and was destroyed. However, Wade's own aircraft (X4618) was damaged by a 109 forcing him to make a landing at Gravesend. This ended Wade's Battle period, what would 1941 bring?

* * *

Wimpy was still with 92 Squadron in 1941. The RAF was about to launch itself onto the offensive by flying missions over northern France. As the year progressed more and more demands were made on the RAF in general and Fighter Command in particular, as other hotspots of the war began to flare up, such as the defence of Malta, and the war in the North African desert. There could only be limited response to being aggressive over France, and as Fighter Command quickly discovered, the German fighter pilots had little need to 'come up and fight' as Hurricanes and Spitfires flying above the French countryside posed no danger. The plan changed by sending small formations of light bombers – Blenheims – out to attack targets, such as aerodromes, power stations, railways, small factories, etc, which would to some extent force German pilots to react and engage these intrusions. They became known as Circus operations, supported by large numbers of RAF fighters in Wings, either in direct escort or by flying fighter sweeps nearby, to 'sweep-up' any fighters that did rise to the bait. This, overall, is a simplistic view, but that is roughly how 1941 developed on the Western Front.

Wade's squadron was now flying Spitfire Mark V fighters and, still being based at Biggin Hill, 92 became part of the Biggin Hill Wing, led by Wing Commander A G Malan DSO DFC, along with 609 and 74 Squadrons, but on 8 May, the next time Wimpy saw fighter action, 92 were sent aloft on their own to intercept a German fighter sweep over Kent. Between Dungeness and Ashford they engaged 109s and claimed to have shot down two, one falling to Wimpy.

On 16 May it was during another patrol, over the Channel this time, that they met Me109s in the early evening. The CO, Squadron Leader Jamie Rankin, and three of his pilots, Flying Officer A R Wright DFC, Flight Sergeant D E Kingaby DFM, and Wimpy, shared the destruction of one fighter, fifteen miles south of Dover. He was not so fortunate on 28 May, as an entry in Pilot Officer Neville Duke's personal diary shows:

'609, 74 and us, plus Hornchurch Wing, off on a Sweep over France. I had to return as I could not turn the oxygen on. Damn and blast! Wimpy Wade was shot-up a bit by a 109. Got cannon shell and m.g. in the wings. Went down out of control in weird spin. Spun for 15,000 ft but landed OK at Manston.'

Operations continued and on 16 June, 92 and 74 Squadrons providing an offensive sweep between Le Touquet, St Omer and Gravelines, in support of Circus 14, a raid against the gas works at Boulogne. By this stage 92 were flying in sections of four, and three such sections crossed the French coast at 24,000 feet just north of Le Touquet, patrolling about ten miles inland. 74 Squadron encountered four Me109F fighters 2,000 feet above them, then a further twelve 109Fs, which dived towards the Spitfires. Individual combats developed as 92, also aware of 109s above them, got into combat. Both squadrons made claims for 109s shot down, one going to Wimpy Wade. The only damage to the RAF was one Spitfire of 74 forced to crash-land near Hawkinge on the way home.

The following came from the report made out by Wimpy:

'P/O Wade, after being himself attacked 2 or 3 times, got in a number of bursts at an E/A which was attacking F/L Kingcome, from varying angles and ranges varying from 200 to 50 yards. After his final burst the port side of the E/As engine caught fire, it dived steeply and rolling on its back, crashed into the sea; he was then engaged by another, and getting into a position to fire from above, found his ammunition exhausted.'

On the 21st, the Biggin Hill Wing flew as one of two Target Support Wings, all three squadrons being involved. This was Circus 17 and Malan led the

Wing. They were engaged by Me109s as the bombers reached the target, Devres Aerodrome, and a fight developed with three Messerschmitts. Two were shot down, one by the CO, Rankin, the second shared between Rankin and Wimpy, south of Boulogne.

The next day, 22 June, the war changed significantly as Germany invaded Russia and it was not long before the Russian leader, Joseph Stalin, was calling upon Britain's prime minister to open a second front in the west in order to relieve the pressure on his own country. Obviously there was no way Britain could have made any such attempt at invading France, the only way that help could be given was to ramp up the pressure on the Luftwaffe in the west so that it would bring back some fighter units from the Russian front. At this stage only two German fighter groups were in the west, JG2 and JG26 and they were more than capable of containing whatever the RAF could range against them. RAF operations did increase, but it made no difference to German operations on the Russian front.

However, Wimpy was not destined to see any of these future operations. On the 23rd, on Circus 19, the Biggin Hill Wing was part of the Target Support Wing, against the Kuhlmann chemical works and power station at Chocques. There were plenty of combats, but Wade made no claims. During a late afternoon sweep, more 109s were engaged briefly and once again Wade was flying on Jamie Rankin's wing and they had a scrap with 109s south-east of Boulogne. Rankin claimed two 109s; Wade fired at one trying to get behind the CO, but was only able to claim a probable.

Wade became tour-expired and was sent to join 123 Squadron at Turnhouse where he received notification he had been awarded the Distinguished Flying Cross. The following citation was promulgated in the *London Gazette* on 15 July 1941:

> *This officer has displayed great skill and determination in his numerous engagements against the enemy and has destroyed at least six of their aircraft. His efforts have contributed materially to the success achieved by the squadron.*

In the meantime, Wimpy was married to Josephine on 2 August, at Oxted, with many of the Biggin Hill crowd attending. The reception afterwards was held at Biggin's now famous watering hole the *White Hart* at nearby Brasted, Surrey.

In September Wade was posted to 602 Squadron at RAF Kenley, as a flight commander, to gain some up-to-date experience. In an attack on the Marquise Shell factory on the afternoon of the 17th, the squadron had a fight with some 109s and lost one pilot, but claimed two Messerschmitts. Wade apparently received a wound this date, but as no other Spitfires were reported lost, he must have returned safely.

Upon recovery he was sent to the Central Flying School to complete an instructors' course, following which he went to the Central Gunnery School at RAF Sutton Bridge, as a gunnery instructor. His next posting was to No. 9 Group Headquarters where he was made the group's gunnery instructor, responsible for gunnery instruction at various Operational Training Units.

In late 1943 Wade was appointed officer commanding at AFDU (Air Fighting Development Unit), testing captured enemy aircraft, reporting on their performance and characteristics, and at the same time making comparisons to Allied aircraft they would meet in combat. For this work he received the Air Force Cross in September 1944. Early the following year he was sent to the United States where he tested captured Japanese fighter aircraft while also gaining experience on the latest American fighter types, including the early jets.

Back in England he left the RAF in 1946 and joined the editorial staff of *The Aeroplane*, reporting the testing of new civil light aeroplanes. Then in 1947 he was given the job of assistant test pilot at Hawker Aircraft, and within a few months he took over as Chief Test Pilot, flying the latest jets. He then had a period in America during an exchange scheme, returning to resume his job at Hawker. At this time his number two was Neville Duke DSO DFC & 2 Bars, who had been on 92 Squadron with him in 1941. The main aircraft types they were working on were the Hawker Fury, Tempest IIs and the new jet, the P1040.

It was an interesting time in aviation in the immediate post-war era. All the major aircraft companies were entering the jet age with all their various designs and all were in a race to produce the most effective for RAF service. At Hawker they were working on the P1040, which became the P1072 when fitted with the Armstrong-Siddeley '*Snarler*' rocket motor, fuelled with

Three of Wade's comrades in 1941, turning up for his wedding in August 1941. Left to right: Flight Lieutenant Jamie Rankin, Flying Officer Phil Archer (KIA 1942), and Pilot Officer Neville Duke.

Trevor 'Wimpy' Wade DFC AFC, test pilot.

liquid oxygen. There were also the air displays where the industry could show off its newest designs, and Wimpy was amongst the likes of John Derry, John Cunningham and Neville Duke giving superb flying displays to delight the crowds, all eager to see the latest types in action. In May 1949, Wimpy set a speed record, flying between London and Paris in the P1052, the speed was logged at 617.87 mph.

The Hawker team were working hard, developing the P1042 into the P1052, and then came the P1081. The Royal Australian Air Force was eager to have a new jet fighter to replace their aging Mustangs. Hawker

The P1081 (VX279) in which Wade was killed in 1951.

put forward a proposal for their new swept-wing fighter, the P1081. Once ready, it was handed over to the Royal Aircraft Establishment to work on. Wimpy was used as its test pilot, flying it successfully until 3 April 1950. On another air test something went very wrong, and control with VX279 was lost. Wimpy ejected from it, but he did not survive the fall. The aircraft crashed at Ringmer, near Lewes, Sussex. Wimpy was only 30 years old.

Neville Duke, together with Hawker's secretary, broke the news to his wife Josephine. They had three children, and the sadness was compounded a short time later with the sudden death of one of them, Michael. Neville succeeded Wimpy as Hawker's chief test pilot. As Neville once told me: 'It was a tremendous privilege to hold this post, but I would have preferred to have got it in better circumstances.' 'Wimpy,' he said, 'was a first rate pilot and a tremendous personality, and fun to be with. His work at Hawkers contributed greatly to the early work the company was doing which resulted in the production of the famous Hawker Hunter [P1067].'

Index